Dear Reader:

The book you are about to read is the latest bestseller from the St. Martin's True Crime Library, the imprint the *New York Times* calls "the leader in true crime!" Each month, we offer you a fascinating account of the latest, most sensational crime that has captured the national attention. St. Martin's is the publisher of perennial bestselling true crime author Jack Olsen, whose SALT OF THE EARTH is the true story of one woman's triumph over life-shattering violence; Joseph Wambaugh called it "powerful and absorbing." Fannie Weinstein and Melinda Wilson tell the story of a beautiful honors student who was lured into the dark world of sex for hire in THE COED CALL GIRL MURDER. St. Martin's is also proud to publish two-time Edgar Award-winning author Carlton Stowers, whose TO THE LAST BREATH recounts a two-year-old girl's mysterious death, and the dogged investigation that led loved ones to the most unlikely murderer: her own father. In the book you now hold, BORN EVIL, critically acclaimed author Adrian Havill investigates the life and crimes of one of the most extreme serial killers of all time.

St. Martin's True Crime Library gives you the stories *behind* the headlines. Our authors take you right to the scene of the crime and into the minds of the most notorious murderers to show you what really makes them tick. St. Martin's True Crime Library paperbacks are better than the most terrifying thriller, because it's all true! The next time you want a crackling good read, make sure it's got the St. Martin's True Crime Library logo on the spine—you'll be up all night!

P9-BZZ-699

Charles E. Spicer, Jr.
Executive Editor, St. Martin's True Crime Library

PRAISE FOR ADRIAN HAVILL AND HIS TRUE CRIME BOOKS

WHILE INNOCENTS SLEPT

"Written with compelling detail, WHILE INNOCENTS SLEPT plunges readers into the murky world of Sudden Infant Death Syndrome. Adrian Havill's fair-minded reporting keeps you guessing about a syndrome that can easily destroy an innocent parent's reputation or serve as a perfect mask for the cruelest of murders. Havill's thoroughly written account is a scientific spellbinder—a heart-beating mystery that is even more frightening because it is true."
>—Pete Earley, Edgar Award-winning author of
>CONFESSIONS OF A SPY and THE HOT HOUSE

"In WHILE INNOCENTS SLEPT, Adrian Havill offers up one of the most chilling and evil characters in the long, dark history of true crime writing. People will be talking about this book for some time—as well they should!"
>—Carlton Stowers, Edgar Award-winning author of
>TO THE LAST BREATH

"The best accounts of murder are those that read like mystery novels you can't put down. Adrian Havill has done just that in WHILE INNOCENTS SLEPT, a riveting read that I couldn't put down. Did Garrett Wilson murder two innocent babies and cover the crimes up with a convenient medical diagnosis? Or was he the target of a witch-hunt? The book works like a pot of strong coffee, with rich, fully drawn personalities to keep you awake until the jury reaches its verdict on the final page."
>—Robert K. Ressler,
>one of America's foremost criminologists and author of
>I HAVE LIVED IN THE MONSTER

Turn the page for more acclaim . . .

THE MOTHER, THE SON, AND THE SOCIALITE

"An instant true-crime classic! Gritty and riveting."
—*New York Post*

"Crime journalism at its best! Well-written, carefully researched."   —Jack Olsen, bestselling author of
SALT OF THE EARTH

"The book's catalog of doctored passports and errant blood drops [offers] an engrossing account."
—*Time* magazine

ALSO BY ADRIAN HAVILL

The Last Mogul
The Unauthorized Biography of Jack Kent Cooke

Deep Truth
The Lives of Bob Woodward and Carl Bernstein

Man of Steel
The Career and Courage of Christopher Reeve

The Mother, the Son, and the Socialite
The True Story of a Mother–Son Crime Spree

While Innocents Slept
A Story of Revenge, Murder, and SIDS

The Spy Who Stayed Out in the Cold
The Secret Life of FBI Double Agent Robert Hanssen

AS A CONTRIBUTING AUTHOR

Juice
The O. J. Simpson Tragedy

BORN EVIL

ADRIAN HAVILL

St. Martin's Paperbacks

BORN EVIL

Copyright © 2001 by Adrian Havill.

Cover photograph courtesy Montgomery County Sheriff's Department.

For information address St. Martin's Press, 175 Fifth Avenue, New York, N.Y. 10010.

ISBN: 0-312-97890-1
EAN: 80312-97890-7

Printed in the United States of America

St. Martin's Paperbacks edition/December 2001

20 19 18 17 16 15 14 13 12

THIS BOOK IS FOR
NORAH HARDING

NOTES ON SOURCES AND ACKNOWLEDGMENTS

Hadden Clark was a source for this account. He both called or wrote to me from prison during the writing of this book, where I often interviewed him in person. He was also asked more intimate questions by me through his cellmate, a convict known in this book as "Jesus." I either visited, wrote to Jesus, spoke to him by phone or had messages passed by his wife in order to pose some of the more delicate queries I wanted Hadden to answer. Other quotes by Mr. Clark are from a long interview he gave to Detective Edward Tarney of the Montgomery County Police Department in September of 1998.

Many people helped me in this work but I would particularly like to thank Tim Morgan and Brian Rossman, who were my eyes and ears in California. Chase Culeman-Beckman gathered information for me in Connecticut and Rhode Island. Cassie Trace did the same in White Plains, New York. Terry Lane was most helpful in Maryland. Certain police and prosecution sources cooperated on a confidential basis.

My wife, Georgiana, was my right hand and best critic. Several of her photos are in the center section of the book. Of course, this account would not be possible without the help of two fine editors, Dorsey Mills and Charlie Spicer. My agent, Jane Dystel, has represented me well from the beginning.

Real names are used throughout the book except for the children of Geoffrey Clark. Geoff's progeny were innocents when these events occurred and I have used pseudonyms for them.

The interrogation of Hadden Clark that takes place in Chapters Ten and Eleven has been condensed.

BORN EVIL

Serial and mass murder, defined as the taking of three or more lives through premeditated homicide, is perplexing to law enforcement agencies. As of yet, the perpetrator who might commit these heinous acts cannot be detected in advance. One cannot forecast when or how the quirky neighbor next door will become a methodical planner who plots the death of different people, either sequentially over months and years, or who ends the lives of several within a few short minutes. There are, however, many childhood behavioral patterns shared by these killers.

Experts on multiple murder agree that there are certain precursors that predestine this type of criminal. They will tell you, for instance, that most serial killers practice by tormenting household pets as children. They usually cite Edmund Kemper III as their first example.

Ed Kemper liked to tear his sister's dolls apart at the neck to see what was inside, a practice he continued with young women as an adult. He began his criminal career in 1964 by executing both of his grandparents when he was fifteen. He then killed six young women after being released from the juvenile facility where he had been sent for murdering the family elders. Before being arrested, he also took the life of his mother and a family friend. He tried to cover up those two murders by putting parts of their bodies down an electric sink disposal.

The giant, six-foot-nine-inch Kemper was a frightening animal abuser. As a child, he tortured the family cat by burying it alive. He later dug the dead feline's body back up in order to behead it.

Not that cats are the only pets targeted. The Milwaukee,

Wisconsin, serial cannibal, Jeffrey Dahmer, decapitated dogs as a child. He also fashioned them into trophies by placing their heads on poles in the woods behind his home. Several years later the police found human heads inside Dahmer's refrigerator.

Former FBI agent and noted crime expert Robert Ressler calls animal abuse a sort of feedback system. Since most animals cannot verbally or even physically defend themselves, the budding murderers begin to believe they are entitled to act barbarically forever. When this happens, Ressler says, the torturing of animals eventually escalates to similar behavior against humans. Unless the pattern is stopped early, either by legal authorities or through mental health counseling, the person becomes an unrepentant killer.

This theory, though, is far from foolproof. Not every serialist abuses animals. In fact, often the opposite is found. British murderer Dennis Nilsen, who specialized in the torture and death of gay young men—fifteen of them—was extremely upset when apprehended, but not for the reason one might conclude. A lifelong animal lover, he worried that his beloved dog, Bleep, would be traumatized by being separated from him. The canine was forced to survive without his owner. A judge gave Nilsen a life sentence for his bloody acts.

Besides the torture of animals, a killer's family and his childhood can produce this extreme behavioral pattern. Warning signals can come in clusters. They include adolescent pyromania, bedwetting, and alcoholic parents who practice physical and sexual abuse on their child. It is estimated that six of ten serial killers have been incontinent, regularly soiling their sheets as children and into their teens. As a youth, David Berkowitz, the New York postal worker and serial killer responsible for the phrase "Son of Sam" was an active pyromaniac who set more than 1400 illegal fires. But that crime, believed to have sexually stimulated the fire-starter, appears to be far from universal among those with abnormal deviant personalities. Childhood abuse appears to be the one common thread that defines the early years of a serial killer. It is the one segment of their life histories that sequential murderers always have in common with one another.

These offenses come in many forms. Sexual molestation, incest with either a sibling, the mother or father, or both, frequent physical beatings that could be defined as torture, and mental terrorism are some of the chief varieties. Bullying in school or being ostracized by classmates also contribute.

Sante Kimes and her son Kenny, who killed a wealthy New York widow and may have done away with as many as four people acting in concert, often shared a bedroom together. In my 1999 book on the two, *The Mother, the Son, and the Socialite*, Sante is chronicled as co-hosting a beer keg party with her son to celebrate his second year of college after twenty years of a smothering and sometimes sexual relationship. Offering her son kinky favors was one of the ways she controlled him and molded him into a murderer.

Abusive mother-and-son relationships are often the genesis of a serial killer. A sort of poetic vengeance is wrought when the murderer begins or ends his homicidal spree by killing his mother and often, both parents.

"I wanted my mom to have the same kind of quiet easy death like everyone else," Ed Kemper told the cops. His idea of a peaceful demise, however, was different from what most of us expect. After decapitating and then raping his mother, he placed her head on the living room mantel and reportedly used it as a dartboard. A police investigation later showed that the Kemper matriarch was far from a perfect parent. When her son became too tall for her liking she locked him up in the basement. Her reason: his height was frightening his sisters. Yet Kemper continued to live with his mother as an adult. Like Kenny Kimes, he could never completely extricate himself from her control.

The list of these matricides appears to be endless. Charles Whitman, the twenty-five-year-old killer of sixteen, who also left twenty-nine students wounded in a 1966 rampage on the University of Texas campus in Austin, began the bloody day by stabbing and shooting his mother to death. More recently, in 1998, a fifteen-year-old Oregon youth, Kip Kinkel, murdered both his parents before heading off to high school where he shot two classmates dead and then wounded twenty-two others.

Are the mothers sometimes to blame for these outrageous deeds? Charles Manson's prostitute mom refused to give him a name when he was born and was said to have once traded him away for a pitcher of beer. Later in his childhood, Manson lived with an aunt and uncle who told him he was a sissy, sending him off to school dressed like a girl. They were fortunate to escape retribution from the mass-murdering Manson family years later.

Confusing little boys by dressing them in female clothing or repressing their heterosexual desires is prevalent among parents of mass murderers and serial killers. Joseph Kallinger, a killer of the 1970s who murdered young boys, including his thirteen-year-old son, was adopted early in his life by sadistic stepparents. After a hernia operation at the age of six his mother told him the surgery had been performed to keep his penis from growing. Kallinger believed the appendage was stunted his entire life. The adoptive mom also forced him to hold his hand over flames, beating him when he cried out.

The inspiration for Anthony Perkins' character in the movie *Psycho*, adapted from Robert Bloch's book, was a serial killer of the 1950s by the name of Edward Gein. Gein's fanatical mother, Augusta, preached to him that women were synonymous with sin and that they would give him a disfiguring disease if he ever had sex with them. So he never did. She died of a stroke but her son stayed close to her after death by skinning and preserving much of her body. He literally wore the outer portions of her most intimate organs under his clothing. Gein killed fifteen other women this way, his remote Wisconsin farmhouse becoming a grim, human butcher's shop of the macabre. When the police finally caught on they arrived at this home to find bowls made from skulls and chairs with seats fashioned from human skin. Several other household objects had been carved from body parts by Gein. He was judged criminally insane, and was sent to a state mental hospital, where he died of cancer in 1984 at the advanced age of seventy-eight.

In *The Killers Among Us*, criminology professor Steven Egger confirms the above: "Serial murderers are frequently found to have unusual or unnatural relationships with their mothers." While this is largely true, fathers have sometimes played a part, mostly by physically mistreating their sons.

John Wayne Gacy, Jr., the Illinois building contractor who seduced, tortured, and killed at least thirty-three young men, burying twenty-nine of them under the floorboards of his Chicago home, was badly abused by his alcoholic father. John Sr.'s favorite names for his son were slurs like "sissy" and "queer." The elder Gacy also beat his wife as the boy looked on, and when he was fourteen, shot the family dog in front of him as a punishment for what he viewed as bad behavior by his namesake.

Albert DeSalvo, who confessed to murdering eleven women in the early 1960s, is better known as The Boston Strangler. He watched his father break his mother's fingers one at a time. His dad sold him and his siblings as slaves to a Maine farmer while he was still a young child.

"Papa was a plumber," DeSalvo once said. "One time he smashed me across the back with a metal pipe because I didn't move fast enough."

Some experts are skeptical and discount the claims of

killers like DeSalvo. They believe that serial murderers often exaggerate both their childhood abuse and their body counts in order to gain notoriety and thus enlarge their own importance. Henry Lee Lucas, the Blacksburg, Virginia–born drifter and serial killer of the 1980s, actually claimed more than 600 victims, including his mother. He also told disbelieving authorities that it was he who had put the poison in the Kool-Aid used in the Jonestown, Guyana, massacre. The number of deaths in the Lucas case is undoubtedly inflated, but police departments in several states did close the books on 214 murders because of credible information he provided.

"Serial killers are pathological liars," says James Alan Fox, a criminal justice professor at Northeastern University in Boston. "You have to take everything they say not with a grain of salt, but with the whole shaker."

The parental mistreatment experienced by DeSalvo and others like him eventually forces future serial and mass murderers to seek forms of escape: They usually accomplish this by trying to become someone else. Multiple personalities, schizophrenia, the wearing of disguises, transvestitism, and impersonating others are common.

John Gacy dressed up as a clown called Pogo, visiting young children in hospitals in the costume. California's Zodiac Killer, who has yet to be identified after thirty years, sometimes wears a bizarre executioner's ensemble when he commits his crimes. Ted Bundy, who raped, tortured, and killed women on both coasts of the United States, liked to win the confidence of his victims by telling them he was a counselor at a rape crisis center, or by impersonating a law enforcement officer, and sometimes even an attorney.

Multiple personality disorders in serial and mass murderers are suspect with court prosecutors. Is the claim simply an easy prelude for a plea of insanity and thus, is the assertion genuine? The psychiatric profession believes that spreading the abuse one experiences to several characters inside a deranged mind offers a measure of relief.

A California killer, Herbert Mullin, killed thirteen men and women over a five-month period in the early 1970s. After his bloody spree he confessed his crimes to a priest. While receiving his penance for the murders he dragged the cleric out of the confessional and stabbed him to death. When he was arrested, Mullin said he heard voices in his head that ordered him to kill. He also made the bizarre claim that his murders had prevented earthquakes, an argument which failed to win the sympathy of the jurors, despite the trial's close proximity to San Francisco.

"A mind can be evil without being abnormal," admitted the British killer of fifteen, Dennis Nilsen. Others disagree. How could someone slaughter another person for sheer enjoyment? Yet many crimes are planned by serial killers as intricately as military maneuvers, giving credence to the argument of depraved normalcy.

The subject of this book, Hadden Irving Clark, has many of the attributes that have been discussed here. He does not quite fit the profile of the classic serial killer even though he undoubtedly received sexual thrills from killing young girls and women. (This pleasure was repeated later by reliving the crimes in his mind.) Some of his murders were planned but others were quite spontaneous. A defense attorney or psychotherapist would plead that Hadden Clark be spared from prison and instead be hospitalized because he is simply insane. A prosecutor would respond by saying Hadden is as evil as Satan himself.

On a social level, Hadden Clark is also a bit different from most of the murderers who have gone before him. Generally, serial killers come from the lower half of society. This slayer of as many as a dozen young women can claim to be a true blueblood, someone who is able to trace his roots back nearly 400 years, to the voyage of the *May-*

flower, and later to ancestors who fought in the American Revolution. Additionally, Hadden Clark has a brother who committed murders and mutilated women with a knife much the same way as he did, while living more than 3,000 miles away.

The very worst kind of killers can come from the very best of families. Mothers and fathers can go bad, despite their illustrious ancestors, and spawn demon seeds that they unknowingly nurture into depraved adults. These facts are even more chilling when, as in this account, so many good and innocent lives are destroyed.

PART ONE

Imagine if, at the end of The Silence of the Lambs, *the psychopathic killer had been imprisoned for a mere eleven to thirty years rather than being blown away by the movie's heroine. The string of gruesome, cold-blooded murders we know Hadden Clark has committed makes such an ending unthinkable.*

Yet this is no movie—this is real life—and the unthinkable has happened. Hadden Clark is a serial killer, a man who murders for the bizarre high it gives him. And because he has been so clever and premeditative, he has not left behind enough traces of his actions for us to confront him with a sentence appropriate to their magnitude.

The mother of the woman he murdered, Penny Houghteling, when questioned as to whether or not she thinks he'd kill again given the chance replied, "Oh, yes he would definitely kill again. He won't kill me. But he'll definitely kill again." What if it's you next time? Or your daughter?

For what he has done, and would thrill to do again, he deserves the death penalty or a life sentence without parole.

Somewhere out there is his next victim.

> —A LETTER TO THE JUDGE FROM A FRIEND
> OF THE FAMILY URGING THE MAXIMUM
> SENTENCE FOR HADDEN CLARK.

PROLOGUE

The prison's setting could have been a splendid site for a ski resort. On this sunny May Saturday in the first year of the new century, after exiting Interstate 68 onto Route 220, just past the town of Cumberland in the Maryland panhandle, you drive past a tattoo and piercing parlor, then Shooter's Bar, before arriving in a lush valley dominated by a tall green mountain. Western Correctional Institution or WCI, is nestled against that peak. If they wish, many of the 1,780 convicts inside its boundaries can stand in their cells and view not only the mountain through their smudged safety glass slit of a window, but a sliver of a stream that is the beginning of the 330-mile-long Potomac River.

Western Correctional Institution is one of the largest employers in western Maryland. There is a staff of 580 to control the inmates. This sparsely populated, largely forgotten area has nine percent unemployment, more than double the national rate. Factories close here more often than open and the institution was welcomed with open arms and great fanfare by the local politicians when it was finished in late 1998. These elected officials, knowing that a more desirable computer chip plant was not a realistic possibility for their depressed region, smiled bravely for the cameras as they cut a big ribbon in front of the entrance. The complex that would be the culmination of bad news for its future inhabitants, was very good news indeed for the out-of-work but law-abiding citizens who lived nearby and were more than willing to accept the prison's modest, but dependable, salaries.

WCI appears to be vast, like a large factory complex. Its many buildings are low and long. They go on and on, down the highway for almost a mile, stopping only when they reach the boundaries of a village with the unfortunate name of Cresaptown. Except for the water and guard towers, no structure is higher than two stories. From the road, the view of the prison is slightly obscured behind two layers of a high chain-link fence. The inside enclosure curves inward like an inverted C and has razor-sharp barbed wire on top. The outside barrier has nine coils of high-tech barbed wires woven through the chain links. The layers are laid from top to bottom and loosely pulled from left to right. They resemble giant spiked Slinkys. The enclosure is designed for maximum-risk inmates, though the penal institution itself has been rated as a medium-security facility by the state. When one adds the guard towers and the spotlights that flood the valley with light each night, the max classification is easy to understand. Modern technology may have at last created the perfect penal environment. It is certainly a fact that nobody yet has ever come close to escaping from this cruel, forbidding place.

Inside these walls on this sunny afternoon one first sees acre upon acre of athletic fields. There is a baseball park, an open-air gym with free-weights, and several basketball courts that have paved asphalt flooring and dozens of hoops, enough to make an NBA team envious.

Only African-American men are playing the game this day. Men of color made up seventy-four percent of the inmate population at WCI at the turn of the new century. At the edge of the action, a few wan-looking white men watch the spirited action. Their nervous, frightened faces mark them. They are the black men's bitches, a term used for those weaker inmates who serve their more powerful counterparts by providing them with sexual favors upon demand. The supplicants do this in exchange for protection. It is a master-and-slave relationship, an ironic flip-flop in a cruel place where racial history has been turned upside down. Life is brutal and mean inside these walls. Survival for these frailer convicts requires compromise.

Still, homosexuality in prisons is not as rampant as the outside world believes. It is certainly present and rapes do occur but in the inmate world it is illegal drugs, rather than sex, that is more sought after on most days. Small amounts of cocaine make their way in between the layers of Polaroid pictures or under postage stamps. Six letters from the right source and you are high, say the recipients. Affluent inmates see to it that guards are paid well to bring them packages of illicit substances. They sell cocaine or the other banned narcotics they don't use to the prison population— this time dealing drugs from inside rather than outside the walls. For these elite inmates, little has changed. More than half the prisoners here committed their crimes while high on drugs or because they needed to get money to continue their addiction. In this walled universe, they need their drugs even more than before.

Cocaine and sex are just the beginning of the perks available at WCI. There is this truism among inmates: "If you have money, you can get anything in prison except a car."

To the right of the recreation areas are five orange brick, two-tiered residences that house and shelter the men. There are other buildings—dining halls, a supply warehouse, and a furniture factory that is still under construction. When completed, the convicts will be able to turn out desks and chairs for state offices and police departments at a salary which will start at eighty-five cents and, in a few years, top out at $1.25. A day. The irony, which has not gone unnoticed, is that a cabinet craftsman at WCI could soon be creating a fine mahogany desk for the very officer of the law responsible for sending him here.

One of the residences is known as Cellblock Four. This building houses those who are isolated from the general population—officially called Administrative Segregation but referred to by others as "solitary." Inmates who live here are kept inside their cells twenty-three hours of every day. Most have neither money nor power. The two men being visited in Cellblock Four on this Saturday in May are let out of their eight-by-ten-foot homes an hour before midnight. Twice each week they are allowed to use part of the hour to shower. They can also make collect phone calls. Or they can walk outside in what has been dubbed "the dog run," a long cage inside an enclosure where the moon and stars can be glimpsed only through a latticed chain-link–and–barbed-wire ceiling.

This is the American prison system at its most confining. Those incarcerated here often become insane within a year, though at least one of these two inmates has already reached that state.

The claustrophobia-inducing cells of these men are numbered nine and ten. They don't have the beauty of the mountain view. These side-by-side rooms on the lower level face out towards Route 220. From their slitted windows the men can see cars gliding down the highway and sometimes people entering the physical therapy center across the road. To them, the busy vista is an improvement over the pastoral but static green scenery afforded by the mountain.

Each of their cells has an upper and lower bunk but only the lower one has a two-inch-thick, fire-retardant mattress that has been stuffed with glass fiber. The mattress and a thin blanket are placed over a hard steel slab. The higher bunk is used to store toiletries and personal items. There is a metal toilet and a sink placed against a rough off-white concrete wall with two buttons on the sink that produce water when they are pushed. An identical lukewarm liquid spews forth from each, no matter which control is used. Books are offered from a cart once a day with a single volume at a time allowed to be checked in through the slot in the door. Each man has a television set and a radio. The electronics are usually the best way to shave a few hours from each day. The prison has a satellite dish which sweeps the heavens and finds them a limited supply of local and basic cable stations.

The man in cell number ten is named Hadden Irving Clark but these days he sometimes believes he is someone else, usually a woman. The female name he answers to most often is Kristen Bluefin, who he says is thirty-seven years old. There is also a sixteen-year-old girl named Nicole inside of him and when he is in her persona, his assertion is that she is Kristen's evil daughter.

"Hadden Clark never murdered nobody," he will whine in a sing-song voice when he returns to a semblance of normalcy. "It's the ladies who killed them. I didn't kill anybody."

Speaking from the depths of this paranoid dementia he claims that it was Kristen who killed Laura Bettis Houghteling and that it was that nasty little Nicole who cut Michele Lee Dorr from stem to stern and held her down while she bled to death.

In Hadden's world, his other personalities are the murderers. He might cry out again unexpectedly in a female voice just to show his listener that he still can be prim, proper, and moral.

"And I'm not a lesbian. Don't ever call me a lesbian."

Nobody ever has.

Hadden plays this feminine role seriously. He only urinates sitting down when he imagines himself a woman and will often flirt coquettishly, batting his blue eyes at anyone he comes into contact with, disregarding the consequences.

He is rarely in his right mind these days. You can see that today by just peering into the interior of the cell. Hadden has taken the fried sausage links that came on his breakfast tray and suspended them from dental floss in the window of his cell to age. He imagines he is a hunter in a campsite where winter is coming and there could be a food shortage. When he has cured and dried this meat, with the shriveled sausage becoming furry with mold, he will cock his head to the side. Then, as if he is a baby bird about to receive a worm from its mother, Hadden will leap at one of the brown casings, snapping the shrunken, brittle tubes in half with his teeth, and eating them as an afternoon snack.

He has similar fun with his other food. Hadden will empty and scrape a half grapefruit down to the white of the rind, then fill it with bread or anything else that's edible and cover it with paper. Turning it upside down he will hide it in a corner of his cell for a week or so and then consume the fuzzy mass. Hadden also likes to stuff food inside small plastic-coated milk cartons and play the same game.

Sometimes he forgets to eat his stash. His cell's odor becomes rank and gets to the point where a rookie guard will be ordered to enter his quarters to remove the rotting food. It is not an assignment that correctional officers vie for.

None of this bacteria-infested feasting is healthy. Despite carrying a lean and hard 165 pounds stretched over a six-foot-two frame, Hadden is often sick. His hair is all but gone. Not that it matters. He shaves both his head and his eyebrows. He also vomits easily and spends many of his waking hours hunched over the toilet with diarrhea. He denies it is his diet which causes these frequent discomforts.

A visitor's emotions will volley back-and-forth between sympathy and revulsion. There is suspicion too. Hadden Clark can be a shrewd and calculating man who can easily beat most players at a serious game of chess. Hadden plays expertly and is a member of both the U.S. Chess Federation and its Massachusetts state chapter. He has a long-term subscription to a chess magazine and opts to read *The Washington Times* over *The Washington Post* just because it offers David Sands' weekly chess column.

Hadden's highs run off-and-on. He is at last a celebrity, someone who gets fan mail delivered to his cell and endless letters from writers and television news crews who all say they just want to talk to him. He has just been the subject of a *Dateline* piece on NBC. The prison tried to stop him from watching the show by turning off the television reception on the Tuesday night it was broadcast. Hadden was angry with the censorship but a week later he was flipping around the dial and there was the same *Dateline* piece on Channel 28, MSNBC. It was being rebroadcast, repackaged as *Weekend Edition* and no less than Stone Phillips introduced him. They showed it again a few nights later. Both Hadden and Kristen were thrilled. Attention was being paid.

He knows that the *New Yorker* piece by Alec Wilkinson will be coming out soon. A few days ago he gave an interview by telephone to Juju Chang. She is the new Connie Chung on *20/20* except she is Korean and not Chinese like Connie. Juju told him his story is so special it might even be a two-parter. He is famous, creating enough memories to last a lifetime. This is important to Hadden because, after all this is over, he will be spending the rest of his days alone, confined to an eight-by-ten cell much like the one he occupies now. The monotony will not be broken by visits from friends or family. These have long stopped, probably forever.

Out of nowhere, Hadden begins singing. He does this often and the effect is disturbing. The songs are always biblical hymns, the innocent, simple tunes from his youth:

> "Jesus loves me! This I know,
> for the Bible tells me so . . ."

His favorite seems to be this one, a religious ditty that seems to partly absolve him of his sins:

"He's still working on me,
Making me what I ought to be.
Took just a week to make the moon and the stars,
Sun and Earth, Jupiter and Mars.
How loving and patient he must be,
He's still working on me."

When he offers these devotions, they come out sounding sinister. Hadden's singing voice is a nasal falsetto. It has an ominous ring.

Next door in cell number nine is a man whom Hadden believes is Jesus Christ. Of course he is not Jesus. His real name is John Patrick Truitt, and though the first two sound saintly, Jesus has been inside the Maryland prison system continuously since 1974, more than half his life. He is a convicted murderer and kidnapper. Jesus has been eligible for parole for more than a decade but the people who decide these things have not listened to his pleas despite a record of exemplary behavior. Hadden Clark, nutty, crazy Hadden Clark, may be his last chance to walk free.

Jesus does look amazingly like the popular paintings which depict Christ. But this Jesus is forty-seven and a bit pudgy. His hair is long and parted in the middle with his beard and mustache containing streaks of gray. The beard is nearly two years old and it tapers to a point naturally, just above the second button of his denim shirt. His trousers are not what you might expect of a holy man either. They are gray athletic sweat pants and on the left thigh there is a logo that says *Race for the Cure*. Since he has never run a 5K or suffered from breast cancer it is safe to assume they were given to him rather than awarded as a prize.

On one of his fingers is an intricate silver wedding ring. Jesus looks forward to visits from his wife on Fridays, even though—they were married inside a prison—the union has never been consummated. Visiting days for men in solitary confinement are restricted to Monday and Friday mornings but Jesus is only allowed to shower on Monday and Thursday nights. That presents a problem. Fastidious to a fault, he wants to look clean for his spouse. Come only on Fridays, he tells her.

He has always resembled God's son. There is a photograph of him taken in June of 1974 that appeared on the front page of his local newspaper just after he was arrested for pumping four bullets into a man he didn't like. The picture shows him nearly nude and barefoot wearing only a tiny pair of white denim shorts. He is handcuffed, his hands manacled in front, surrounded by an angry mob of police and onlookers. In the photo he looks directly into the camera's lens, so thin from drug use, his ribs protrude. The same shoulder-length hair is there and the photograph *is* a bit startling. It may be blasphemous to think such thoughts, but the image can be seen as Christ being led away to be crucified.

Jesus has served as a living confessional to Hadden since November 1999. His new position at the prison is to coax words from him that detail his crimes. He is to do whatever it takes to make Hadden focus on this project, putting his bloody biography on paper. The FBI wants it all in writing. They're interested in every murder he's ever committed, every name he can remember contacting. So far Hadden, with the help of Jesus, has filled 203 pages in a series of notebooks. Many are drawings. He fancies himself an artist and likes to illustrate his murders, showing himself as the aggressor, knife in hand, reenacting a crime. The killing scenes are colored in red with Hadden sometimes using his own blood as ink to emphasize the gore.

When Hadden writes or says something revealing, Jesus will go to the phone in the middle of the night and punch in a special number that goes to an FBI serial murder team in Baltimore, Maryland. Jesus has been told that when all this is over he might be paroled because of his services. On the other hand, if he's not released he could soon be dead. His duties for the Feds on the matter of Hadden Clark are dangerous. Jesus is taking a serious life-or-death risk. Nobody likes a snitch. In prison, there is a code that says those who tell tales to cops wind up with blades sticking out of their backs.

Truth be told, Hadden Clark disgusts him. It is one thing to kill a man over a monetary dispute or to shoot a woman who cheated on you, but cutting up and raping innocent little girls is beyond the pale. He has had to listen to Hadden rambling on about how sweet human flesh is to eat and how he likes to suck the blood from a just-amputated finger.

"People taste like veal," Hadden has said, with an unholy pleasure in his voice.

Then there is all this transgender business. Jesus can't play chess very well so Hadden plays checkers with him instead. Midway through the game he might become Kristen. Then he begins flirting outrageously, and, like a girl on a date, lets Jesus win. This feminine side of Hadden creeps him out.

Parts of Hadden's life story seem over the top. Like when he told Jesus he had an intimate relationship with his sister or that it was his father who taught him to kill, first by hunting animals and then real people. Can this be true? That's for the FBI to sort through. Jesus is just doing his job.

Most of this intelligence was gathered for the Bureau months ago, before Jesus and Hadden were separated into these side-by-side cells. Hadden now confides in him by whispering through the heating and air-conditioning vents or when they are let out together at midnight. The two lived large back then, housed in comparatively plush quarters, in a wing of the prison's hospital. Hadden was with him all day long, and at night Jesus could still go into his own room and lock the door. He slept safe. That was important because he felt there was always a chance Hadden could zap out—the prison term for insane behavior—and attack him while he slept. His charge has told him many times he is not yet finished dealing with his enemies.

"When I get out, the first thing I'm going to do is find Geoff and Alison and cut them up," he will rant in his Hadden voice. The two names are those of his brother and sister. Geoff once wore a wire into the prison when he visited him, Hadden has learned. Alison testified against her sibling at one of his murder trials. In his mind, slaying them both is easily justified.

When they lived in the hospital, Jesus and Hadden would be taken out on field trips with the FBI serial killer team and two Montgomery County, Maryland, detectives, Edward Tarney and Michael Garvey. Both cops had been after Hadden for years and were jointly responsible for his two murder convictions. The odd couple would be put in leg irons and handcuffed with their hands in front for comfort. Then they would drive up Interstate 95 in a black, smoked-glass Chevy Suburban, with Hadden sitting in the front and Jesus relaxing in the back.

The trips to New England, where Hadden claimed he buried most of his victims, were grand, luxurious by prison standards. They would stop at Burger Kings to eat, though frankly neither one liked the fast food very much. Hadden ideally prefers his chow raw, bloody, and rotten and that certainly wasn't Burger King's usual style. Jesus is a vegetarian, partly because he has a lifetime medical problem called hemachromatosis. With an oversupply of iron in his blood he has to either lay off the meat or go to the doctor and be bled—almost like medics did centuries ago with leeches—and in a prison, well, the medics don't always take requests like that as seriously as they should.

For Jesus, the journeys were a window to a world and a life that had passed him by. He had not been out of the state of Maryland for more than twenty-five years and was outside the walls of a prison only when he was being transferred from one penal institution to another. Finally, he saw a little of America again, and in style, sitting high up in the new SUV, looking through the one-way windows. Hadden had told the cops he wouldn't go anywhere without his lord and personal savior, and if he were going to find bodies for them they had better let Jesus come along. Besides, when they found the bodies, he explained, Jesus would be there to bring them back from the dead.

The law treated him like the crazed superstar serial killer he was and Hadden played the role to an outrageous hilt. He got away with it—some of his victims were thought to be the daughters of the rich and powerful, who wanted some final closure. His demands required that he wear female clothing when he looked for the bodies. So six cops had to go out and get him some panties, stockings, and a bra to wear beneath the sweater and skirt they had purchased for him at a Cape Cod Kmart. They had made a spectacle of themselves at the discount store, awkwardly pawing through racks of ladies' wear. Hadden wouldn't wear the skirt, saying it was the wrong style and too big for his frame. He opted for slacks. On top of his nearly bald head he wore a ghastly red acrylic wig with bangs. It was cheap and any self-respecting drag queen would have turned it down. With the hairpiece on, Hadden resembled an evil Ginger, the character Tina Louise played on *Gilligan's Island*.

On one such tour, he amazed Jesus. Hadden left his reading glasses behind at WCI and without them could not read a newspaper. But when he was given a New England daily he seemed to have no problem with the small print. Jesus reasoned that since he was in his full Kristen persona and thus a decade younger, his brain must be processing his sight differently. It was a phenomenal incident, he believed.

On one of the four-day excursions, when Hadden was in his Kristen personality he expressed a schoolgirl crush for both Tarney and one of the FBI agents, Desiree Skinner. It didn't seem to make sense to Jesus when he first thought about it but he later guessed that the female side of Hadden yearned for both. With Tarney it was unrequited romance. And he wanted the FBI gal to be his sister.

The road trips had them looking for bodies in Connecticut and Pennsylvania, and in Massachusetts, on the northern tip of Cape Cod. At the Barnstable police station Jesus was given a polygraph test to see whether he was telling the truth about some of Hadden's claims. Most of the readings were inconclusive. Every time Hadden's name was mentioned his heart began beating rapidly. Jesus had to admit his fear. He was often afraid of Hadden Clark, he told the cops.

It was an eleven-hour drive to Cape Cod from WCI. It may have been cheaper to fly, but Jesus, who knew his limits, wasn't about to get on any commercial airline jet.

"All the Xanax in the world couldn't get me on a plane," he told them.

The first time they drove up it was the middle of January, two weeks after the Millennium celebration. A blizzard had rolled in from the Atlantic. They couldn't find anything in that sea of white, especially with the cadaver-sniffing dogs neutralized because of the frozen ground. They made another trip in April and this time cops flagged two areas on the Cape but wouldn't dig because there was too much press around. The spectre of a victim's skeleton being raised and caught by a telescopic lens from one of the media helicopters was too much to risk and worse yet, an empty hole could be even more embarrassing. Wait until the cameras were gone and then we will bring in the shovels, was the consensus.

So everyone was playing a waiting game, with Hadden and Jesus sent to the purgatory of Cellblock Four. Keeping Hadden and Jesus in their hospital suite had been costly for WCI. The penal staff was out-sourced in that part of the prison and the staff was forced to bring in part-time employees just for them. The warden, Jon Galley, had put the pair there at the request of Tarney and Garvey. Galley used to be a Montgomery County prison executive and was buddies with Garvey from way back. The added expenditures made him go over the prison's budget and so he was forced to move the odd couple closer to hell.

All this worried Jesus. If the FBI gave up on finding the bodies Hadden was just a nasty killer again, convicted of murdering a cute six-year-old girl and a beautiful twenty-three-year-old woman, burying them, and then trying to curry favor with the cops by telling them where the bodies could be found. Jesus' own, maybe last, attempt at freedom would be jeopardized. The scheme he had for getting rich by putting Hadden's memoirs up on a Website and charging ten dollars to read it, and then another ten to view the killer's artwork, would never happen. Hadden would be sent out into the general population to be executed by an inmate while the guards looked the other way, just like Jeffrey Dahmer. It would be prison justice—everyone inside had no use for someone who raped and murdered little girls. Who would Jesus be then? He would be the snitch who cozied up to a child molester and ratted him out, that's who. Certainly that is how it would be seen, no matter how he tried to explain it. He would wind up like Hadden if the cops forgot him.

These are perilous times. Jesus knows that he will need all of the wisdom he has gained in the Maryland prison system to survive the months ahead. Getting out, which seemed so close just a short time ago, now appears illusory, as far away as the moon.

1

THE STORY OF JESUS

The Delmarva peninsula south of New Jersey is flat and fertile. The land is named for Delaware, Maryland, and Virginia, as all have portions of their states within its boundaries. Delmarva's western border stops at the shore of the Chesapeake Bay and on the east, the Atlantic Ocean. On that coast some of the finest beaches in the Middle Atlantic region beckon those who worship the sun.

Near the waters of the Chesapeake live gentlemen farmers. It is they who own the prime properties that jut into deep, brackish harbors. The fingers of fertile brown earth come with patches of virgin forest still intact. These old-money nobles have migrated to Delmarva in great numbers. They use their thousand-acre farms for pheasant hunting during the fall months employing the dogs of locals to fetch their prey. The colorful plumed birds are more often stuffed than eaten. They serve as trophies to be placed on mantelpieces or displayed mounted on the old oak wall paneling of their libraries. Summers are reserved for sailing, with scores of graceful white yachts dotting the great Bay, the winged vessels seemingly as abundant as seagulls. It is a good life for those who are born so privileged.

The gulf between rich and poor in Delmarva is wide. The land owners of the region have long learned to be discreet. They keep their holdings hidden behind modestly worded markers that quietly herald the entrances to their estates. The poor here are equally invisible. They eke out livings mostly by working on chicken farms. Delmarva is the headquarters of the Perdue poultry empire and Perdue kills several million of these birds each year. The other choice for the impoverished is a life on the Bay, as oystermen or crabbers, or at waterside shelling the day's catch inside a canning factory. With decades of declining harvests, a job with a fishing crew on the Chesapeake is harsh and risky. The promise of a decent monetary reward at day's end is more than often broken.

Jesus grew up within ten miles of a Perdue plant. In 1960, a few weeks before his eighth birthday, he was hit hard in the head with a baseball bat by an adult. The accident required doctors to give him more than 200 stitches. After being discharged from the hospital he had seizures and severe headaches that lasted for weeks. His parents were poor and becoming more so—his father's heavy drinking had contributed to the family downfall. There were three other children to worry about and his parents were unable to afford the after-care program or the prescriptions the nurses said their son needed. Jesus quickly learned to improvise, dulling the pain by smoking locally grown marijuana and ingesting other, more powerful illegal substances before he was ten.

If he had the ability to learn in a structured environment it was never apparent. In the county schools he attended near the southern tip of Delmarva, he failed the fourth, sixth, seventh, and eighth grades. He dropped out in the ninth.

According to a report later filed by a psychotherapist, Lawrence Donner, PhD, of Baltimore, Jesus confessed that his mother had once engaged in a long, intimate relationship with him. She sought to continue her sexual hold on him when he reached his teens by forbidding him to date girls. To drive home the point, she once pointed a loaded gun at him when she discovered him with a young girl in the family home. When his mother threatened to kill Jesus with the weapon, he fled the premises, leaving the stunned date to deal with his pistol-wielding parent alone.

*   *   *

In his teens and without an education, Jesus tried working on a crew that paved highways. It was hard, unrewarding toil so Jesus decided to become an entrepreneur of sorts. As the cannabis he smoked grew more and more expensive he began his own pot farm in a rural area far away from the roads and the prying eyes of the local police department. Soon there were acres of hemp that was two feet high and he was shipping the weed into several nearby states. There are those who say that Jesus once offered a mellow smoke that was unmatched on the Eastern Seaboard.

Part of the profits were used to finance rock bands where he either sang, played guitar, or, sometimes, banged on the drums. The first group was a dressed-up, ten-piece show band called Soul Expressions. The next one was a more down-to-earth hard rock combo named Wrangler. Jesus performed at clubs in nearby Ocean City and as far away as Baltimore. He cut demo records, and dreamt of a day when he would perform in stadiums like The Rolling Stones and The Beatles. It was the beginning of a new decade, the 1970s, and he was young. Anything seemed possible.

By then, Jesus wasn't consuming much of his own crop. He had moved on to stronger substances. His favorite was homemade phencyclidine, or PCP, a hallucinogen made from parsley and a horse tranquilizer. He smoked or sometimes chewed the mixture. In those days Jesus didn't know the clinical term for the drug. He was first told it was called "angel dust," which he abbreviated by calling it simply "dust." The pharmaceutical firm Parke-Davis had once manufactured PCP, marketing it to humans, but had taken it off the market after determining that it was dangerous. Jesus loved the drug, though one wondered why. Following his long highs, a type of paranoia would set in. He would hallucinate and suffer panic attacks, which were followed by deep anxiety spells.

Though drugs were consuming him, Jesus found time to father both a boy and a girl by the time he was twenty-one. He lived with the mother of one of his children, and called her his wife.

On June 28, 1974, five months before his twenty-second birthday, he was entering the third week of a PCP high. It was hot that Friday in Salisbury, Maryland, with an on-and-off misting rain. Still, Jesus wasn't wearing shoes when he walked into a saddle shop at noon near the county trash dump with a .25 caliber handgun in one hand. He wore a Halloween mask, the plastic face of a cat. He kept the disguise on by pulling a woman's nylon stocking over both his face and the mask. The costume was accented with a green Army fatigue jacket, bell-bottom denim dungarees, and, despite the heat, orange gloves. With him was a pal he called Bruce who was not wearing anything to hide his appearance.

The owner of the shop, Edwin Franklin Rice, was said to owe him a lot of cash. Rice had purchased drugs from him on credit. Still, he did not appear overly concerned about the menacing appearance of the two men.

"What about my money?" Jesus asked the twenty-seven-year-old Rice.

"Sonny, I'll have it for you," Rice told Jesus, dismissing him by waving his hands in the air.

Jesus was so high on drugs he didn't notice at first that there was another witness present. The onlooker, a truck driver by the name of Paul E. Trivits, was at the side of the shop, trying to select a shirt to go with the pair of boots he had just purchased. He dove to the ground when the first shots were fired.

The trigger of the gun was pulled twice, with each bullet entering the chest of the store's proprietor. This caused Rice to fall face first onto the floor of the shop. As he fell, his eyeglasses came loose and fell off. A witness would testify that Jesus walked forward, stood over him, and began going through his pockets. When he found no money there, he began running his fingers down along the inside of the dying man's cowboy boots. When he finished searching the body he fired another round into Rice's back which lodged in a lung. Then, standing over him, the blood making his feet wet, Jesus fired another round from close range into the head, the bullet entering the brain. He next pointed the gun at Trivits, who was cowering on his knees behind the shirt rack.

Jesus thrust the gun up close, right into Trivits' face. The customer faced the man in the mask, trying to remain calm. The killer, though, seemed ready to explode at any moment.

"Be cool or I'll blow your goddamned head off."

He ejected a copper shell. The casing landed with a metallic clink at Trivits' feet.

"You're driving me out of here," he told him. The shopper, who a few minutes before had been lazily looking for a country-styled shirt, did not argue with him. With Jesus pushing the gun into the small of Trivits' back, the two men went outside where Trivits' Chevy El Camino pickup truck was parked in front of the store. Bruce was left behind to fend for himself.

"Where are we headed?" Trivits asked as they got into the cab.

"Out to the highway, then go towards Ocean City."

With Jesus in the passenger seat pointing the handgun towards him, Trivits drove back out Brickiln Road onto another street until he reached Route 50, the main highway that took tourist traffic into nearby Ocean City. It was one in the afternoon.

Before leaving the city limits, they stopped at a red light. Across the road was a local police car. Just in case the cop inside it looked their way, Jesus removed the Halloween mask and nylon stocking. Trivits got a good look at the man waving a gun in his direction. He decided to become bolder.

"You're making me nervous with that gun. You're going to have to put it away or get out," he said. The police car had turned around and was behind them now and Trivits thought he might pull them over. But at the next light, the black-and-white went around his truck, sped through the yellow warning signal, and pulled away. Trivits again tried to talk to the man with the gun.

"Your problems are your problems. I've got problems of my own and I don't want your problems to be mine," he told Jesus.

"I have no problem. I've just taken care of my problem," Jesus responded.

"Well, I still have plenty of problems," Trivits said. "Why don't you go your way and I'll go my way? I didn't see nothing and I don't know nothing."

Jesus surprised Trivits by taking him up on his offer.

"Thank you, brother," he told Trivits and offered him his hand. Trivits shook it as if the two were departing friends.

"I'm going to get out right here at the corner."

Trivits was in the passing lane but was so happy his high-on-drugs passenger wanted to leave his truck that he swerved through two lanes of traffic just to get to the curb. The El Camino stopped directly in front of a Perdue chicken plant and Jesus hopped out. Trivits then turned the vehicle around and sped towards the nearest police station.

Back at the saddlery shop, Rice's sister had shown up, seen her brother's body, and called the police. The county coroner arrived first. He later described discovering Rice as lying face down, his head turned sideways. He had crushed his eyeglasses when he fell on them. His left arm was tucked under him and his right hand was turned palm up. There were puddles of blood around his neck and head with holes visible in the back of the shirt that the coroner described as "the size of silver dollars." Rice's eyes were open and when the pulse was checked and the fingers squeezed, with no rush of blood forthcoming, he was pronounced dead.

When Trivits told the police how he had just spent his lunch hour, the cops pulled out 100 mug shots and scattered them on a desk, asking him if one of them was his abductor. Trivits looked through the selection and found no matches. He described the murderer for them, noting to the cops that there was an angry red pimple on the side of the killer's face. He was then presented with another selection, but this time was given just fifty photos to choose from. On the twenty-ninth photo, he identified the face of Jesus as the man who had shot and killed the saddlery shop owner, and then kidnapped him at gunpoint.

"That's your boy. That's the guy," Trivits said. The image looked a lot like a sketch that a police artist had just drawn of the killer.

The local cops knew the suspect and they knew where to find him. They arrested Jesus just after four o'clock the next day at a Penguin Drive apartment in Ocean City, Maryland. With him was his common-law wife and their infant son. Jesus was charged with murder and kidnapping. After patting down his wife, the cops charged her with drug possession.

During his first interrogation, Jesus said he had tossed the murder weapon into the ocean. In November at trial, Jesus had a different spin on the shooting entirely. He was innocent, his public defender told the court in an opening statement. The prosecution's case was one of identity and they were mistaken. It was his friend Bruce who had shot Edwin Rice. Jesus had sold Bruce the handgun in exchange for drugs, he admitted, but it was Bruce who'd killed the store owner. Jesus had been somewhere in the area, a little high on PCP perhaps, but not in the shop when Rice was killed. His pal Bruce had dropped him off at a gas station, then driven off to murder the owner of the saddlery shop, was the claim. He had hitchhiked to Ocean City later that afternoon for a weekend at the beach. One of his chief contentions was that the mug shots taken after his arrest showed no evidence of any red pimple on the face.

That was his story. He stuck to it throughout the trial.

The prosecution retaliated by attempting to make the murder sound even more sinister. They implied that the motivation for Rice's murder was that Jesus and Bruce believed he was an undercover police agent in the narcotics division of the Maryland State Patrol by the name of George Spicer. Thus, they were able to paint Jesus as a cop killer throughout the trial rather than as a drug dealer who had murdered a client because he fell behind on a drug debt.

"He's our man. He's Spicer. And he's going to be dead," a witness testified he heard Jesus say before the murder.

At the trial, Jesus took the stand in his own defense. The move was a mistake. His testimony contained so much crime jargon that jurors might be forgiven if they began to roll their eyes and convict him even before the closing arguments were given.

"What do you mean by 'split'?"

"I mean I bucked. I left. You know? All I could do, you know. He was flipping me out. I mean, I was flipped out, you know. As far as the drugs, he had given me something, you know—and you know, kept giving me something and I just couldn't handle it, you know."

"Now you say you rode around and he was trying to rap you into doing something. What does 'rap you into doing something' means?"

"Well, like previously to the—couple of weeks ago we had been smoking dust . . . ?"

"Dust is PCP?"

"It's parsley—some kind of drug. He got me into smoking it. I was smoking it pretty heavy."

"Were you smoking or chewing dust that day?"

"Yes, I was."

After Jesus answered the public defender's questions, the prosecution used its opportunity to destroy him. Jesus didn't stand a chance. He looked silly trying to spar with the prosecutor.

"Have you ever been convicted of any violation of the criminal law when you were represented by an attorney or had willingly waived the right to be represented by an attorney?"

"You mean . . . sentenced?"

"Have you ever been convicted of any crime when you were represented by an attorney or had willingly and effectively waived your right to be represented by an attorney?"

"I don't more or less understand you. Sorry."

"Have you ever been convicted of a crime before?"

"Convicted? Do you mean sentenced?"

"I mean convicted. Have you ever been found guilty?"

"Marijuana."

"How long have you been using drugs?"

"Since I was eight. If you want to term marijuana drugs."

Though Jesus took the stand in his own behalf, and pled not guilty to four different charges, his entire trial took less than one day. The jury was even briefer, adjourning to deliberate at 4:06 and returning a guilty verdict on all counts at 4:20, giving everyone plenty of time to be home for the early news. At the time it was said to have been the shortest murder trial in modern Maryland history. At his sentencing on November 27, 1974, the prosecutor, Fulton Jeffers, continued to press the point that Jesus was a cop killer, even though Jesus had more than likely shot an active drug user who wasn't paying his bills. Jeffers laid it on thick.

We have before us a case of deliberate, premeditated, malicious killing of a person who was believed to be a state trooper. This is a case which shocks me. It is a serious, horrendous offense. Not only was it an effort to kill an undercover state trooper who was investigating drugs, but it was a double tragedy through the error in identification in which an innocent third person was killed.

Then we have the kidnapping, completely unrelated to the murder, of an innocent person who just happened to be at that location, underscoring this tragic event. I think this justifies the maximum sentence.

Jesus was asked by the judge, Richard Pollitt, if he had anything to say for himself. He did.

"I'm not guilty of these crimes. I hope that I'm the only person left that is sentenced for something he didn't do. That's it."

The judge followed the statement by making a long speech about the tragedy of what happens to young people when they become influenced by drugs. He said people who use and deal hallucinatory drugs belong in prison.

He gave Jesus life for the murder of Edwin Rice. On the kidnapping charge he added a fifteen-year term, to be served consecutively, after the life sentence. There was also a ten-year sentence for carrying a handgun in the commission of a felony, but that was concurrent, with the time allowed to run side-by-side with the life sentence. The fourth charge, carrying a gun without a permit, was ignored by the judge. Under the laws of the time, Jesus was to have been eligible for parole in fifteen years, or the summer of

1989. A few months later, Jesus's friend Bruce received a thirty-year sentence after pleading guilty to second-degree murder.

Jesus soon learned to be an excellent jailhouse lawyer. By the time his appeal on the murder and kidnapping was heard he had come up with six points of contention that he said warranted a new trial. He reiterated his public defender's court argument that he should have been allowed to sit in the courtroom between two plainclothes detectives as part of the identification process. Jesus also contended that the court had allowed repetitive testimony in its rebuttal; that it allowed a statement into evidence that he had given before he received his Miranda warning; and that a state trooper was allowed to testify as a drug expert even though he wasn't. The other two points of appeal were that the evidence was insufficient to go to trial and that the court had received improper evidence when a motion was made for a new trial.

The appeals were quickly rejected. A state trooper said Jesus did not appear to be high when he gave them a statement and it was ruled that since it was not objected to at the time he gave it in court, it was now too late to do so. None of this stopped Jesus. He continued to appeal, coming up with new reasons the courts should grant him a new trial. One was that a juror had worked at Montgomery Ward with Edwin Rice and was virtually a friend. Those facts should have been considered when they were choosing the jury, Jesus said. He again revisited Trivits' statement to the police that his abductor had a big pimple on his face when, in fact, the mug shots showed none. In Jesus's mind, he had been convicted simply because he was involved in drugs and the police wanted him locked up. In 1977, his mother wrote a letter to an appeals court judge, echoing those thoughts, and asking for a new trial.

I know my son did not commit murder. He was deeply involved with a dope ring and was framed to get him off the streets. At the same time my son was arrested, the son of a high ranking city police official and the son of a very prominent lawyer were involved with the same ring.

A judge told me that he had never in his life witnessed a murder trial that took less than four hours, including the selection of the jury. At the trial, the jury was not questioned or interviewed.

My son has been in the penitentiary four years. He is sick and needs help from the head injury he received when he was eight.

My husband and myself need our son very much. He has kicked his dope habit and can make a living with his music.

His mother went on to list other irregularities that occurred in the trial and finished by begging the judge for a personal meeting. She didn't get it. And though Jesus continued to seek new lines of appeal, they were always quickly rejected.

In 1989, after fifteen years of serving time in several Maryland prisons, Jesus became eligible for parole for the first time. It had been a difficult period. According to prison records, he was sexually assaulted on the first day inside prison and was placed in solitary confinement at his own request. After venturing out again into the general population Jesus appears to have adjusted to life behind bars. He became a prison artist and eventually his paintings were selected to be exhibited at the NAACP's national headquarters in Baltimore.

He used this talent to build a cottage industry inside the walls by becoming its resident tattoo technician. His price was a pack of cigarettes. He would scrape the black rubber off an old boot, melt it into goo, and jab the molten mess into skin with the stiff wire gleaned from a guitar.

There were few infractions on his record and by 1989 he had earned 874 days of good conduct time by doing charitable work like reading books into a microphone that were being taped for the blind.

Jesus was ready for the parole board. He had documents showing he had earned his high school diploma in prison, learned several trades, and had a job offer in writing from a paving contractor that would pay him seven dollars an hour. He also had a permanent place to live upon release. The residence was offered by Josephine Ball, a psychiatric clinical nurse he had met during his years inside. Ms. Ball claimed to be his fiancée and offered her own letter in support of his parole, describing Jesus as a changed man.

> I have observed him mature into a personable, intelligent man with good judgment and insight. I have had the opportunity and great pleasure to look at him objectively, when I worked as a nurse, and personally, when I fell in love with him. We are planning to marry as soon as he's free. He has a lot of support from me and my family. He has agreed to see a therapist who will assist him with community adjustment. He is a remarkable man who deserves a chance.

In spite of these pleas and the outstanding record he had compiled in prison, Jesus was not released. There are three main criteria most parole boards look at when considering to let a man walk free. The first is the severity of the crime itself. The second is the prison record. And the third is the remorse expressed by the prisoner during the interview with parole board members. It was the first indelible mark, made by the crime itself, that kept him from being allowed back on the streets.

After continuing to be denied parole, Jesus grew desperate. When the former football player and television celebrity, O. J. Simpson, was accused of murder, Jesus watched the trial unfold from his cell and grew to admire Simpson's defense team. Soon he was firing off long letters to Robert Shapiro, Johnnie Cochran, and one of the trial's broadcast commentators, lawyer Gerry Spence. He asked them to help him gain a writ of habeas corpus. Shapiro wrote back saying he was committed to the Simpson trial for its duration, and Cochran wrote essentially the same letter. Only Spence seemed to offer encouragement.

"One of the things that make me feel badly is that is impossible for us to help everybody," Spence wrote. "Sometimes I feel guilty about that. I want you to know that if we could help you we would, but I can't take your case. I also want you to know how complimented I am that you cared enough to contact us. My wishes go out to you for good success in your endeavor to get justice. It's hard. Don't give up."

Jesus took Gerry Spence's advice to heart, though his new, self-composed legal briefs became increasingly shrill, with his protestations of innocence in the petitions typed in sentences that used only capital letters. His relationship with the prison nurse, Josephine Ball, ended, but one had to be amazed by Jesus's romantic skills from behind bars. By 1994, there was a new love, a woman named Jackie whom his son introduced to him over the phone. At the end of the year, they married in prison, though their love remained unconsummated. His wife became his paralegal researcher, gathering documents for new appeals.

By now he was citing declining health as one reason for his release. A 1997 petition that was denied claimed he had experienced, among other ailments: "A change in mental status, myoclonus of the upper and lower extremities . . . a history of seizures, a history of hemochromatosis, and a lipoma in the pineal region of the brain."

He continued to assert his innocence. In one letter to the

Maryland Court of Special Appeals he summarized the turn of events that had locked him away for more than two decades.

> They wanted me off the streets, they wanted my connections and I would not give them what they wanted because I knew those people would go after my family and do them great harm. I had two small children, their mothers, and my own mother and father to think about. I could not let anything happen to them.
>
> I have been to hell and back again the past twenty-three years, and I have made great changes in my life all for the better. I have a new wife that I would like to spend time with outside of these walls. I am not a well man these days. I am not a threat to anyone. All I want is a chance to start my life over again and help young adults to learn that drugs are not something that they should get involved in, and if they are involved that there is help for them if they need it.
>
> I have paid dearly with my life for something I did not do, please help me!

The emotional appeals were increasingly ignored with terse, one-word denials. There was no longer any light at the end of the tunnel for Jesus. Part of this was due to Maryland's new governor, Parris Glendening. The new chief executive for the state was a Democrat who believed in the platforms of the liberal Democratic Party, except for one. He was exceedingly tough on crime and was determined never to parole any prisoner who had been convicted of a serious offense.

"Do not even recommend, nor send to my desk, any request for parole for murderers and rapists," he publicly told the state's parole commission in September of 1995. According to the new chief state executive, and his assistant attorney general, Richard Rosenblatt, who often spoke for him, "Life means life, and if you are sentenced to life, you are going to serve substantial time in incarceration."

The edict did not go unnoticed by the nearly 2,000 men serving such terms in Maryland. Up until Governor Glendening began living in the executive mansion, the average time served by a lifer had been twenty-two years. These prisoners began to believe the new governor would happily extend their time to infinity. Four prison guards at the Jessup Correctional Institution were quickly attacked by inmates. The governor's new policy was cited as the reason for the eruption.

"You had better get ready for more of that if you're going to put a lot of offenders in and then tell them: 'You are never going to get out until you are ready to die,' " said David Wright of the Prison Rights Information System in a press conference.

Glendening responded by building the state's first "Supermax" controlled confinement facility in Baltimore. Conservative columnist George Will wrote a column that praised the forbidding structure. The new prison housed 1300, mostly lifers and prisoners considered too violent to be housed in other Maryland prisons. Here they would spend twenty-three hours a day in solitary confinement for years. Radios and television sets, the one narcotic that could numb their loneliness, took months and sometimes years to be earned.

Jesus's illnesses and relatively clean record spared him from Baltimore's Supermax. Instead he was sent to another newly built prison, Roxbury Correctional Institute, just below the Catoctin Mountain Range near Hagerstown. Over the years, he had served time in nearly every correctional institution in Maryland. The state's policy for inmates serving long sentences was to keep moving them around. The theory held that such men should not be allowed time to bond with their guards, who then might provide them with contraband or look the other way if they made an escape

attempt. The new prison was 200 miles west from Delmarva, which made it difficult for his new wife and children
to visit as often as they might like. Both of his parents were
long deceased and now Jesus thought that it might only be
when he was ready to join his mother and father in death
that the Department of Corrections would finally release
him.

Jesus got more bad news during November of 1999. He
was to be moved yet again, this time to Cumberland, Maryland, where his home would be inside the state's newly
completed Western Correctional Institution. This expanded
the distance of the trip for his family to more than 300
miles each way, but it was easy freeway driving, the state
of Maryland told Jackie and the other inmates' families
when they complained.

Jesus was put in leg irons and handcuffs for the transfer.
Five other men went with him, and all were chained together until they got inside the vehicle that would take them
there. One of them appeared to be genuinely insane, a real
zap-out. The crazed prisoner grinned at Jesus throughout
the trip, and continued to stare steadily at him as they were
driven west through carved-from-dynamic mountain passes.

"I know who you are, you're Jesus Christ," Hadden
Clark said as they sped down the interstate.

Yeah, whatever, Jesus thought. He kept his mouth shut
and tried to think of other topics, but Hadden stuck to the
subject.

"Please swear on the Bible that you're him," he asked
Jesus. Hadden had a paperback edition of the Good Book
with him and waved it his way. Jesus didn't bite.

They got to WCI, were processed, and Jesus was walked
to a cell. Sitting on the bunk, patiently waiting for him, was
Hadden Clark. Oh God, Jesus thought, I don't need this.
Hadden Clark continued to babble.

"I knew you would come. I know who you are."

Hadden said that God had visited him in his cell back in Hagerstown and told him he would soon be sending his only son in human form to live with him. Jesus ignored it all until Hadden began telling him the details of how he had cut six-year-old Michele Dorr's throat and where he had buried her. He also told Jesus he had buried other bodies and had collected pieces of jewelry from women he killed up in New England. The trinkets were in a bucket on the property of his grandfather, he claimed. Jesus called Jackie, who called the local police. They called the FBI and soon they were digging up little Michele's body and finally having a funeral, nearly fourteen years after Hadden had murdered her with a very large and very long butcher knife.

Jesus was frank with Hadden from the start. "You know, someday I might have to testify against you in court," he told him.

If that were to happen, that will be the Lord's will, Hadden said. He continued to be forthcoming with details about his murders. Jesus began to believe that this time, the way the wind was blowing, maybe this crazy Hadden Clark would be the one who would finally punch his ticket to freedom.

2

A GOOD FAMILY GOES BAD

Silas Skidmore Clark loved a good fight. He was the star running back and team leader of the Wesleyan University Crimson football eleven in his senior year, 1914, and looked forward to butting helmets with the gridiron powers of the day. Opponents like Yale and Columbia may have been bigger schools but little Wesleyan of Middletown, Connecticut, always gave a good account of itself with young Clark leading the charge.

College football in the early years of the twentieth century was far more dangerous than today. An article in *The New York Times* that October noted fourteen deaths on the nation's playing fields with the season yet to reach its midway point. It was due to the lack of sophisticated protective gear. Kicks to the head were common and the medical profession was unable to deal with head traumas the way it does today. Silas Clark himself suffered a concussion that year, which effectively ended his playing days well before Wesleyan completed its nine-game schedule.

Silas was popular, a member of the athletic fraternity, Delta Kappa Epsilon. DKE would one day spawn two Presidents, Gerald Ford and George Bush. Si Clark was already a Republican and there was no doubt in anyone's mind that he was going to be a lawyer, like his father, Frederick. The Clark patriarch already had law offices in two cities in the state of New York, Mount Vernon and White Plains, and had just run for mayor of Mount Vernon, losing by a small margin. As a consolation prize he had been named corporation counsel for the city. It was expected that Silas would join his father just as soon as he was out of school and had a few years of legal seasoning.

Silas entered New York University law school in 1915 but quickly surprised his family by delaying his legal education for a far more dangerous adventure. In 1916 he enlisted with the U.S. Army's Seventh Regiment, specifically to serve under his idol, General John J. "Black Jack" Pershing. The promised hell-raising experience seemed too exciting to miss. Pershing was down on the Mexican border, assembling an armed group of 10,000 men to go south into the state of Chihuahua and hunt down Francisco "Pancho" Villa, the revolutionary and bandit adored by the country's peasants. Villa's army had recently crossed the line by raiding Columbus, New Mexico, and reportedly killing eighteen U.S. civilians.

What redblooded young man could resist the chance to battle sombrero-wearing bandits? How heroic it seemed, to ride on horseback into an enemy stronghold alongside a famous military hero! Pershing was already legendary for capturing Geronimo and storming San Juan Hill with Teddy Roosevelt. This was irresistible for someone like Si Clark. The Mexican president, Venustiano Carranza, had just broken ties with Villa and was encouraging President Woodrow Wilson to either capture or kill his former ally in northern Mexico. Wilson believed that the military expedition would serve as a toughening exercise for American troops. The U.S. leader had by now determined that America's entrance into the European conflict, where most of the countries were already at war, was inevitable.

Pershing's army failed to capture Villa in 1916. The legendary guerrilla leader holed up in a cave part of that year, leaving his cavalry, *Los Dorados*, to do battle in his name. Pershing and his men, including twenty-three-year-old Lieutenant Si Clark, did advance some 350 miles into Mexico. They fought several battles, but never killed more than forty men in Villa's cavalry at any one time.

He returned to New York. But in May of 1917, a few days after graduating from law school, Silas left to fight again. This time there was a real war. President Wilson said "the world must be made safe for democracy." Once more Si linked up with Pershing. He was with him when the first American troops landed in France that June. Pershing rushed his American Expeditionary Forces to the Chateau Thierry area to help stem the German offensive. The ensuing hand-to-hand struggle, with Si Clark on the winning side, was one of the turning points of the first World War.

As an infantry lieutenant, Silas fought in several bayonet battles. He was on the front lines in Flanders and Saint-Mihiel—almost forgotten names in the twenty-first century—but as hallowed in that time as Iwo Jima or the Invasion of Normandy would be twenty-five years later.

Silas came back to his hometown of White Plains in New York's Westchester County in March of 1919, but wasn't yet ready to begin practicing law. Instead, he decompressed from the two conflicts by romancing a tall, blue-eyed young woman he met on a blind date. Edith Helene Hadden was just over six feet—an inch higher than he was. The pair's first outing was to a Rye, New York, beach for a moonlit swim. Si Clark knew what he wanted and he acted fast. Within months he had an engagement ring on the willowy blonde's finger. A formal wedding at the Hitchcock Memorial Presbyterian Church in Scarsdale took place the next June.

His bride had the requisite pedigree. She was a founder of Sigma Kappa, a perfect match for a DKE. Silas Clark could trace his lineage all the way back to the voyage of the *Mayflower* but Edith Hadden was no slouch in the ancestry department. She was a direct descendant of John Alvord, one of the heroes of the American Revolution.

Edith Hadden was a professional dancer in her youth, attending the Chalif School of Dance in New York where she was a featured ballerina between 1916 and 1918 at Carnegie Hall. After marrying Si Clark, she opened a children's dance studio in her parents' home in Scarsdale. Even there, her husband's World War I heroism seemed very much on her mind.

"Mother played my accompaniments," she told a local newspaper years later. "I organized a troupe of child performers which put on recitals for patriotic organizations. We had a program called 'Dances of the Allied Nations' which featured the Sailor's Hornpipe, the Highland Fling, an Irish Jig, the Tarantella, and an English Maypole number."

Silas Clark began practicing law in 1920. He spent two years with the New York Title Insurance Company and then clerked for a New York State Supreme Court Justice, Frederick Close. He joined his father at the family law firm in 1923.

During the 1920s, Si and Edith had three children, all boys. The first was named Raymond Shelton Clark; the second, Theodore Willes Clark; and the youngest, born in 1929, was baptized Hadden. Unlike his two brothers, the third son received no middle name.

When America's entry into the second great war of the century began in December of 1941, Si Clark was eager to send his boys into battle. He was the commander of a Westchester County American Legion post and during World War II chaired the local draft board, where he hosted Godspeed parties, going-away celebrations for local youths headed to the front. Raymond and Ted both entered the war as officers, becoming pilots in the branch of the service then known as the Army Air Force. Raymond, who was called Shelly, flew a C-46 in the European Theater of Operations. Young Hadden was a bit different. Aided by his father, he lied about his age to get into the war. He was sixteen when he was shipped off to China as a private, spending most of his time in Shanghai. Friends thought it somewhat unusual that he stayed on until late 1946 in Asia, long after the war was over. Hadden could have returned home much earlier.

In 1946, Silas Clark was elected Mayor of White Plains on the Republican ticket. The victory partially atoned for the defeat of his father, Frederick, who had lost in his run for the same office in nearby Mount Vernon. Si Clark was a strong office-holder, responsible for enticing the first Macy's department store to town, eliminating many of White Plains' slums, and redeeming some of the city's unsavory reputation.

In a long, positive profile of him in 1947, *The New York Times* described White Plains as a city with "legalistic tangles by notables involved in ugly murders and lively peccadillos." Silas was called a "foe of civic lethargy" by the newspaper and was described as working seven-day weeks even though the salary was a mere $2500 a year.

According to the *Times*, Silas Clark was "regarded as resembling a combined La Guardia and Moses, minus the fire of Fiorello and Robert, but not their stamina."

Continuing his positive assessment, the *Times* reporter wrote, "he has gained the reputation as a ubiquitous and inexhaustible mayor with a philosophical purpose. Beyond the borders of his home he is becoming known as an innovator of systems for promoting neighborliness, civic beauty, traffic and parking controls, and a modern and rapidly growing shopping area."

Edith Clark seemed happy in her role as first lady of White Plains, delighted to motor around town in a big Buick with its official license plate that read WP1. From their large home on Ridgeway Circle she chaired meetings of the DAR and hosted bridge evenings for wives of city leaders.

In 1950, just after his term as Mayor expired, Silas and Edith decided to retire and leave White Plains forever. During the oversubscribed going-away dinner, the townspeople gave them a plaque and a Rembrandt brand television set following testimonials that went on for hours.

Silas Clark was just fifty-seven, a bit young to be walking away from a successful legal practice. His political career might have eventually gone all the way to the governor's mansion. But Silas and Edith were grandparents by now. It was time to move on.

Silas had fallen in love with an isolated estate on seven-and-a-half acres of land in Massachusetts. He had vacationed in Truro, on the north forearm of Cape Cod, all his life, and the property was in nearby Wellfleet. It was just off Pamet Point Road and located on a high bluff. Silas had become an active horticulturist, and the house had once been owned by a florist. There were already terraced gardens and rare plants. Best of all, the land was surrounded by several hundred acres of pine woods that had been mandated as protected park land by the federal government. The Clarks would be able to stay secluded forever.

Their children were leaving White Plains to seek their own destinies. Shelly had relocated to Arizona and only Ted was nearby, in Connecticut. Hadden, in the best Clark military tradition, was off to war again. This time he was fighting in Korea, even though he was now married and had a son.

Hadden's bride, Flavia Ann Scranton, was a Connecticut Yankee from Meriden, just north of New Haven. Her wedding dress had been made from the silk of a parachute her husband had picked up in the Pacific. Friends often called her Flivver, a moniker given to her when she spent summers as a counselor at Camp Ohuivo in Oxford, Maine, though her closest friends sometimes shortened it to Fliv.

Flavia's lineage rivaled her husband's. Her father, Maynard Bailey Scranton, a piano tuner, and her mother, Flavia Harvest Bloxham, could also trace their descendants back to the seventeenth century and claimed several statesmen among their forebears. She had been given an upper-crust, single-sex education that began at the Northfield Seminary School for Young Ladies in Massachusetts followed by Wells College, a women's school on the banks of Cayuga

Lake in upstate New York. By now, her husband had more diplomas than the number of wars he had fought in. He had already earned a degree in languages at Vermont's historic Middlebury College, followed by an MBA, and finally, a PhD in chemistry at the prestigious Rensselaer Polytechnic Institute in Troy, New York. As the youngest of Silas Clark's three sons, Hadden was by far the most promising, though like many brilliant men he quickly grew impatient for the rewards and recognition he felt due him in the workplace.

Hadden and his outgoing, talkative, redheaded bride produced four children in the 1950s in spite of the Korean War, the college studies, and moving from town to town like overeducated gypsies. Their eldest was born in October of 1950. He was baptized Bradfield Hadden—the first name was the same as Flavia's older brother. A year later there was a second son they christened Hadden Irving. Hadden's middle name was one that had been given to his grandmother's father and carried with it much tradition and pride. Since there were now three Haddens in the family, one could easily assume there might have been a fourth; common sense prevailed with Flavia insisting on Geoffrey Scranton. He was born in April of 1955. There was a girl, too, Alison, born in 1959.

It was far from an easy life for the Clark children, despite the elder Hadden's genius and earning power. He saw to that by forcing Flavia and the four children to move constantly, often twice a year. Flavia's husband was never satisfied with his employers. He was furious when he improved the cling in plastic wrap for for a major petroleum company and then made several advances in fire-retardant carpeting for Celanese, only to find out there would be no royalties. His contracts had a clause saying he was "work for hire" and so he was out in the cold for the big money.

Flavia Clark seemed to give birth to a new baby in each city they lived in. Bradfield Hadden was born in Southbury,

Connecticut. Hadden Irving entered the world in Troy, while his father was writing his PhD thesis at Rensselaer. She delivered Geoffrey Scranton in Stamford, Connecticut, and Alison in Warren Township, New Jersey. There were other towns in between—New Canaan, Darien, and Flavia's hometown of Meriden, all posh Connecticut bedroom communities. The Clark elder always seemed to believe there was greener grass over the next ridge. Warren Township, in Somerset County's Watchung Hills, and within commuting distance of New York City, was the longest the Clarks would live in any one place, and that stay was just over five years.

By the time they moved to Warren, Flavia had begun to suspect there might be something wrong with her children. Her eldest son Brad had become as mean as a rattlesnake and he angered easily. He began stealing to buy drugs before he reached his teens and once shot out the windows of a neighbor's car just for the fun of it. Despite this, an extroverted Flavia continued to masquerade as the model mother who busied herself in the PTA and the Boy Scouts. In private she would drink glass after glass of hard liquor. Her excuse was that she needed the alcohol to help her fall asleep.

"Flivver was always a little hyper to say the least," said Lydia LaVine, a contemporary of Flavia's, who lived down the street from Flavia and Hadden's two-story, traditional colonial home in Warren, which backed into woods.

If Brad was a handful, Hadden seemed to have been born evil. He liked to hurt people, striking out physically when things didn't go his way. The other children in Warren began to run in the opposite direction when young Hadden showed up. Tony Quaglia, who with his wife would sometimes entertain the Clarks at neighborhood dinner parties, had no problem recalling Hadden Clark's childhood behavior.

"He would get angry and go into a corner and pout all

the time. The kids didn't want to play with him," Quaglia said.

His younger brother, Geoff, remembered that the young Hadden was unable to discern right from wrong. Geoff later claimed that several scars on his body were from injuries inflicted by his brother. Several were caused when the two of them were learning to ride bicycles without using their hands. Suddenly Hadden gripped his handlebars and deliberately swerved into him. Geoff crashed to the ground headfirst. When his brother asked for help, Hadden turned and rode away leaving his brother bleeding profusely and lying on the sidewalk. Arriving home he reported the accident to his mother, but the first words out of his mouth seemed inappropriate for the occasion.

"There's been an accident," he said, "but don't worry, the bike's okay."

"My brother's sense of reality was always a little askew," Geoff recalled.

Hadden's mother began to blame his strange behavior on a bad forceps delivery which she said had given him a head injury. She claimed that by the time other children had progressed to reading and writing he was still unable to talk in sentences. He couldn't walk very well either, at first tripping on carpets because the patterns confused his brain. His mother's remedy was to put padded tape around his head to prevent concussions. The larger, tougher kids in Warren who weren't afraid of him, taunted him cruelly. For these boys, Hadden Clark was the neighborhood freak. Hadden's usual mode of revenge was to kidnap their family pets. Days later, the cat or dog would be placed bloodied and dead on the owner's front porch.

"Sometimes, he just couldn't control himself," said Toni Munzipapo, a former neighborhood friend. "If something didn't go his way, he'd get very upset. He angered easily and you could hear him yelling. The other kids would walk away and wait for him to calm down."

Munzipapo also remembered the entire Clark family as being a bit strange. Like others, she started to avoid them.

Hadden found some relief in the Baptist church on Sundays. "God loves everyone," the pastor preached. "Love him and he'll love you right back. Do something wrong and you can ask for forgiveness. If you mean it, everything will be all right. Now let's sing a hymn." And Hadden would sing away at the top of his lungs.

Flavia brought her son to Yale University's Child Study Center when he was four. A doctor told her that Hadden had cerebral palsy and perhaps some mild brain damage. His father began to call his son "the retard." Years later, Hadden would tell a psychiatrist that he once thought "retard" was part of his actual name.

Both Brad and young Hadden were trouble on two feet. Drunken fighting between Flavia and her husband didn't help the family's private agonies. Much of it was played out in front of the children, beginning with arguments and often advancing to a bout of mutual slapping and punching until one of them became injured.

Their father taught Brad how to shoot and gut deer and bring down game birds on the fly, and capture animals alive by using traps. Young Hadden, who wasn't allowed on the hunting trips, took to the trapping lessons and soon had a zoo that included squirrels, raccoons, opossums—even a skunk. The menagerie had a high mortality rate. Hadden killed and dissected most of them within a month. One animal he did keep around for a while was a raccoon that had been hit by a car. He taught it to sit on top of his head while he rode his bicycle, offering the neighbors a strange sight as he pedaled through the streets with the live Davey Crockett coonskin hat clinging to his neck and scalp.

Flavia kept shuttling her problem son back and forth between the private Jiminy Cricket Academy and a public elementary school, with twice-a-week visits to mental

health clinics squeezed in. In elementary school he failed
two grades. By now, the younger Clark children, Geoff and
Alison, had become jealous of the amount of attention Hadden was getting. Alison reacted by running away, and was
placed in a psychiatric hospital for months. Years later, as
an adult, she was asked to talk about her early life as a
member of the Clark household. She began with this bitter
answer:

"I never had a family."

Hadden's care was expensive and the Clarks felt it fi-
nancially. The private schools and therapists became a burden though their family income was among the highest in
Warren. By now Hadden's father, in addition to his alcoholism, was diagnosed as manic-depressive. He controlled
the disease with lithium.

The elder Hadden was either unable or unwilling to
show a normal degree of empathy towards his troubled
sons. A social worker wrote this report when Hadden was
fifteen:

> His father is a chemist with a Ph.D. degree, and his
> mother is a college graduate. As part of Hadden's record
> is a detailed report of his life written by his father. It
> reads like a scientific treatise and is objective and in-
> formative, but one is impressed with the lack of any
> emotional feeling. His observations and facts are re-
> corded as one would record the results of an experiment
> with chemicals.

Hadden, as the next to be born after Brad, was expected to
be a girl. Certainly, his mother dressed him that way from
the start—in pink dresses and frilly underwear—until he
began attending elementary school. The taste for female
garments was implanted by then. And his father was already alternating the "retard" nickname with the name he
had first chosen for his second born—Kristen. Hadden had

disappointed him by being a boy when he'd expected a girl.

During his teens Hadden's fondness for female attire came out in the open. After mowing the lawn for a neighbor he was found in her bedroom wearing a nightgown. Both Flavia and Alison began to notice that their own lingerie were missing. Hadden also stole his sister's dolls. He was eventually discovered by both of his parents wearing adult women's clothing. Hadden wasn't a bit embarrassed. "You're not going to change me, so leave me alone," he told them.

Weeks later Hadden was involved in a Peeping Tom incident that resulted in a police charge. When Flavia asked a psychiatrist what to do about it, she was warned not to challenge the boy. He would grow out of it, she was told. Flavia heeded the therapist's advice.

"When you're paying someone a lot of dollars, you listen," she said.

His father tried to change him. With beatings. He liked to use a belt on his son when he emerged vulnerable and naked from the bathtub. The corporal punishment was useless and failed to change Hadden's behavior.

Hadden's father was a man wearing a mask, his namesake would later say. The respectable corporate chemist was his public face. A tortured, unbalanced alcoholic was the one he wore in private. According to Hadden, he came home one afternoon and found his father alone in the house with a young neighborhood girl who had once been Hadden's babysitter. The two were copulating on a sofa, and they barely looked up when he discovered them. His father told him to keep his mouth shut about it and he did.

Hadden has claimed to have murdered his first victim, a boy, when he was fourteen. He now says his father knew about it and helped to cover up the crime.

As he neared the end of his adolescence Hadden still had no social skills, nor any sense of politeness. Flavia once remembered his teenaged behavior with a sense of frustration. "He would want to get to the sink and you'd be standing there already and so you'd get an 'Excuse me' and a body block both at the same time," she recalled.

On one occasion Hadden told Flavia that his brother had sexually assaulted him in a treehouse. After Brad denied it, Flavia ignored the allegation.

Yet Hadden was not mentally deficient, according to several intelligence tests he was given. He always scored as at least borderline average or in the low average range. While that was not enough to get him into a major university, it certainly didn't doom him to a life of dependency. And while he often acted like a small child emotionally, lashing out when he was publicly criticized, he could appear to be a genius when it came to chess, a game that required thinking and concentration.

One place where Hadden found a degree of normalcy in his troubled life was on his grandfather's retirement estate on Cape Cod. He spent part of each summer there as a boy, treated with affection by Silas and Edith Clark. Here there was peace, without the tension created by his mother and father's alcohol-fueled fights. He learned to fish from shore on rocky points of land. He was told that the biggest fish were caught when there were major thunderstorms containing lightning—the noise and the flashes woke them up. The tale may have been true. Hadden once reeled in a striped bass weighing fifty-seven pounds while surf fishing in a driving nor'easter, one of the proudest moments of his life.

Nobody called him a retard on Cape Cod. Hadden thought of Silas and Edith's home as a special place, a spot that came as close to heaven as he would ever find on earth. His brother agreed.

"The days we spent there were the most wonderful time of Hadden's life," Geoff has said. "It was for all of us."

*   *   *

By 1962 the Clarks were on the move again. This time it was over the New Jersey line into Pennsylvania. First it was Morrisville, then Yardley, in Bucks County, another upscale bedroom community which at first welcomed the affluent but dysfunctional family into its bosom. Hadden was placed in a boarding school for the learning-disabled for three years and there reached a level of stability, enough to place him back into a public middle school by 1967. He was far from a model student but muddled through well enough to enter Yardley's Pennsbury High School. He alternated between Pennsbury and nearby Bucks County Technical School where he took commercial cooking courses. When he finally graduated in 1972, he was almost twenty, the oldest student in his class.

Hadden lived with family friends his last year in Yardley. His mother and father had relocated again, this time just outside Cleveland, Ohio, in the village of Chagrin Falls. His father was now employed by W. R. Grace, the giant chemical conglomerate.

Everyone in the Clark family was expected to get a college degree. Brad was already at Rider College (now Rider University), near Princeton, majoring in management. He would receive a Bachelor of Science degree in commerce from Rider in June of 1973. Geoffrey, the youngest, would be admitted to Michigan State University the year Brad graduated. His major was biochemistry, a choice that undoubtedly pleased his father. Alison was trying to have as little as possible to do with her family. That left the big question hanging. What would they do with Hadden?

Their strange son had asked his father if he could start a bakery and operate it out of the basement of the Chagrin Falls house. Flavia decided if he had that much interest in baking she would send him to a cooking college, the best one she could find. She helped him get a scholarship from a group of Philadelphia hotels to enter a two-year program at the prestigious Culinary Institute of America in Hyde Park, New York. At the school, Hadden demonstrated a real talent for carving ice sculptures and figures from tallow or hardened salt. He became adept at fashioning flowers from vegetables and spinning swans from sugar. Enthused by the recognition of a talent, he began to collect every type of kitchen knife made, engraving his name on the blades, sharpening them personally to a razor edge and storing them in a long metal box. Hadden proudly called them the tools of his new trade.

The stay at the school was not without incident. On one occasion he urinated into a vat of mashed potatoes after he became angry. He didn't reveal the secret until weeks later.

Surprisingly, considering his academic history, he eventually passed enough of the school's courses to graduate, receiving an associate degree from the culinary college in January of 1974. In a rare show of unification, every member of the Clark family showed up for the commencement ceremonies.

A degree from the top cooking school in the country can land you a chef's job almost anywhere. At first, Hadden got choice positions, but he was only able to last a short time with each of his employers. He was eagerly chosen in the spring of 1974 as the new chef at The Moors, a Provincetown, Massachusetts, restaurant but was fired within days because of his strange behavior, which included, among other culinary sins, chugging beef blood on the job. After several such episodes on the Cape he was hired as a chef on a cruise ship, the *SS Norway*, in 1979. At more than 1000 feet long and weighing 76,000 tons, it was then the largest pleasure boat sailing to ports of call in the West Indies. Hadden claimed he didn't like taking orders from the non–English-speaking Korean chefs, the dominant nationality in the *Norway*'s huge, sweaty kitchens. His stay aboard lasted less than a year. "There were so many languages being spoken, it sounded like a crowded chicken coop," Hadden said.

He carved ice sculptures for banquet halls on Long Island and at the 1980 Olympics in Lake Placid, New York, a six-week assignment, winning a best-in-show ribbon for his efforts. The next year he became a *sous*-chef at the historic Brown Palace hotel in Denver, Colorado. That position didn't take, either. In all, Hadden would hold fourteen different jobs between 1974 and 1982.

His family was disintegrating. Silas Clark died in March of 1975 after a stroke, his remains buried a short distance away at Wellfleet's Pleasant Hill Cemetery. His three sons inherited the property but sold it in 1982 for $165,000. Edith, confined to a wheelchair, was relegated to the Kathryn Barton Nursing Home in Wayland, a far western suburb of Boston. Hadden's special haven, whose terraced flower gardens were once considered so beautiful that they were featured in national magazines, was no more. The year also marked the beginning of his parents' marital separation. His father lived on the Wellfleet estate for a while before it was sold, then married a younger woman named Sandy, who had a son from a first marriage. Flavia did not make the divorce easy on him.

Hadden blamed his mother for the breakup. "My mother didn't like it. She had problems, but she didn't want to admit her problems. A lot of people close to my mom, well, they only saw the good side. When you don't live with a person, you don't see the other side."

Hadden philosophized about Flavia's alcoholism in disjointed, cryptic terms. "Marriage is a partnership. When you have a problem, you have to admit you have a problem. The reason you have a lot of problems is because people won't admit their problems."

Flavia had always blamed young Hadden for her binge drinking. "It's you who made me drink and smoke and now

I can't stop. It's all your fault," she had tearfully complained to him when he was in his teens.

Flavia and his father were still fighting through their divorce when Hadden returned from Denver in January of 1982. Hadden sought lodging with her. His mother was alone, with neither children nor a husband, living in a house on Yale Avenue, in her hometown of Meriden. She was spending most of each day there providing nursing care for her dying father, Maynard Scranton. Flavia told Hadden he could stay for free as long as he mowed the lawn and did household maintenance chores. But Hadden's presence in the household increased tensions. On March 31, 1982, he attacked his mother without explanation, kicking her at first and then beating her up. A frightened Flavia went to the local police, who charged Hadden with assault and battery. A few months later, a court chose not to prosecute the case. Despite attacking his mother, Maynard still left Hadden $500 in his will when he died a few months later.

In 1978, following her marital separation, Flavia's brother and his wife had purchased a cottage in partnership with her on Block Island. The eleven-square-mile summer vacation destination was a favorite of New Englanders and lay twelve miles off the coast of Rhode Island.

The house, in an area called Calico Hill, had once belonged to Flavia's parents. The price for the residence and its acre of land was $53,000. Her sibling, Brad Scranton, was a vice-president of Becton, Dickinson, the medical supplies company. Like his sister, he was an alcoholic.

In 1983, Flavia bought her brother's share of the property with the proceeds from her divorce. Her children, now adults, had yet to self-destruct. She was determined to make the final chapter of her life a happy one.

Flavia had loved Block Island living since childhood, when she began vacationing there with her family. As an adult she would rent places on the island for brief summer getaways. Despite her fights with young Hadden she continued to allow him to stay on her property whenever he showed up. But Flavia would no longer allow him to live in the house. Instead, Hadden was made to sleep in the barn out back or at other sites on the property. One island resident remembers him living in a pump house in front of the house, next to the well. There Hadden bunked down on a small, spartan cot. What struck observers as bizarre and created island gossip was that rotting turtle shells surrounded his bed and put out a scent one could smell a hundred feet away.

Flavia took a job with the state of Rhode Island as a park naturalist, leading visitors on tours through the woods and dunes. She also purchased part of an island gift shop. The lifestyle seemed to suit her.

"I love my job," she once told her friend Claire McQueeny, the publisher of the *Block Island Beacon*. "I just walk around and pick up trash on the trails which is what I like to do anyway."

Flavia considered herself a thrifty Yankee. She would rent the house out to summer tourists at a hefty price and then live elsewhere. Once, when her tenants left, she wrote a letter of complaint to the island's water company. Her gripe: Since she conserved water when living there, consuming less than the minimum, she shouldn't be charged for her tenants who had squandered her surplus by taking too many baths and running up her bill.

Mentally, Hadden was unraveling each day. With his family's encouragement, he sought what would be a last chance for a normal life. He joined the Navy, intending to make a career of it. Despite his mental history, checkered employment background, and being just a month shy of the maximum enlistment age of thirty, the seagoing branch of the U.S. Armed Forces had no problem welcoming him to its ranks. Within months after signing on, Hadden would complain he had been deceived by the Navy recruiters.

"They screwed me good," he said.

Hadden claimed the Navy promised him schooling that would have given him a new skill. He had chosen a classification known as "aviation storekeeper." Hadden said he was planning to use this knowledge when he left the military. The training would take place on the East Coast, he was assured. Instead, he remembered, he was sent to the Great Lakes Naval Training Center, thirty-five miles north of Chicago. There he did a few months of basic training and was sent off to sea, assigned to be a cook again.

"See, I was supposed to go in the Navy in July," Hadden recalled. "I was working in Maryland and I lost my job there. I told my boss, 'I'm going in the Navy in July.' But the Navy changed their plans and I had already given my notice. Boom! Then they tell me I can't go until November.

"So I drive up to Block Island and work for about three months until November comes on. The Navy drives me to Baltimore and we were supposed to leave at five in the morning to go to Great Lakes but we didn't leave until pretty near five in the evening. I said, 'Where's my stuff, my guarantee?' and they said, 'You'll get it when you get there.' I never got it. They stole my school from me."

His first assignment was aboard a new nuclear aircraft carrier, the *USS Carl Vinson*, named for the veteran Georgia congressman and military expert. Because it was nuclear, all Navy men and women serving on the ship were supposed to have classified clearances. Somehow, Hadden went on board without one.

Hadden's letters to Flavia and Geoffrey at first showed exhilaration at docking in exotic ports of call, such as African cities in the Mediterranean Sea, Asian hot spots like Hong Kong, and harbors in Korea that were part of the *Carl Vinson*'s worldwide tour. Then he began to complain about his shipmates. Homophobic sailors were not pleased to discover that the line cook they sometimes showered with, and who served them surf 'n' turf on Saturday nights, also wore frilly ladies' panties under his uniform. This led to beatings by his peers and counseling sessions with his chaplain. Once he was locked in a large meat freezer for hours. It wasn't long before he was deemed disruptive to the ship and transferred to a nearly identical vessel, the just-christened *USS Theodore Roosevelt.*

There, Hadden's troubles intensified. In late 1984 several sailors waited for him to finish his duties, ambushed him in the dark, and beat him so severely he was hospitalized.

"They smashed my head against the deck several times," he told a Navy doctor. Hadden also said his shipmates had attacked him because they were jealous of his cooking skills.

"When I came to I was in a hospital. I'm on a ship one minute and I wake up and I'm in a hospital," he said in typically disjointed prose. "All these windows are around me, that's why I knew it was a hospital. Navy ships don't have windows. Just portholes."

Hadden was put off the *Roosevelt* and assigned to a smaller, non-nuclear carrier, the *USS Iwo Jima.* The ship was classified as an amphibious assault vessel with more Marines aboard than sailors. The persecution by his peers continued and within weeks he was medically evaluated, declared unfit for duty, and admitted to another Naval Hospital in Portsmouth, Virginia. The doctors took X-rays of his skull which came back negative, but they did provide a written diagnosis that said he had experienced an acute psychotic episode aboard ship. Now, it seemed, every time he went onto shore there were incidents. He was stopped in an airport, then at a local department store. Both reports were nearly identical: "Acting in a bizarre manner, destroying property," were some of the descriptions. Hadden told the military police he had blacked out and couldn't remember what had happened.

The Navy psychiatrists made a final evaluation. If the military wanted him out, the psychiatrists' documents certainly paved the way.

"He suffers from schizophrenia. He is paranoid, with manifestations of persecution and grandiose delusions," the report read. On June 22, 1985, Hadden received an honorable discharge for medical reasons with a thirty percent disability status. The pronouncement qualified him for a small pension.

Days after his discharge Hadden showed up at his brother Geoffrey's rented house in a Maryland suburb of Washington, D.C. Geoff gave him the basement of the house to live in for $450 a month, with some food included. Hadden found a cook's position at a restaurant, but after living with his brother for two months was arrested for shoplifting panties and bras at a local department store. Geoff hurried to the police station to bail him out.

When Geoff talked to Flavia he expressed concern. His brother's stint in the service hadn't cured his problems, but only aggravated them, he told his mother.

"As bad as he was before the Navy, he was worse when he got out," Geoff said.

3

FIRST BROTHER FREAKS OUT

Of the four children whom Hadden and Flavia Clark produced, their eldest son had always been considered the brightest and the most promising, despite his early problems. At six feet tall, with regular features and his grandmother's blue eyes, Bradfield Clark was considered the handsome one in the Clark family. He did not disappoint them in his schooling. After receiving his undergraduate education at Rider College, he went directly to Temple University in Philadelphia. In August of 1976 he received a Masters of Business Administration in management and organization, an advanced degree that not only distinguished him, but virtually guaranteed an interview over lunch with any of the *Fortune* 500 companies. Brad didn't stop his academic studies there. By the early 1980s he had only to give a dissertation to get his PhD. The doctorate was to be in social psychology, which would have furthered his understanding of dynamics in the workplace. Compared to Hadden, Brad seemed to have straightened out, with only blue skies ahead.

Brad had looked into the future and correctly deduced that computers, with all their soon-to-be-realized applications, would shortly become the fastest-growing industry in America. In the 1970s, Boston, with companies like Wang Labs and Data General, was one of the centers for the new technology. Brad moved there, but had fallen in love with a Rider College coed, Linda Kay Elwood. She was a year younger than Brad, both smart and beautiful. There was a small wedding in August of 1977 in Bucks County, but the marriage was doomed from the start, and it quickly fell apart. Brad alleged that the cause was adultery by Linda.

The two separated in November of 1980 and in January of 1981 Brad filed for divorce, charging Linda with "cruel and abusive treatment toward the plaintiff on August 24, 1980 and on other dates and in other places."

Linda did not dispute Brad's charges. Both wanted out quickly. Since there were no children or property to divide, a quick divorce was possible.

"Serious and irreconcilable differences have arisen between the husband and the wife and they acknowledge there has been an irretrievable breakdown of the marriage. The parties have been living apart since November 30, 1980, are now living separately, have agreed to live apart, and this agreement is binding on the parties," the separation papers read when they were filed in January of 1981.

The couple divided up their belongings with Brad acquiring possession of their one asset that had substantial value, a red Datsun 280 ZX sports car. He paid Linda two thousand dollars for the privilege of retaining it. No alimony was requested by either party.

After their divorce became final in March of 1981, Brad left Boston and began driving west. He settled in Los Gatos, California, at the near epicenter of another, even faster-growing high-tech enclave, Silicon Valley. Brad was hired as a software specialist for Tymshare, Inc., a computer network manufacturer. Because of his MBA in management the company sometimes sent him to other cities as a troubleshooter and problem solver.

On one such trip, to Chicago, Brad met a woman, Carolyn Calzavara, and began a romance with her that lasted just over a year. Carolyn was a Tymshare technical manager for Chicago and parts of the Midwest. She was of Italian descent, both affectionate and beautiful. In June of 1984 she had second thoughts and broke off the affair. Within days, say his former co-workers, Brad began behaving strangely at Tymshare's Cupertino, California, headquarters. He strongly suggested that his office mates read

John Champlin Gardner's book, *Grendel*, a 1971 cult classic about a half-human monster who is unusually close to
his mother and enjoys eating people. Brad began to mumble
under his breath and his speech became garbled.

Tymshare employees were deserting the company in
droves in mid-1984. The rumor sweeping the company was
that the McDonnell Douglas corporation was about to buy
the company and jobs would be eliminated in the process.
In fact, the aerospace giant soon did, and one of those prescient opportunists jumping ship in advance of the takeover
was a twenty-nine-year-old woman, Patricia Mak, whom
Brad Clark had just begun to think of romantically. The
two had engaged in some heavy office petting at Tymshare
when others weren't around, but had never consummated
the relationship. It was just as well. Trish Mak had been
married for eight years and her husband Sidney was not
aware of his wife's near-infidelity inside the company offices on Valley Green Drive.

Mak, despite her attraction to the handsome Brad Clark,
wasn't about to leave her husband. The couple had just
moved into a new, luxurious $150,000 two-story stucco
home in nearby Union City and were looking forward to
decorating their dream house.

Trish Mak, though, was more than willing to continue
the serious flirtation, and perhaps curious enough to day-
dream about an extramarital relationship with her former
office mate. After leaving Tymshare, she had landed at
Hewlett Packard in Palo Alto where a product manager's
position had opened. Brad was looking for a new company
himself. A sexual encounter now appeared possible since
neither would be seeing each other in the workplace anymore.

On Friday, July 20, 1984, at six o'clock, immediately after arriving home from work, Brad telephoned his conquest-
to-be. He invited both Trish and Sid Mak to dinner that night
at his six-hundred-dollar-a-month second-floor Los Gatos

garden apartment on Riviera Terrace Drive. The Maks had been over once before as a couple. But the cookout invitation, which appeared to be on the spur of the moment, was a bit disingenuous. Brad was gambling that Trish would come by herself. He knew her husband was out of town and probably wouldn't be back in time to make the dinner.

Brad's guess was right and certainly Trish seemed to have no problem accepting even though it meant having dinner with him alone and without her husband. She was there by eight, wearing a thin cotton blouse and tight jeans that made her appear even younger than her twenty-nine years. When Trish had spoken to him on the phone she asked if she could bring some food to help out.

"I said, 'Well, I'm fixing lamb,'" Brad remembered. "Then I called her back and said, 'I need a fresh veggie and potatoes,' and told her to bring a bathing suit."

Mak drove over in her white Mazda bringing a bag of russet potatoes and some fresh broccoli. Brad foil-wrapped the potatoes to oven-bake them while Trish cut and prepared the broccoli. The two bantered and talked about their computer careers. While the dinner was cooking and Brad's marinated leg of lamb barbecued slowly on his balcony grill, they began to do some serious drinking.

Brad had drunk a couple of beers before Trish arrived and would later estimate his beer consumption that night at either four or six. Additionally he drank two scotch and sodas which he described as making in "very large glasses." Trish Mak stuck with gin and tonics served in the same tall tumblers, with the estimate later put at four. Brad and Trish also opened and polished off a straw-covered bottle of Banfi Chianti, which Brad insisted on pouring into a pair of massive pewter goblets. Brad, a budding wine connoisseur, explained to Trish that the harsh red wine went well with flavorful meat. After dinner the two took the rest of the wine and went down to sit around the swimming pool.

They never entered the water but instead began some nuzzling that progressed to necking. None of the petting was that serious, partly due to the very public nature of the area. It was nearly eleven o'clock.

They went back inside the apartment and continued the kissing and fondling on the couch. Brad took off his aviator-style glasses and then his guest's blouse followed by her bra. He began kissing her breasts, his thick mustache tickling the skin. The kissing soon turned to nibbles and then sharp bites. Trish didn't want teeth marks on her breasts that her husband might see and tried to push him away. When he continued she slapped him. That's when Brad Clark put his mouth over Trish Mak's nipple and bit into the protusion so hard he severed it. The tip of her breast was now in his mouth, he was still on the couch, and Trish Mak was down on the floor of his apartment screaming in agony.

Margaret Landa, who lived directly above Brad Clark, was one of many residents of the Riviera Terrace Apartments who heard Trish Mak's cry of help that night. She did nothing. She couldn't even tell the police what she heard days later.

"I was going to tell the detectives about it," she would tell the San Jose *Mercury News*. "But I was so scared, I couldn't. I couldn't have even given them my name. They would have thought I was nuts."

It would have probably been too late. Though Trish Mak tried to push and slap a crazed Brad Clark away after he bit off part of her breast, he began hitting her with his fists and soon had both hands around her neck, choking her. As she weakened, she fell against a sharp corner of his desk, cutting herself. He then pushed her into a corner where there were gray cinder blocks that had once been used to make a bookcase. He banged her head viciously against the bricks until she was unconscious. At that point blood began flowing from the back of her head.

The apartment became silent. Trish Mak was on her back on the floor motionless, blood puddling around her head. Brad thought she might be dead. He didn't know what to do next. Certainly, he never entertained any thought of calling an ambulance or the police. Instead, he took a pack of cigarettes and his keys, and left the apartment. For the next hour Brad Clark went for a relaxing stroll through the Los Gatos Old Town section a few blocks away to ponder his predicament while Trish Mak lay on his living room floor, slowly bleeding to death.

When he returned, it was past midnight. During the walk, Brad had made his decision and knew what he was going to do next. What he did that night, say members of the Los Gatos Police Department who know the case, is perhaps the most grisly chapter in their department's homicide files.

Brad Clark removed the rest of Trish Mak's clothing and dragged her into the bathroom. He placed her on her back in the bathtub. His first act was to completely cut off the breast that no longer had a nipple, and take it out to the still-hot barbecue grill on the balcony. He cooked it until it was black, ate part of it, and pushed the remainder between Trish Mak's legs and down the drain of the bathtub. The nipple, which he had not eaten, was picked off the floor and flushed down the toilet. Whether or not she was still alive when he removed the rest of her breast is undetermined, but blood did squirt onto the bathroom walls when he cut into it, a sign of life.

He then went into the bathroom medicine cabinet and found a bottle of rubbing alcohol. Brad poured the contents over Trish Mak's pubic hair, lit a match, and set her genitals on fire. Then he took off his clothes, put on a pair of old cutoff jeans, and went to the kitchen. In an act that would later be compared to some of Hadden's he found a long butcher knife and a seven-inch de-boning knife that he had recently bought on sale at a supermarket. Walking back into the bathroom, he began the gruesome work of dismembering the young and lovely body of Patricia Mak.

The bloody job took until dawn. Using the deer-hunting and slaughtering skills he had learned from his father, Brad was careful to make incisions into the joints rather than try to saw directly into bone. After cutting completely around an appendage he would twist it off, with the bones and cartilage often making crunching and snapping sounds. The legs were sliced and trimmed neatly into two pieces as were the arms and the torso, which he divided horizontally. The head was removed as well. The bloody business of human butchery sometimes got to him and he vomited.

"I was less than thrilled by the whole experience," Brad would say in a matter-of-fact voice later. "I would work at it for a bit, get sick for a little bit, and work at it a little bit more."

The vomiting was done leaning over the toilet, next to the tub. When the job was complete it was dawn and Patricia Mak was in eleven pieces. Her remains and clothing, together with Brad's gore-stained cutoff jeans were placed in six green plastic trash bags and sealed with gold-colored metal ties. Since it was now daylight, Brad didn't want to be seen carrying out the remains of a body, no matter how opaque the containers. He stashed the sacks in his bedroom closet, intending to take them out to his car the next evening, drive into the nearby Santa Cruz mountains, and bury the remains during the night.

Trish Mak's white Mazda was still in front of his apartment's carport. Something had to be done about that. Brad took her keys, drove the Mazda to a Safeway store on North Santa Cruz Avenue, and parked it on the side of the building. He then went inside the market and purchased a box of Spic and Span and some sponges. Walking back to his apartment, he went directly to the bathroom and scrubbed it clean, removing all signs of blood. After cleaning all of the tile surfaces he stepped into the tub and treated himself to a long hot shower. About that time he got a telephone call from Sidney Mak, wanting to know if his wife was there. Brad said she wasn't.

"I told him Trish was a no-show," he would tell the police.

Finally Brad Clark slept, but not before inviting two more young women, a Debbie and a Sharon, both employees of Tymshare, to his apartment for a grilled chicken dinner that evening in what promised to be a reprise of the previous night. Debbie was a secretary for Brad's software group and Sharon was the executive assistant to a Tymshare vice-president. Both arrived early, just after five on Saturday afternoon.

The cookout didn't go smoothly. Brad felt queasy with Debbie and Sharon chattering merrily away, sitting on a sofa that was stained with splotches of freshly dried blood, with their feet often resting on more of the same. Trish Mak's much-divided body was stacked just inches away inside the bedroom closet. He later said that he thought the two women assumed the blood to be red wine spills and that they saw him as the typical messy bachelor.

Brad managed to prepare dinner for the pair, serving everyone on foldout TV trays, but found eating the food made him sick. He told the women he had a flu bug and went into the bathroom to vomit loudly, which certainly put a damper on the evening. His guests left a few minutes later. Brad made the most of the opportunity provided by the women's early departure. He began taking out Trish Mak's body to the his little sports car bag by bag. The car's trunk was small and when he noticed one of the plastic sacks leaked, he placed that one inside a yellow plastic cooler on the back seat. Some of the bags were pushed out inside a wheeled grocery cart. It soon became apparent that it was impossible to crowd all of Trish Mak's body parts into the rear storage area of the little Datsun with its Massachusetts plate, 29GPG, still on the bumpers. So Brad tossed one of the bags into a trash can near his car and then walked to the other end of the apartment complex where he put another sack containing the now-crimson-tinged knives and blood-soaked sponges into a second receptacle.

At one in the afternoon the next day, a pair of Union City detectives knocked on the door of his apartment. Sidney Mak had reported his wife's disappearance to the police and after asking a few questions, Brad's apartment seemed a good place to start their search. Like Sid Mak, they wanted to know if he had seen Trish. Brad said he hadn't and when the cops asked him if they could look around he motioned them inside. They did a cursory search, opening the doors of the closets and looking under the bed, but somehow failed to notice the red stains on the carpet and couch. To be fair, much of the gore on the upholstery had been scrubbed away by Brad before they arrived after noticing Debbie and Sharon eyeing it. He did the job right by first walking back to Safeway and purchasing a spray can of Woolite carpet cleaner.

The two police detectives questioned him about Trish Mak and their relationship for more than an hour, then handed him their business cards and left. By now Brad Clark was feeling pressured. He began to wonder if he would really be able to get away with the murder.

"Finally I just said the hell with it," Brad recalled later. "I just didn't care anymore. I couldn't live with this and it didn't really matter if they found out. When the Union City police showed up I lied to them to give myself another twenty-four hours so I could get up enough courage to do myself in."

Brad Clark made his suicide attempt an hour after the Union City cops left. He began by stabbing himself repeatedly in several parts of his body. However, Los Gatos Police Detective Tim Morgan, among the first police officers to arrive on the scene, said only a single wound in the stomach was serious. The others, small stabs throughout the body, were superficial. When questioned, Brad had a hard time remembering when exactly he had begun the attempt to end his life.

"I inflicted the belly wounds around . . . uh, I'm not sure," he would tell Morgan. "I stabbed myself twice and took a shot at my arm and passed out and was hoping not to wake up. Well I did and at that point didn't have enough strength to do another major cut so I found a razor blade and tried to slit an artery on the side of my neck. I passed out again and when I woke up it was one of those things where I wasn't passed out, I was just fading in and out. I could hardly move and so I was figuring that I had gone through enough pain and I was ready to call this one a failure."

Brad called a hospital ambulance just after six the next morning and told them he had tried to kill himself but failed. The hospital called the police, who instantly matched the name of the man who had called in a suicide attempt with the missing Patricia Mak. With that link established, more than the usual number of cops arrived at Brad's apartment complex minutes after the ambulance. The police at first thought the man in the T-shirt and shorts might be dying and if he was, they wanted to get a quick interview that might explain her disappearance. Los Gatos Police Lieutenant Art Roy's first question to Brad resulted in this exchange, which immediately cleared up the mystery of the missing woman's whereabouts.

"Do you know a Patricia Mak?"
"She's dead. Her body is in the trunk of my car."

Brad Clark was placed under arrest, charged with murder and then taken to Los Gatos Community Hospital in the ambulance. Before the doctors operated on the deep wound where he had pierced his abdomen, the Los Gatos Police Department's Tim Morgan had an initial conversation with Brad. What immediately struck Morgan was how matter-of-factly the suspect spoke about his crime and how little, if any, remorse was shown. At times, despite the pain and the enormity of his act, Brad Clark was able to laugh at some of the questions, and willing to correct Morgan on some of his presumptions about body dismemberment. Brad told Morgan he had freaked out, but when Morgan gave him the opportunity to make a statement, he seemed to want to talk more about himself than what happened to Trish Mak.

"This is your time, I'm giving you the opportunity to say anything you like. I want to treat you fair."

"Well, it is definitely is the strangest thing that I ever had happen to me or . . . I can say that has happened to me."

It became clear to the police that Trish Mak had fought hard for her life. In his first of three separate confessions, the murderer gave this blow-by-blow account to Tim Morgan, saying she had struck the first blow:

"So I slapped her back."

"Open-handed or closed?"

"Open hand."

"You slapped her in the face?"

"Yes, I slapped her on the cheek, well, I slapped her, you know, low on the cheek."

"Okay."

"Not real hard. I mean, I didn't spin her head or anything, and then she hauled off and tried to punch me."

"Uh huh."

"So I hauled off and punched her. That's how it all started."

"When you hit her, you hit her with a closed fist. Did she lose consciousness or anything like that? Did she bleed at all when you hit her?"

"I'm not sure."

"Okay."

"But it was a close-fisted punch."

"Then what happened, Brad, what happened after that?"

"It just went rapidly downhill from there."

"Can you go through it once for me?"

"She swung at me, I swung at her. I think when it really got out of control is when she started to scream and I grabbed her by the throat."

"Did you grab her with one hand or two hands?"

"If I remember correctly I originally grabbed her with one hand and when she broke that I then grabbed her with two hands."

"How did she break it, did she knock your hand away?"

"Knocked my hand away."

"Okay, after you choked her you said she looked like she was dead. How did you determine that you had killed her, how did you figure that?"

"She wasn't moving."

"She wasn't moving at all, nothing?"

"Nothing."

Officers from the Los Gatos Police Department went into Brad Clark's apartment and searched it. They found small quantities of hashish and two kinds of hallucinogens in the living room. They also confiscated a chart that listed a number of illegal drugs and the type of effect each substance had on a person. Of particular interest were some

Heavy Metal magazines, one of which had special interest for the police.

"Do you remember anything in those magazines about an octopus, chasing and grabbing the women?"

"Uh, yeah, that was a strange cartoon."

"Did you read what it said at the end, when the alien is talking to the other alien about the women they captured, remember what they did?"

"Oh wow, yeah, they cut her up. I remember reading that story."

"That kind of shocks you if you say, 'Oh, wow,' you know."

"I, I never made the connection."

Within twenty-four hours the Santa Clara County Coroner determined that Patricia Mak had died of both strangulation and stabbing from a knife. Because of her wounds Brad Clark was initially charged with both first-degree murder and the infliction of torture, upon the belief that Brad had begun dismembering Trish while she was still alive. By mid-1985, prosecutors would withdraw the torture charge and change it to that of mutilating human remains. Prosecutors thought the actual time of death might be hard to prove in court and the resulting press coverage detailing the torture would be too hard for the Mak family to endure. Since Brad had both confessed and pled guilty, his sentence was fifteen years to life with three years added for the mutilation of Trish's body. If he had been convicted of a torture charge, he could have faced the death penalty.

What puzzled the police officers who investigated the murder was that there was never a moment during Brad Clark's several confessions where he expressed contrition or offered an apology to the family of Patricia Mak. In conversations he had with several police officers while he was in the hospital, he found time to complain several times about his own pain, or talked about how angry she had made him by slapping him. Based on this behavior, Sergeant Michael Yorks of the Los Gatos Police Department was surprised to learn that Brad came from a large family.

"Clark reminded me of the type of person who has no brothers or sisters," he said. "He was the loner type."

What was Brad's mother's reaction to learning her son was charged with murdering Trish Mak? Flavia kept calling it "that mess in California." She was fighting to keep what remained of her sanity, having just heard of Hadden's beatings in the Navy. Hadden heard about it from his mother, which couldn't have helped his mental state. Brad was sentenced at the same time Hadden was given his military discharge, diagnosed by the Navy as a paranoid schizophrenic.

Doctors insisted Brad be kept in the hospital for three weeks. After that he was arraigned and imprisoned within the Santa Clara County judicial system. By the time they took his booking photo at the county jail he had grown a full beard.

As part of his pre-sentencing investigation, most of the people in Brad's past were interviewed. According to Los Gatos Detective Tim Morgan, his former wife, Linda spoke to Brad by telephone several times in 1984 while he was in custody awaiting sentencing. During one conversation Brad confessed to her that he had murdered three other people and mutilated their corpses, in much the same way he had killed Trish Mak. Two of the murders were in Massachusetts, he said, and the other took place in New York State. Linda told the police about Brad's additional revelations. Morgan recalled that the appropriate jurisdictions were notified of Linda's allegations but both replied they were too busy with other homicides to pursue her information.

Like Jesus, Brad Clark spent time in penal institutions throughout California. He is presently incarcerated at Pleasant Valley State Prison near the town of Coalinga. PVSP, as it is known by inmates, opened the same year as WCI but has double the inmate population. Penal sources say Brad is a model prisoner who likes to study Jewish philosophy and mysticism. He has worked as a clerk for the institution's communications office, but is not allowed access to any computers.

"Too dangerous," said a PVSP guard. "He knows too much about them." Brad Clark is presently eligible for parole, though he has no illusions about being released.

"The California Board of Prison Terms may never find me suitable for parole," Brad Clark wrote last year. "I am doing well in prison and am way better than reasonably happy."

He also admitted his actions had caused pain for many families.

"I have done enough damage in this lifetime. I do not want to do anything that might conceivably do more harm."

Why did he do it? Not because of drugs, he said.

"I was abusing alcohol back then. I don't remember anything about the crime," Brad Clark claimed.

Detective Tim Morgan has been unable to forget it. He remembers having had nightmares about the murder for some four years after listening to Brad Clark's confessions.

4

SECOND BROTHER WITH PROBLEMS

Of the three Clark boys, Geoffrey could be called the runt of the family. While Hadden and Bradfield grew to more than six feet tall, Geoff would barely reach five foot-nine. Brad was considered the brainy one, with Hadden and Geoff appearing to be more interested in sports. Hadden became an avid New York Islanders hockey fan while Geoff was a soccer player. He continued to play as an adult and became a coach of neighborhood youth teams. Still, Geoff shared many of his family's more disturbing traits. Like his father, Geoff was diagnosed as a manic-depressive who controlled his illness with drugs. Like his brother Brad, Geoff was a recreational user of marijuana. And like his brother Hadden, Geoff had a temper which at times could veer out of control. With the ponytail he affected and wore through the end of the last century, he gave the appearance of being from an earlier, more gentle era. Geoffrey Scranton Clark appeared to be the personification of a passive flower-child of the seventies who had been frozen in time. His outward appearance belied the terrible truths of a family in trouble.

Geoff met his first wife, Marcia Kay, in Chagrin Falls where her father was a local cop. During the first half of 1975, just after Silas Clark's death and during the time his parents were separating, the two married. Both dropped out of college and were wed on June fourteenth in the Cleveland, Ohio suburb. Geoff stayed out of college a year and then finished two years later, earning a degree in microbiology at Ohio State in Columbus in 1977. Marcia did not immediately return to school, working instead. Since Geoff was a resident of Ohio, he received the in-state tuition rate, which reduced his financial burden.

After receiving his diploma, Geoff was able to land a government job as a microbiologist with the Food and Drug Administration in Bethesda, Maryland, just outside the nation's capital. He was assigned to the Bureau of Medical Devices.

Bethesda was in the heart of Montgomery County, one of the richest counties in America. Montgomery was huge, with urban cities on its eastern borders and dairy farms in the west, though rural holdings were giving way to town home developments as the wealthy suburb continued to grow. Living was expensive, with housing so costly that school teachers and police officers had to be subsidized. Perhaps it was the combination of living in costly Montgomery County and a fertile wife that doomed Geoff Clark's marriage despite his earning a substantial salary.

Geoff and Marcia had three children in quick succession. The eldest, John Scott, was born in April of 1978. There was a second son, Jacob Stuart, born in August of 1979, and finally, a daughter, Eliza Rose, whom Marcia delivered in January of 1981. Having three children did not provide the glue that generally keeps couples together. They agreed to separate and end their seven-year marriage in late 1982. After much negotiating, Marcia Clark moved out of the house they were renting at 9125 Sudbury Road in Silver Spring, Maryland, on the first day of 1983. The three children remained with Geoff at the house, three miles outside the Washington, D.C., line.

Marcia Clark claimed that she had no choice as far as the children were concerned. She said she had no means of supporting them and that Geoff had told her he wouldn't pay a penny towards their care if she took them with her. Before she moved out, she asserted, Geoff made her sign a joint custody agreement he had written. If she hadn't, Geoff would not only have had total custody of the three, but it would have looked like she had abandoned them. During the first year of their separation, according to Geoff's contract, Marcia was allowed to have the children over for dinner one night during the week and had full custody on most weekends.

Geoff put the children into the Tumble Inn Daycare Center while he worked at his government job. In December of 1983, a teacher at the nursery school, Susan Cahill, observed an unsettling incident between Geoff and his four-year-old son, Jacob. She was one of three witnesses who would later testify about his temper.

It was late in the afternoon, about 5:45 and Mr. Clark came in. He apparently was in a hurry and asked for his son. He told his son to get ready, because he wanted to leave right away.

Jacob was making something with some Play-Doh. He did not want to leave at that time, so he sort of went down in his chair and whined a little bit. Right after that, like I say, everything happened and it was very abrupt. Geoff took Jacob by the collar forcefully . . . the chair went flying across the room to where my bulletin board is . . . Jacob was up in the air, Geoff shook him and kept on yelling, "You are not going to do this to me anymore, you are not going to do this to me anymore."

Cahill was then asked to describe the tone and loudness of Geoff's voice.

"It was unbelievable. The whole room came to a standstill. I think that everybody was appalled by the behavior."

What happened after Geoff shook Jacob?

"He was still shaking the child and repeating that going out of the room. It was dark outside. I heard a very loud noise, a banging."

Another witness to the incident, Joanne Christenson, who was deaf, described the event this way.

> I am very sensitive to vibrations. I felt something moving, vibrating, and I looked and saw Mr. Clark, saw him pick up Jacob, and he was shaking him in the air and immediately Mr. Clark and Jacob walked out without closing the door.

Geoff denied the allegations of abuse in a deposition this way:

> When the other witnesses testified that the violent manner in which you picked your son up and yelled at him, were they inaccurate?
>   Well, the fact that there are three accounts require they be inaccurate. Because they could not all three be accurate and be as different as they are.

Another incident in 1983 involved his oldest son, John, then five. Geoff had come to pick up his son from Marcia's house. Both his soon-to-be former wife and her housemate, Beverly Thomas, witnessed the event. The women's testimony was substantially the same. The following is that of Ms. Thomas:

> I was sitting in the living room and Mr. Clark came to pick up the children and John could not find his coat or was dawdling about trying to find a coat. Mr. Clark told John that if he did not get his coat on he was leaving him behind. He proceeded to go out and get in the car, start it, and back down the driveway, leaving the five-year-old child standing on the porch crying, "Daddy, Daddy, wait." Marcia found John's coat and put it on him and took him out to the car. Mr. Clark had backed his car out and was already at the end of the driveway.

Geoff did not dispute the testimony. Instead, he excused his actions with this answer:

And your child was screaming and crying because you weren't taking him with you?

I had explained to the children more than once . . .

A third episode involved Eliza, his daughter, then two. The witness to the event was Lisa Guerra, a woman renting a room from Geoff at the Sudbury Road address. The unusual event took place on Easter Sunday.

"I was upstairs. He was upstairs having Eliza change her clothes," she recalled. "Eliza did not want to change her clothes. She was making a large fuss about it. He kept telling her to change her clothes. He was yelling. I then heard a bang and I hear Eliza cry. What happened, I don't know."

Geoff admitted that Guerra was accurate in her report but then she added that he had kicked one of the boys on the leg when he became angry. There was also testimony about Geoff physically disciplining other neighborhood children.

By far the most damaging information, which would soon reverse the child custodial duties of Geoff and Marcia, were eight witnesses who all testified about Geoff's use of illegal substances. They said that they not only saw Geoff use marijuana during the time he was taking care of his three offspring, but that it appeared he would sometimes smoke marijuana in the car while picking up or delivering his children to daycare. Geoff never denied the charges, though his answers were evasive, and at times, could be called Clintonesque.

Did you hear the testimony of Kim Shirley as to the number of times that she saw you under the influence of marijuana?

No, I don't recall that part of her testimony.

Would it refresh your recollection if I told you that what she testified to was that she frequently saw you under the influence of marijuana?

That could have been what she said.

Would she have been accurate when she said that?

I would have to ask somebody to define the word *frequently*. That can vary.

There was other testimony that made Geoff look unfit to care for his three children. Though John, at five, was extremely sexually precocious, Geoff had allowed him to tape photos of scantily clad or semi-nude women on the refrigerator door. John had already displayed signs of inheriting the Clark family's temper problems. He had begun striking his two siblings and throwing objects at the slightest provocation. At times he would try to talk by using animal noises. There were witnesses who claimed Geoff often left the children alone in the house while he went over to a neighbor's to play with a new computer.

Though the bitter, ugly divorce wasn't yet final, the children began to live with Marcia. It was Geoff who had custody on weekends now with the holidays divided between them. After more negotiations, seven amendments were added, making even the lawyers impatient. One would write this to the judge overseeing the case:

I insist that Mr. Clark's attempt to avoid paying child support during the last two weeks of the summer is also inconsistent with the terms of the order. What I think everyone would agree to is that this matter needs to come to an end. We ask that you act promptly on the orders prepared and proposed.

Much of the dispute was centered around money. Geoff would make more than $36,000 a year in 1984 but had paid just $250 a month in child support. By 1988 that would be increased to $450 a month paid over nine months of the school year with Geoff still allowed to have the majority of their custody during the summer months.

Marcia and Geoff's divorce went into effect in July of 1986. Geoff had already met another woman, Stephanie Matchette, whom he married soon after the document was finalized. Marcia matched Geoff's nuptials tit for tat. She wed a Thomas Shields at nearly the same time. While there would be successful second marriages for the two couples, the legal wrangling between Marcia and Geoff seemed endless. There were frequent threats by Marcia to garnish Geoff's wages when he missed his child support payments, while Geoff's attorneys continued to lobby with the courts for an increase in his custody days. Lawyers would either resign or be fired, with disputes often breaking out over hourly billing practices that Marcia deemed excessive. In all, there would be nearly 150 separate filings by attorneys on their divorce or the long running fight for the children.

It shouldn't have been surprising when their battle culminated in violence. Battery charges were filed by Marcia for a beating Geoff gave her in the kitchen of her home. Her former husband received a twenty-four-month suspended prison term for the assault. During the two years Geoff was on probation he was under a court order to stay away from Marcia and her residence. When the probation was over, Marcia sought a sheriff's order that would have a third party pick up and deliver the children to and from her home. The request was granted, though Marcia claimed Geoff often ignored the edict.

Marcia's concern may have been justified. Just two months after Geoff's probation ended she again charged him with attacking her, this time during a PTA back-to-school night.

According to Marcia, Geoff came out of a classroom, saw her and "in passing me in the hallway, slugged me with his elbow and arm into my upper right arm. Mr. Clark is under a 'no contact' order from Judge Mitchell . . ." the court documents claimed. Geoff drew a ninety-day suspended sentence but appealed the verdict to a higher court and was acquitted.

The rancorous struggle between the two parents could be expected to have a disastrous effect on the children. It did. Besides being diagnosed with Attention Deficit Disorder and prescribed Ritalin, their eldest son would be called "severely depressed and suicidal" by a therapist as early as the age of ten. During one summer, Geoff refused custody of John because of the behavior problems.

When Geoffrey's children reached their teens Marcia would see her eldest son psychiatrically hospitalized at Maryland's Potomac Ridge Treatment Center. According to legal papers filed by Marcia, John told a therapist there he had been physically and sexually abused by his father. Their other son, Jacob, was in therapy at the same time with Marcia stating that Geoff had abused him, too, and that he "recently exhibited troubling behavior at school, such as setting fires, and has begun to act out aggressively at home. There is substantial evidence that the defendant has seriously mistreated and neglected his children in the past." Their daughter, Eliza, according to independent observations by both boys, had also been sexually abused by Geoff, Marcia claimed. Geoff denied all the allegations of physical and sexual abuse against his children.

Marcia said that John's psychological condition remained serious since he had been institutionalized and that his treatment would require hospitalization or residential care for one full year. She asked that Geoff be denied all visitation rights permanently though a partial prohibition was already in effect.

"The children are in severe emotional and psychological trauma," wrote Marcia's latest lawyer, Judith A. Wolfer. "This court should not vacate any order without a full hearing from the children's therapists and psychiatrists about what is causing their difficulties and what is in their best interests."

Geoff denied everything and a court eventually found the charges to be unsubstantiated. He continued his limited visitations. A judge did find "neglect, which reflects the emotional abuse and trauma that the children have experienced." Monetarily the legal system raised Geoff's monthly child support payments to a new high of $1,610 a month and garnished his government wages for arrearages on other past-due children's bills. Both parties were forced to pay their eldest son's doctor and special schooling fees in percentages that corresponded with their annual incomes.

One curious order set down by the court involved Silas Clark's widow, Edith. A judge barred Geoff and Marcia's children from having any contact with her at all times. Geoff was prohibited from discussing or explaining her exile from the children.

Hadden's arrival on the doorstep of Geoff's home in mid-1985 certainly didn't calm things down at the Clark residence on Sudbury Roads. The side street was several blocks off Georgia Avenue, the main thoroughfare that ran north-to-south through Silver Spring and connected with the Capital Beltway. Sudbury Road was a narrow strip of asphalt with mature trees and lookalike older brick homes on each side. Nearly all the houses were two-stories tall. A long jumble of cars parked out on the curb or in driveways was Sudbury's most distinctive feature. Many of the garages had long been converted into extra rooms.

Geoff's home was typical for the street: an upstairs, downstairs, and a basement. The bedrooms and a single bathroom were on the top floor. Geoff had the largest, his two sons shared another, and Eliza had the smallest, which was not much larger than a walk-in closet and not much more than twelve feet in depth.

The brotherly presence in Geoff's household was welcomed. Hadden had been frugal, husbanding his small inheritances and saving part of his salary during his years on cruise ships and Navy vessels. By 1985, he had amassed a tidy sum of $40,000. Hadden could pay his way and Geoff needed money for child support. Nearly $500 a month for room and board, which was defined as the run of the basement and the privilege to put food in the refrigerator, seemed steep but Hadden didn't seem to mind. He used his cooking school credentials and found a job as a chef close by at the Chevy Chase Country Club. Hadden purchased both a used 1983 white Datsun pickup truck and a bicycle for transportation.

At first, his presence seemed needed. One of Geoff's legal responses on a child custody filing informed Marcia's lawyers that his brother Hadden had begun residing with him. So, he said, there was now a trusted sibling who would spell him from time-to-time with the chores of delivering and picking up the children from nursery school. The two brothers had reason to bond. Just after Hadden arrived, they learned that their father had pancreatic cancer. A terminal diagnosis had been given. Alison, who tried to have as little to do with her family as possible, cared for him during his last months. Flavia, in a display of decency considering the past, sometimes visited with him during his final days. The elder Hadden passed away at Alison's home in Rhode Island during September of 1986. He was fifty-seven.

Their father was cremated, his ashes eventually buried near Silas by Hadden himself in Wellfleet. Hadden attended a private memorial service wearing his sailor's uniform even though his disastrous Navy stint had ended a year before. Edith Clark had died of a stroke at her nursing home the year before. She was interred in the Clark family plot. It was filling up rapidly.

*   *   *

Hadden liked playing with his nephews and niece. Geoff said that mentally, his brother was a child.

"Here was this six-foot-two-inch-tall man who was their emotional age," he once told the *Washingtonian* magazine. "He was a playmate, but a playmate who could drive a truck to the park and choose the biggest swing. Hadden was a playmate who had money to buy them candy and who taught them how to kill, skin, butcher, and cook the rabbits he raised in our back-yard pen. He was an adult, with the social skills of an eight- to-ten-year-old child."

The rough play with the children came with a price. Hadden once claimed one of the boys had kicked him in his testicles, hard enough to make him writhe on the ground in pain. Instead of striking back at the boys, he tackled a neighborhood little girl, pinning her to the ground on her back. He liked that part of the physical play best.

And Hadden wasn't *that* much of a manchild. He loaned Geoff $11,025 in 1986 to put a down payment on the Sudbury Road house, which was about to be put on the market for $84,000. His brother was supposed to pay him back at the rate of $168.75 every three months with a balloon payment of $9,000 due in June of 1989. Geoff paid the first two installments and then stopped. According to Hadden, his brother raised his rent in order to make the payments. Luckily there was a written agreement. Hadden went to the courthouse and sued his brother, asking that the full amount be returned to him. There is no record that he was ever paid.

During the first week of May in 1986 Geoff asked Hadden to move out. His brother had masturbated in front of the children, and, while killing and skinning rabbits in front of them could be seen as disturbing, sexual behavior of that kind was not welcome in the Clark household, no matter how dysfunctional their family had become. Besides, Geoff was eager to marry Stephanie Matchette and have her move into the house. Stephanie loathed Hadden and thought he was weird. She had a small son of her own and worried about what might happen with Hadden around. Geoff told his brother he had to leave by the end of the month.

Hadden's feelings were hurt, but not enough to drive him over the edge. Being rejected was something that had become part of his life. Certainly when it came right from a family member, he felt more pain than when it came from strangers. He would get his revenge one day, Geoff could be sure of that. His brother's charges for the basement were too much anyway, he reasoned. He quickly found a $150-a-month room a few miles away and began moving out his possessions a little bit at a time, in cardboard boxes.

There was *another* incident that *had* made him boil over with rage. It had more to do with Eliza than Geoff. Towards the end of May he had substituted for his brother and had gone to Eliza's daycare center to pick the little girl up and drive her home. But Eliza had been bratty, playing games with his head and telling the teacher's aide she didn't know him. They had refused to release her. Geoff had had to come and had then told the teacher's assistant that he was "Eliza's retarded uncle." "Retarded" was the word his father once used.

Hadden hated Eliza for starting that up again. He hated her so much he would have killed her if given the opportunity.

On Saturday, May 31, Hadden drove to the Sudbury Road house during the noon hour to get the last of his things. It was a hot, humid day, already ninety degrees, and the kind of weather that could rile you up if you stood around outside and let the sun beat down on you. Geoff and Stephanie had his boys and her son that weekend and were already off to the soccer fields. Eliza was spending the night with a school chum. The house was empty and hot as hell inside. Nobody had bothered to write him a goodbye note.

Hadden brought some more boxes up from the basement

and stood leaning against his truck sweating, feeling sorry for himself. Geoff's family was out having fun and he had to be in a steamy kitchen by the middle of the afternoon, toiling away for eight hours and dishing out plates of fancy food to rich people.

A little girl walked up to him. She looked to be six years old, with shoulder-length hair and blue eyes, just like Hadden's. Her bangs needed cutting and the freckles over the bridge of her nose were prominent, a sign she had already spent some time out in the sun that year. When she opened her mouth to talk Hadden could see a missing upper baby tooth in front.

Hadden thought he had seen the tyke before. She was Eliza's friend but only seemed to show up on weekends. What was her name—Shelly? Kelly? Michele? It was something like that. She was wearing a wet, hot-pink one-piece swimsuit covered with tiny white polka dots only slightly larger than pinholes. A cute half-circle of ruffles was sewn on each hip. Her feet were bare and she dragged a bath towel on the ground. She wanted to know if Eliza was inside. Hadden didn't want to hear that name—he had not forgotten what Eliza had done a few days before. He told her he thought she might be in the kitchen or upstairs in her room. Go on in, he said. She's playing there or maybe eating some cereal. The little girl wearing the swimsuit went into the house and was soon walking up to Eliza's bedroom.

When she was inside the house Hadden walked casually to the back of his truck and selected a sharp-as-a-razor, twelve-inch-long butcher knife from the metal box that contained his culinary tools. He put the handle around his right hand and went inside Geoff's house. Hadden waited a moment and then took the steps up to Eliza's bedroom two at a time, treading as lightly as he knew how. The little girl was playing with a doll. "Where's Eliza?" she asked him.

Hadden didn't answer. Instead he gripped the knife more tightly.

This was his time to get back at Eliza. This was the way to do it.

PART TWO

My name is Michele Lee Dorr and I'm six. October twelfth is my birthday. I like being six because I like being big.

I live in Gaithersburg with my mom and Tina, two roommates and two cats.

My mom is a nurse. I don't know what hospital she goes to but she takes care of sick and hurt people. I think she likes to do that. When she comes home she has a little bit of quiet in her room. Sunday we went to get my superstar cake.

Tina is a teenager, I think. She goes to Martin Luther King. She likes school a little. She likes to play outside with her friends.

My dad works on cars. He paints them, too. Sometimes I spend the night at his house. That's lots of fun. We go to the park and 7–11.

My cats are J. J. and Fuzz. I love them. They eat tuna fish and sleep wherever they want to.

When I grow up I want to be a teacher. I'm really happy.

— A SCHOOL ESSAY
WRITTEN BY MICHELE
LEE DORR, AGE SIX.

5

DEE DEE AND CARL DORR

If Geoff and Marcia Clark's endless bickering over their three children had created a private hell, the marriage, separation, divorce, and ensuing custody battles between Carl David Dorr and his wife, Dorothy Jean, were on the way to being its mirror image in 1986. Their six-year-old daughter, Michele Lee, had not escaped unharmed. She was well aware of the enmity that existed between the two and, like many children of divorce, she suffered.

Carl and Dorothy—she was Dorothy McDowell back then—had met in the seventies while Carl was at the University of Maryland in College Park trying to earn his third college degree, this time in management. The first two, one in economics and another in psychology, hadn't done a lot for him. After college, he worked as a body shop manager in a Maryland auto dealership—a place called Reed Brothers Dodge—for seven years and then had been fired. An assembly line job at a car coloring place called Paint Masters lasted a few months. By May of 1986 he was painting vehicles at another shop, Classic Auto Body, working on commission. Maybe it was his size. Carl was just five-foot-five and 135 pounds. You could add an inch to that if you included his thick, bushy hair. But despite a rakish full mustache, Carl Dorr didn't exactly cut an imposing figure.

Dorothy's résumé wasn't much better. She had dropped out of high school, had been married and divorced, and was struggling to raise her daughter Tina by ringing up the cash register in a grocery store. Dorothy was a close-cropped brunette with bad teeth when she met Carl. She was two or three inches taller than he was and when she wore heels she towered over him. Still, there was chemistry between them from the start. "My friends call me Dee Dee," she told him coquettishly the day they met.

They married in 1978 on the last day of September. She was twenty-seven then, a year older than Carl. Michele was born a year later and after that their union began falling apart. They separated in 1981, got back together, and separated again in 1983. Money wasn't the problem. Both were working and they had moved from a trailer park in the country to a suburban brick town house on Chadburn Place in the upwardly striving new community of Montgomery Village.

Financial success aside, Dee Dee claimed that Carl began beating on her just after Michele was born, sometimes right in front of the children. Those were ugly days. Dee Dee would testify that Carl's abuse had gone on for years.

Police were called more than once when Carl began slapping her around in front of Michele and Tina. There was one winter incident where Carl pushed her to the ground outside their house. The earth was nearly frozen and Michele ran towards her with a cry of "Mommy, Mommy."

The physical fights between the parents were hard on their little girl. She missed several months of kindergarten, began stuttering, and ground her teeth while she slept. Her doctor chalked up the problems to stress, something a child shouldn't have to experience at that age.

"She had seen too much for a six-year-old," Dee Dee would later tell *The Washington Post*.

The biggest battle had taken place on February fourteenth, Valentine's Day. Dee Dee said Carl showed up at the house on Chadburn Place and refused to leave when she asked him. He told her if there was a divorce hearing he'd lie under oath and say she was an adulteress and an unfit mother. In his rage, Carl said she wouldn't be seeing their daughter anymore. He was going to kidnap Michele from the school bus stop.

Carl also claimed he could make just one phone call and

her life would be over. When Dee Dee tried to run into a bedroom, he blocked her way. Then, according to Dee Dee, he threw her up against the wall several times which caused cuts and bruises. After the incident her mother was waiting at the bus stop every time Michele rode it home.

The problem they faced was that neither Dee Dee nor Carl knew how to let go. Carl would move out, then move back in. They would stop having sex, then start again. There was a night when Carl came over and fixed Dee Dee's car, and they had spontaneous sex, with Michele walking in on them. Once, Carl moved back in, and a few days later when Dee Dee told him to leave, he refused so *she* had to move out. Dee Dee had to go to court and get a legal order that forced him to vacate the premises. They couldn't live with each other though there were times it seemed they couldn't live without each other.

There was never enough money. Dee Dee and Carl's legal bills and the cost of maintaining two residences were bringing them down. The electric company took legal action and got a judgment against Dee Dee. She had to pay the utility twenty-five dollars extra a month for a year. Her practical nursing job paid a paltry $8.61 an hour and then Carl said he wouldn't pay her the $500 a month child support money she requested through her lawyer. Dee Dee claimed he told her he would quit his job and collect unemployment if a court ordered him to pay it. The house was in Carl's name and so now it was she who had to pay him rent and when she was late he would send her an overdue notice while at the same time notifying the divorce judge.

What a mess.

"Nothing could be clearer than the rule of the cases that there is no set rule fixing the amount of child support, which must be tailored to meet the circumstances of each case," a judge said, quoting a precedent case. "The interest of the child does not lie in crippling the father when struggling to restore his earning capacity and fortune, so the rate should be practical."

Carl's child support payments were set at $400 a month, a big bump up from the $250 he had been paying. He got visitation rights on alternate weekends, two weeks during the summer, and part of each major holiday.

Though both were setting up their daughter for an adulthood that would likely include regular visits to a psychotherapist, both parents genuinely loved Michele. Carl, in fact, spoiled her in the way most divorced fathers do who only have weekend custodial rights. That certainly was the pattern on the last two days of May in 1986 when Carl had Michele, and Dee Dee took off for Hampton, Virginia, with Tina to visit her mother. Their relationship had deteriorated to a point where his former wife didn't even give Carl a phone number to call in case of an emergency.

"She didn't want to leave me that day," Dee Dee recalled. "She clung to my leg and said she didn't want to go."

Carl and his younger brother Chuck had rented a home two doors down from the Clark family at 9129 Sudbury Road. It was a fifty-year-old colonial almost identical to Geoff's except that some previous owner had become energetic and painted the brick exterior white. The old house's walls were peeling, blistered by too many hot summers. Not that Carl and Chuck cared very much. They were thirty-something bachelors and the old house was their pad.

Carl remembers working that Friday at Classic Auto Body. He got an early start by beating the heart of the rush hour, leaving just after seven and beginning work at 8:15. He could have slept in. There was only one car to do—less than a half-day's work. Carl took an extra long lunch break at a Hardee's hamburger joint, read a magazine, and picked up his paycheck. The amount was $355 and change. After getting back into his old Dodge Colt station wagon, he drove to his former home on Chadburn Place to pick up Michele. A babysitter was there. Dee Dee was already on the road, trying to beat the afternoon traffic. She had dressed Michele in a white blouse and a blue pin-striped skirt with white shoes. Carl thought she looked like a princess.

It was six o'clock and time for dinner when he left Chadburn Place. He took Michele to McDonald's. His daughter had a Happy Meal and played outside in the restaurant's playground. Carl, aware that he was eating at his second fast food place in five hours had a healthy McDLT with his Coke and fries. He bought Michele a sundae when she tired outside and then let her eat the soft ice-cream concoction inside the station wagon. Determined to give Michele anything he could to make her happy, he drove to Erol's, a video-rental store.

"I got *The Little Mermaid* for Michele and *Death Wish 3* for me," Carl recalled. He drove the two of them home to the old house on Sudbury and parked near his other car, an old Chevrolet van that leaked oil badly. Carl rarely drove it.

His brother was there with another couple. They were all going to a Friday night party. Carl watched most of the mermaid movie with Michele and then got her ready for bed in the spare room upstairs. He watched *Death Wish 3*, then the late news. It looked like the beginning of a lazy weekend, the kind where you do nothing and feel good that you did.

"Michele woke me up at nine by coming into my room," he remembered. "She told me she was ready for breakfast. I went and got her favorite cereal, Lucky Charms, and put her down in front of the TV to watch cartoons. While she watched I went back to my room and laid down for an hour. Then I got up and fixed a bowl of cereal for myself. Michele was still watching cartoons and so I watched *Alvin and the Chipmunks* with her."

His brother had come home during the night but was already gone before Michele shook him awake. Chuck sold cars for a living and Saturdays were the most important eight hours of his week.

It was getting warm outside. Carl felt the humid, sub-tropical heat drifting in through an open door, making his forehead glisten with sweat. The old house wasn't air-conditioned and Carl planned for them to both cool down by taking Michele back to Montgomery Village to swim in its Olympic-sized swimming pool in the late afternoon. Michele came down dressed for the day in a flowered jump suit. She was ready to go to the big pool any time, she said.

Carl had anticipated this. He wanted to watch the Indianapolis 500 auto race, which began at noon, first. But there was a round green plastic wading pool decorated with turtles outside. It was waiting for her in the back yard. He had already dragged it from a spot next to the detached garage, found a level spot on the grass, and gotten a hose from the basement going, trying to fill it up for her. It had a small plastic slide that went with it and he thought it would be a fun temporary substitute. The fill-up went slowly. When Michele opened the back screen door to look outside, the bottom was barely covered with water. Carl decided to drive them to a 7-Eleven convenience store and buy his daughter a gift while the plastic pool's water level rose.

"I went inside and got my wallet and car keys about 12:30," he recalled. The drive was a quick one, ten minutes. Everything was normal. Boring, some would say.

"I got a coffee and a newspaper. Michele was looking for a student note book and she complained that they only had kites for boys. I picked up a gallon of milk and told Michele to find a snack instead of a toy. She picked out some candy where the container was shaped like a washing machine and the Sweet Tarts inside looked like laundry. Then she got some Nerds candy in a red and blue box too. I paid for it and we got in the car and left."

The wading pool was over half-full when they got back and Carl put the hose on full force. Michele went upstairs and slipped on her swimsuit. It was a stylish one-piece number by OshKosh B'Gosh that Dee Dee had found at a mall. It was pink, covered in polka dots with ruffles.

By now the pool was almost full but Carl decided to keep the hose running because the pool had a slow leak. He sat on the back steps while his daughter showed him how brave she was, sliding down the slide feet first. After a few minutes Carl went inside and fried up a couple of eggs with some ham for lunch. He remembered checking on Michele every few minutes at first. She wanted to show off some more. "Look," she said. "See how long I can hold my head under the water."

Carl went back inside and read his newspaper. He clicked the television on and turned to the Indianapolis 500 race on ABC. The annual event was supposed to have taken place the week before, on the big three-day Memorial Day holiday but it had been rained out. Carl watched, mesmerized. It was the first year the race was on network television and it looked like it was going down to the wire. Rick Mears was trying to win his third trophy and he was locked in a neck-and-neck struggle with Bobby Rahal and Kevin Cogan. Carl Dorr knew cars even though he couldn't afford to drive a good one. When the announcer said they were averaging 171 miles an hour, he didn't have to tell Carl it was a record pace. But eventually he became bored with the coverage and its frequent cutaways for commercials. He walked away from the set.

He went out to the station wagon and got his checkbook from the glove compartment to pay some bills. He looked into the back yard. The water in the pool was still, barely a ripple from the running hose. His little girl wasn't there. He turned off the water and went back into the house. Carl shrugged. He figured she had probably gone over to the Clarks to play with Eliza.

Carl sat down and wrote checks to American Express and MasterCard, then made the hated child support payment to Dee Dee, and paid the rent for June. He filled out a sweepstakes entry form that a magazine had mailed him. Carl was overdue to get lucky.

What time was it? He wasn't good at keeping track of the hour. Carl thought it was around three. He made his bed, cleaned his bedroom, and took the trash out to the back porch. Carl saw two boys in the Clarks' back yard kicking a soccer ball back and forth. No sign of Geoff or Eliza and Michele. There wasn't anybody in the Binder family's house on the other side. Carl wasn't concerned. He was convinced Michele was inside the Clark home with Eliza.

He turned his attention back to the Indy race. This time it was riveting. Mears, Rahal, and Cogan were still going at it and there were just five laps left. He watched it to the end, watched Rahal win by seconds, watched the victory celebration with the champagne squirting over everyone, and then switched over to a soccer game on NBC. Italy was defending its World Cup crown against Bulgaria in the tournament opener. He soon got bored with that and walked away from the set a second time. Time to get Michele at Geoff Clark's house and go to the pool.

It would be the perfect end to a very good Saturday. A very ordinary day. In Carl's present situation, a day that was ordinary was a very good day indeed.

Hadden threw the little girl to the floor in Eliza's room and was on her so fast she didn't get a chance to scream. The first slash with the butcher knife was backhanded, from left to right across her chest, the second went the other way, almost like Zorro making the Z sign. She fell back in shock and he straddled her, putting his right hand over her mouth. She surprised him by fighting back, biting his hand. Damn!

With his left hand, he plunged the twelve-inch-long knife into her throat.

Blood spurted onto the wooden floor of the little bedroom and it began running, flowing under her bed. The old house wasn't level on the second floor, the room sloped, and the blood sought the lowest point. That was next to the bed, in the corner. Mop it up, Hadden thought frantically, clean the floor and stop the blood. He made a dam with the little girl's beach towel to keep more blood from going under the bed.

Should he do her? Have sex with her? He wanted to, tried to, but couldn't make it work.

He ran downstairs to the kitchen and got some plastic trash bags. He ran out to his truck to get some rags and his old Navy duffel bag. Can't take Geoff's dish cloths, he might miss them. He was back in the house in seconds, running up the stairs to grab the little girl—his prize—and stuff her into the plastic bag. Wipe, wipe it up, he told himself. It's like the Navy where the deck has to be wiped clean. He ran to the bathroom to rinse the rags in the upstairs toilet, flushed it, and rushed back to wipe the floor some more. The floor was coming clean now. You wouldn't suspect anything had happened except Eliza's little cotton throw rug next to her bed was splattered with blood. He pushed the rug into the other plastic bag and then put everything inside the duffel bag. The small carpet wouldn't be missed, he hoped. But hurry, Hadden, hurry, he told himself. Geoff and the boys could come home any minute now. Wash your hands, get the blood off them. His right hand was bleeding where the little brat had bit him. Slap some Band-Aids on it, Hadden, and hope like hell nobody notices. Get it stitched up later. What to do now? Put the plastic bag with the prize inside the duffel bag and into the back of the truck, on the bed underneath the cap, and get to work. Can't afford to miss the shift. That *would* be noticed.

It seemed that he had done this drill before in different ways and different places. Still, it was always a thrill.

Hadden thought as hard as he could. Don't leave the body in the truck at the country club parking lot, he told himself. A snoopy security guard could decide to look inside. He knew how nosy they could be. Hadden drove the Datsun to a deserted construction site and parked it in a corner of the lot behind a bulldozer. Then he pulled his bicycle out of the back of the pickup and pedaled to the Chevy Chase Country Club, pushing his time card into the clock at 2:46. He began the day by carving a double C from ice for the dining room. The frozen water soothed his nerves, let him think. What would he do with the little girl? And how would he remember her? What would he take for a souvenir?

So far, it had not been an ordinary day for Hadden.

Carl avoided going to the Clarks' house until nearly six o'clock. He thought Geoff was a homosexual and tried to stay away from him because of this theory. There was an up side to this kind of thinking. In his mind, Michele was safe from any kind of funny business by Geoff. She was inside with Eliza, watching movies and having a good time. He was sure of it.

Mentally, he scrapped the big pool outing. Carl had gone back to watching the World Cup soccer game, seeing it through to the end. Now it was 5:30 and he hadn't seen Michele for more than five hours. Not that it mattered. She was having a good time, playing with Eliza, he had no doubt. A good time for her was important. There had been so few of them lately.

He had dodged Geoffrey Clark long enough. He walked down the back steps and saw the Clarks in their back yard, barbecuing. Geoff's sons were there with another boy. A woman was there. Eliza was there. But where was Michele?

Geoff said he didn't know, in fact he hadn't seen her all day. Carl didn't believe him.

"I asked Eliza, Where was Michele? She told me she hadn't seen my daughter either. I said I thought I had heard Michele and Eliza laughing together when I was watching the race. Geoff told me to check at John Binder's house and he said to come back if I didn't find her."

Carl walked over to the Binder family's home, directly to the right of his house. John Binder told him they had been out all day, had just returned, but had not seen Michele. Somewhat bewildered, Carl walked to the end of Sudbury and looked in each direction. He grew more perplexed, went back to the Clarks' home and asked for Michele again. Geoff told him to check with the other neighbors. Carl walked the streets in the neighborhood and saw nothing.

He telephoned Dee Dee's house. By now Carl's mind was grasping for anything. He thought that maybe his ex-wife had swooped by, grabbed Michele, and then taken her home without letting him know. That would be just like her. Or maybe Michele had become lost and told an adult to call her mother. She knew that number and she didn't know his. Dee Dee's phone rang and rang. There was no answer. He drove through the neighborhood again. No Michele. Finally, he pointed the car in the direction of the Silver Spring police precinct and reported her missing to the cops.

The moment he did so he became their prime suspect.

6

ALWAYS SUSPECT THE PARENT

Every rookie cop being trained at a police academy is told that when a child disappears or is murdered to look first in the direction of the parents or the caregiver. Federal crime statistics bear this out. Hard numbers say it's a ninety-percent chance that the mother, the father, or both committed the crime. It came as no surprise when the Montgomery County Police Department immediately raised an eyebrow and stared hard in the direction of Carl Dorr after hearing his story of losing and failing to find his daughter.

Mike Garvey, one of the first cops assigned to the case, would say later that eliminating the family as suspects was "page one in the handbook." And the more they looked at Carl, the more he looked like their man. After all, hadn't he threatened Dee Dee, saying he would abduct Michele less than three months before? Hadn't he and Dee Dee been battling over the kid for years? Wasn't Carl the last one to see his daughter? All they had to do was to make him confess. They went right at him, asking him to take a lie detector test the next day.

Less than twenty-four hours after Michele vanished Carl was given the Q and A interrogation by a local fire marshal, the only qualified polygraph examiner available on a Sunday. The fire marshal said the test revealed that Carl might know more about Michele's whereabouts than he was telling them. Uh oh. That was all the cops needed to hear. At nine that evening two detectives, Wayne Farrell and Tom Leonard cornered Carl in a small room at the police precinct and went at him.

"It was good cop, bad cop," Carl told *The Washington*

Post later. "Farrell was the bad cop. And I mean he was right in my face, telling me I had failed the polygraph test; how it's been twenty-four hours and they know she's dead. And he says: 'We're going to find her! We're going to find her body!' And then he says, 'When we find her, I'm coming to get you!' He said he had talked to Dee Dee and knew what I was about."

Farrell had indeed spoken to Dee Dee at her mother's house in southern Virginia. Her first thought was the same as the cops': "Carl did it!" She gave them the dirt on their marriage. Now the police had a motive—a dad who wanted to get out of paying $400 a month child support. Oh, he could do it, the detectives thought, look at his temper outbursts. There was, of course, no physical evidence. So they had to get him to confess.

Carl told them that Dee Dee had exaggerated her court charges and sometimes lied to make him look bad. He never threatened to abduct Michele or to kill Dee Dee, he told them. Never, absolutely, never.

"Besides, I love my daughter," he said.

The cops weren't satisfied with the polygraph results. They told Carl they would pick him up for another test the next day with a different examiner. He agreed to take it and went home. It was nearly midnight and he had not slept for more than a day. Michele had been missing for more than thirty hours.

The nightmare was just beginning. He called the divorce attorney who was representing him and told him what was going on. The lawyer, David Goldberg, told him not to allow himself to be hooked up to a polygraph machine again unless it was administered by an independent examiner. Goldberg advised him that he shouldn't speak to the cops without an attorney present. When a detective showed up at his Sudbury Road address and Carl gave them the news, the cops were furious. They knew Carl had done it, just knew it, and grew even more determined to break him and indict him.

Garvey, a straight-arrow cop with a daughter Michele's age, started a covert surveillance on Carl and his residence immediately after he refused to take a second lie detector test. He also tapped his phone. The device gave him the phone number of every local call dialed out of the Sudbury Road house. Garvey got his long-distance records from the phone company and studied them. Then the cops served both Carl and Chuck Dorr a subpoena which required them to appear before a grand jury on Thursday, five days after Michele had disappeared.

"The summons is an attempt to intimidate and harass me," Carl told a local reporter. "They've accused me point blank of abducting my daughter and killing her. They put me under the gun because they have no clues and nothing to go on."

At the courthouse, Carl frustrated both the grand jury and the cops. On the advice of his lawyer, he said, he would refuse to answer any questions on the grounds that his answers might incriminate him. Pleading the Fifth Amendment did not endear Carl to the Montgomery County Police Department. Chuck testified, but he was no help either. He knew nothing and was selling cars that day, he said. His alibi checked out.

Faced with further harassment and advised by Goldberg that the police now considered him their suspect, Carl caved in. He promised to take another polygraph test. And he agreed to stop pleading the Fifth Amendment.

It was dark, almost black, and moonless when Hadden walked to his bike and pedaled back to his truck after pulling his shift at the country club. It would soon be midnight. First he drove to Bethesda Naval Hospital where he knew they would take care of his bitten right hand. He was a Navy veteran, and was entitled to free medical care. The medics put six stitches in it without asking any questions about how it happened. Hadden left the hospital, drove out Wisconsin Avenue to the Capital Beltway, turned right and drove for ten miles. He wasn't sure where he was going, but he was looking for woods. It was always quiet in the woods. They were good places to bury bodies.

He turned on to old Route 29, now called Columbia Pike because it went through the new town of Columbia, south of Baltimore. He drove slowly until his headlights illuminated a sign that said Paint Branch Park. There was a shoulder to pull off on and he slowly pulled the truck to a stop. Traffic whizzed by. If the cops stopped to see what was up, he would tell him he'd had to pee and couldn't wait. That should satisfy them.

He dragged out the sea bag and a ceremonial silver shovel that Silas had given him. The digging tool had once been used to break ground for the first Macy's department store in White Plains. Tonight it would be used to dispose of a little girl. Hadden took the bag, a flashlight, and the shovel. He stumbled down a ravine. At the base of a tree he dug a grave four feet long, digging down until he hit clay. There, the soil became too hard to penetrate. He took the little girl out of the bag and began to drop her in. Hadden paused. He knew he had to taste her, drink her blood. He couldn't stop himself—it was happening too fast. This would be how he would remember her. Her flesh was his prize, and he had his revenge.

Afterwards, he found an old mattress nearby, and placed it on top of her body. Then he covered the dirt with leaves, scrambled back up the ravine, and drove back to his rented room on Munson Street, five miles from Geoff's house. (*Author's note: Hadden has told me a second version of how Michele Dorr died. He said he accosted his victim, tying her up with duct tape and then abducted her in his truck. He said he took her to a deserted house in Bethesda, Maryland. Hadden claimed to have later killed her in the basement of the house and then took her to the burial site. The act of cannibalism is the same in both stories. Police dismiss the abduction claim because, among other facts, there was no duct tape found with her body. Hadden says he removed it all after she expired.*)

Carl took the second polygraph with a different examiner and passed easily. When he was asked if he had harmed or hurt Michele he said he hadn't and the test administrator told the police he was truthful. That wasn't enough for the Montgomery County Police Department. They still eyed him suspiciously, and knocked on his door with a search warrant on June 9, 1986, finding nothing.

Over the next five years he would attempt to prove his innocence by a number of methods that included submitting to questions after an injection of sodium penathol, the so-called truth serum. Carl underwent hypnosis in another effort to clear his name. Eventually, he became bitter about the experience, upset that the police didn't seem to believe him, despite his jumping through hoops for them whenever they asked.

"The police terrorized me," Carl said. "It's as plain as day I didn't have anything to do with it."

His case wasn't helped when he snapped and had what doctors called an acute psychotic episode less than a week after the second polygraph exam. In his altered mental state, which a psychiatrist said was caused by stress and guilt, he now claimed he *had* abducted and killed his daughter.

"I started hallucinating," he remembered. "I just couldn't take the pressure. I hadn't slept in a week. My brain was soup."

While watching television a week after Michele vanished he began to believe that the people on the show he was viewing were talking about him. He looked behind the set. Then he thought that the cops had altered his television reception.

When he woke up the next morning Carl got into his Dodge station wagon and drove to his father's grave in adjoining Prince George's County. He began speaking to his father's headstone. In his altered mental state, he believed the headstone was talking back to him. He thought he was God's only son.

"I believed that if I could find Michele, I could bring her back to life," Carl said. "And if I was able to do that, then I must be Jesus."

He rushed to his old house in Montgomery Village to pass along this revelation to Dee Dee. The visit was poorly timed. There was a strange man in the house with her, Edward Jagen. He was, he said, a spokesman for something called the National Missing Child Society. The six-foot-five Jagen, a former police officer with ramrod military bearing, was known as a avid publicity-seeker, and at the time Carl arrived, had been attempting to get a donation from her. After Carl told his tale of visiting his father's cemetery plot, Jagen tossed him out.

In his crazed state, Carl had a second epiphany. Jagen was Satan and it was he who had killed Michele. Carl began calling himself the White Messiah. Satan, he said, had hidden her body underneath his bedroom in the basement crawlspace. Jagen's group, not yet knowing that Michele's father was fingering their leader, called the news media and offered a $20,000 reward for information leading to her whereabouts.

Carl came to his former home again the next morning and told Dee Dee the story of Jagen as Satan and the body in the crawlspace. His wife and Jagen both called the police. But by the time the cops showed up on Sudbury Road, the police affidavit had a decidedly different spin from what Carl had told Dee Dee.

"Carl Dorr, father of the missing Michele Lee Dorr stated that he, Carl Dorr, had in fact murdered his child Michele Lee, and buried her under the residence at 9129

Sudbury Road," it read, substituting his name for Jagen's. The police looked and found nothing.

Dee Dee filed a petition to have Carl committed for psychiatric observation. He had to be restrained when taken away and spent seventy-two hours being poked and probed in a hospital. After discharging him the doctors told the cops they shouldn't believe the claims of guilt Carl was spouting. It was fatigue and stress that had made him temporarily insane, their evaluation said. The police wanted to believe Carl's confessions of murder more than anything. He was their prime suspect, and their only one. His lawyer, Dave Goldberg, tried to be optimistic about his client's dilemma.

"He's just lost it, he has had a mental breakdown," Goldberg told reporters. "The accusations being made and the press always being in his face just got to him. He blames himself for her disappearance and has a heavy load of guilt about that. The police have accused him of killing her and have beat up on him psychologically, called him before the grand jury, and given him lie detector tests. It's all just overwhelmed him."

The day Carl was released from the hospital, the police grabbed him again and brought him in for another round of questioning. This time they wanted a minute-by-minute account of his actions for the day his daughter disappeared. Carl Dorr, too ashamed to tell the cops that the last time he had seen Michele was well before one in the afternoon, fudged the timeline.

"At approximately 2:10 P.M., Michele came in and obtained a towel, then went back outside after inquiring if they were still going to the pool in Montgomery Village," Mike Garvey wrote after questioning Carl.

Garvey had been a cop for more than a dozen years. He had started out as a rookie patrolman in 1973, just a few miles away from Geoff's house. After a couple of years in a squad car he became an undercover detective for the narcotics division and stayed there for ten years. He was in a new unit, the homicide and sex division, and he thought he had heard it all. Except now, he thought, maybe he hadn't.

If Carl seemed to have lost his mind, Dee Dee wasn't far behind him. She engaged a psychic named Emily to find her daughter. The seer envisioned the word "Patricia." It only poured fuel on the fire when Carl admitted that Michele's beach towel had the logo "Pat Taylor" printed on the cotton terry cloth. Dee Dee also put a special recording on her phone just in case their daughter telephoned.

"Michele, talk after the beep," the message said. "Look at the number on the phone and read it to Mommy. Remember you can push the *O* and tell the operator where you are. I love you and will come to get you soon."

Dee Dee began sobbing on the six o'clock news. The TV stations in town liked the story so much they usually repeated her tears at eleven. Soon it was Dee Dee who was in the hospital. She told the doctors she had overdosed on alcohol and anti-depressants.

David Goldberg, meanwhile, continued to absolve his client of any involvement, even if the cops weren't so sure. He spoke to the press on Carl's behalf.

"One of the doctors said it was a true schizophrenic episode," he said. "Even his wife says he doesn't have anything to do with Michele's disappearance. He's taken another polygraph and passed with flying colors."

With the investigation of Carl Dorr at a dead end, the cops drew a circle on a map with his home as its center and spread out. On June tenth, five teams of dog handlers from a private organization joined the police in searching the woods and fields near the house on Sudbury Road. The dogs were billed by the press as the animals who had found several victims in the 1985 Mexico City earthquake. This time they found nothing.

"We've searched large expanses of land close to the father's house where a child might have wandered or where there are places you could secrete something," a police spokesman said. They pried open manholes and crawled through the sewers under Sudbury Road. They drove to southern Virginia to talk with Dee Dee's mother. There was nothing.

"We are baffled," Mike Garvey admitted to the press.

The police went through Carl's neighborhood knocking on doors and passing out questionnaires they wanted filled out. A gardener who had mowed the Binders' lawn that Saturday remembered seeing a man outside Geoff Clark's house. When he asked him to use the phone, the yardman said, he observed a little girl who matched Michele's description in the kitchen. The man outside the house the detectives learned, was Hadden Clark, someone the neighbors called strange, a real kook.

Detective Wayne Farrell remembered cruising Sudbury Road the day after Michele vanished. He was grasping for any straw and there was Hadden with his pickup in the Clarks' front yard, working on the truck's engine.

"Were you here yesterday?" he asked him.

"Well, I was here for two or three minutes to feed my rabbits," Hadden said. Farrell told Garvey about the meeting with a tall man in the Clark family's driveway.

"Let's bring him in," Garvey ordered. He wanted to have a talk with this Hadden Clark.

Hadden came in alone at 9:30 on the morning of June 8, 1986. The police had telephoned Geoff Clark looking for him and Geoff had called his brother and told him to go to the police station. Garvey let Hadden cool his heels for ten minutes before going to work on him. At first his suspect talked about being at his brother's house that Saturday except now the amount of time became fifteen minutes—between 1:30 and 1:45 P.M. He reiterated that he had fed his rabbits. He also said he had had a conversation with the Binders' black yardman, O'Neil Camock, and had talked

with him about his native Jamaica. Hadden had traveled
there on the *SS Norway*. Their suspect was carrying a Bible
with him—it was a Sunday—at one point lifting the book
up and quoting scripture from the New Testament. This
made Garvey write "Religion!" on his notepad and under-
line the word. Hadden parroted phrases from the sixteenth
chapter of Matthew. The cops may have missed the hints
in the biblical passages:

> Get thee behind me, Satan: thou art an offense unto me.
> For thou savorest not the things that be of God, but those
> that be of men. . . .
>
> For what is a man profited, if he shall gain the whole
> world, and lose his own soul? . . .
>
> There be some standing here, which shall not taste
> of death, til they see the Son of man coming in his
> kingdom.

The detective asked Hadden who his past employers
were and what people he considered his friends, softening
him up. When he asked him about his relationship with
Geoff, Hadden began complaining about his brother's kids
and how one of the boys had once kicked him in the testicles. Then he slipped and mentioned that he had pinned
small girls to the ground while playing with the youngsters.
Garvey jumped on the admission, interjecting with a quick,
simple question.

"Is that what you did with Michele?" he asked. He
pulled out a photo of Michele Dorr and when he did Hadden began rocking back and forth in his chair. He wouldn't
look at the photo and tears appeared in his eyes. Garvey
inserted the picture of Michele into the pages of the Bible.

"Is that what you did with Michele?"

Hadden wouldn't answer Garvey's repeated question directly, instead mumbling something that sounded garbled.
His response had nothing to do with the question that was

posed. Instead, his behavior became something the cops weren't prepared to handle.

"I feel sick. Do you have a bathroom?" Hadden asked. You couldn't ignore a question like that. He went into the police station's facilities and began vomiting into the toilet. Then he shut the stall and claimed to be having diarrhea as well. The cops, sensing he was being evasive, followed him into the lavatory.

"What did you do?" Garvey shouted through the stall. "The parents need to know. Tell me what happened. They need to bury their child. Was it an accident? Let's talk about it."

Garvey shoved the photo of Michele under the stall door. "What did you do?"

Hadden, heaving his guts out from inside the stall, made what later sounded like a partial confession.

"I may have done something. I don't know. Sometimes I black out and do things I don't remember," he told Garvey. He repeated the statement in a slightly different context when he left the bathroom. They were close. Their suspect was an inch away from giving in and telling them everything.

Instead, Hadden appeared to recover and get a second wind. He said he had worked that day, biking to the country club, and punching himself in at 2:46 in the afternoon. Garvey checked his notes. Carl claimed he had last seen Michele at ten after two. You couldn't kidnap or kill someone, dump or hide a body, and then bicycle five miles in thirty-five minutes. It was impossible. When Hadden asked the Montgomery County cops for both a psychiatrist and a lawyer they allowed him to use a telephone.

"They thought that letting him make the phone call would help the interview continue," a detective remembered. "So they permitted him to phone his doctor, and the doctor turned out to be a female psychiatrist who demanded that we stop the questioning, so that was the end of that."

The police drove to the Chevy Chase Country Club. Hadden had indeed punched in at 2:46. A chef said he had shown up at the country club with a bandaged hand. He had hurt the hand, Hadden told his co-workers, when a car forced him off the road and made him crash his bicycle into a tree on the way to work. The alibi was now firmly established and that was enough for the police. Incredibly, they stopped thinking of Hadden as a suspect.

"I went back to the country club years later," Ed Tarney, a detective who was put on the case in 1992, said. "The manager was still there and one thing I learned is that at one time they were having a problem with people punching each other's card in and out."

Later, not then, was to become the operative word. There would certainly be no arrest then.

"Clark gets upset," Garvey's notes read. "Cries, vomits, and makes statements that he may have blacked out and did something he doesn't remember."

He was released after two hours of questioning. There would be no covert surveillance or telephone monitoring of Hadden Clark like that of Carl Dorr.

"I mean, what could you do?" an embarrassed cop asked. "I mean, you couldn't follow this guy around for the rest of his life."

Hadden went home and called Geoff. He told him about his morning visit with the Montgomery County cops.

"Hadden was in a panic," Geoff recalled.

Carl Dorr never let the police forget that he was still their best suspect. He continued to make himself such a target for murder charges that he might as well have painted a bulls-eye on his body. During the fall of 1987, he suffered another breakdown. He walked into a police precinct and claimed he had the power of resurrection. If he could only find Michele, he said, he would bring her back to life. Garvey showed up an hour later, determined to get a confession out of Carl, despite his passing two polygraph tests.

"Garvey was working on me and at one point he started telling me, 'We know you did it. We have the towel,' " Carl recalled. "And I said, 'What do you mean, you have the towel?' So he said, 'The towel, you left the towel behind when you killed her.' And I said, 'What do you mean? I didn't kill her.' Garvey said, 'Well, we mean when she drowned in the pool. We know she drowned in the pool. We know it wasn't your fault. She just drowned in the pool, right? Where did you take her body?' "

It was a standard interrogation technique right out of a detective's manual. Suggest the suspect was responsible for the death but that it wasn't intentional. Tell him it was an accident. Garvey tried every trick he had ever been taught, playing mind games with Carl for hours. He thought he was just a question away from a full confession, but didn't know the right one to ask. Carl remembered it vividly.

"At one point Garvey says, 'Well, you didn't mean to kill her. You just smothered her. You put your hand over her face, and it just happened, right?' "

Wrong. But they had Carl close to the edge. He was ready to break again.

"I guess after a couple of hours they had me brainwashed, thinking I did kill her. They put these thoughts in my head, and then they got Dee Dee on the phone, and they said, 'Here, talk to Dee Dee.' " Carl talked with Dee Dee and told her that yes, he had smothered Michele, and that yes, her body was in the back of his 1975 Chevy van, the one that he couldn't drive because it leaked oil.

By now even Dee Dee believed Carl was innocent so she screamed "No, no!" into the phone loud enough for Garvey to hear her. Of course, the van was empty when they searched it and the cops felt sucker-punched. The next night when Carl showed up at the police station to tell how he could resurrect dead people they threw him out as if he were a drunk found passed out at the bar after closing time.

A day later he came back again. This time Carl told them he had buried Michele inside his father's coffin at the Fort Lincoln cemetery. Then he said he had held his hand over her mouth until she suffocated, and put her body in a sewer pipe wrapped in a blanket. The cops didn't even bother to look up this time. They were no longer buying the stories, especially after their former suspect got a traffic citation and signed the ticket "God." Carl checked back into another hospital, spending ten days in the psychiatric unit.

When he got out, there was more bad news. The TV show *America's Most Wanted* had featured Michele. The program all but said that Carl was responsible for her disappearance.

The police were beginning to feel that their suspect was now playing with their heads in much the same way they had done with him. In May of 1988, just after *America's Most Wanted* was aired, Carl showed up at a garden apartment complex Dee Dee had moved into, and confessed to killing Michele yet again. The cops barely blinked. His former wife told them that Carl had harassed her when she tried to close the door on him. Carl then went to a bedroom window and, when she tried to shut the window, he broke it, her new charges said.

"He was yelling that he knew where Michele was and that it was his secret and this would burn in my soul," her affidavit stated. Carl was sentenced to three years of unsupervised probation for malicious destruction of property and barred from having any further contact with Dee Dee.

"It was too overwhelming," Carl would say years later. "Everyone was coming at me, the police, the reporters, the subpoenas. And to never see Michele again in the course of all that—well, what a one-two punch. How much did I bring on myself? Quite a bit.

"People were expecting me to solve the case for them. The detectives seemed to be working overtime trying to make me their key suspect."

Carl came to believe that he was a victim of an incompetent criminal justice system. He would have a hard time forgiving the police department's mishandling of Michele's disappearance.

Hadden Clark was never able to come close to committing the perfect murder. He wasn't that smart. Although Michele Dorr wasn't his first or even his second such killing, he had not gotten better with practice. Many of his murders were what the FBI calls a "disorganized crime." The Bureau defines these actions as homicides carried out with little or no advance planning and never the same way twice. When multiple murderers behave this way their crimes are among the hardest to solve. There is no pattern or common thread for law enforcement to follow.

With a faulty timeline giving Hadden an alibi, not to mention Michele's deranged father at times begging to be charged in her death, the police forgot Hadden. Carl Dorr was to be their prime suspect for years despite passing polygraphs, undergoing hypnosis, and taking sodium pentathol. They didn't look much further.

Certainly, Hadden didn't go underground or try to keep a low profile after killing Michele. He maintained his need for revenge, to get back at people he believed had wronged him, no matter how petty the offense. But he didn't always retaliate by murdering. When Geoff didn't settle the $10,000 debt that his sibling still was expecting payment for, Hadden took action, but it wasn't violent.

Geoff's Sudbury Road house was burglarized in 1987. Among the items taken was a landscape of a Block Island scene painted by Flavia's mother. She had given it to Geoff when he graduated from high school. Years later it would be found in a storage locker rented by Hadden. In 1989 Geoff found all the air gone from his car tires after coming out of a movie theater. A friend helped him pump the tires back up and a few weeks later the windshield of *his* friend's car was smashed in. Years later, when Hadden was asked about the stolen landscape and Geoff's suspicions he would give this rambling non-denial:

> He might say that. I don't care what he said. I've heard him say a few other things. There's been some problems between my brother and me that I really don't want to bring up. He did things to me that I don't care to bring up because I know it will probably be in the newspaper. If I start knocking them down, it ain't going to do me any good. I'm trying to build my relationship with my family.

By now, Geoff had ceased having any contact with Hadden. His older brother, though, was just warming up.

7

A WALKING TIME BOMB

There are criminals who manage to fly under the police radar seemingly forever. Hadden Clark, in spite of being stopped by the police for both minor and major legal violations several times each year after he murdered Michele Dorr, is a good example. Looking back with the benefit of hindsight, even his driving was suspect. There were two convictions of speeding over the legal limit by ten miles or more in Montgomery County—one in November of 1987 and the other in March of 1988. A year later he was convicted of running a stop light. And that was the small stuff.

In September of 1988 Hadden returned to Block Island, the summer vacation destination off the coast of Rhode Island, and stayed on Flavia's one-acre property for three months. He got a job with a construction crew as a carpenter's apprentice at twelve dollars an hour. In November there was another altercation with his mother. When she saw him carrying several items from the basement during the night, she screamed at him in anger.

"What are you doing, stealing from me like you did Geoff?" she yelled.

Hadden knocked Flavia down and began kicking her. Then he jumped in his truck, and appeared ready to run her over. His mother leaped aside just in time. The next day she charged him with assault and battery with Hadden eventually pleading no contest to the indictment. A Rhode Island judge gave him a year's probation. There was no jail time.

After their fight Flavia wrote her son a letter. She said she was going to pretend he was dead until he got some help from a veterans' hospital.

"Always remember that your mother and father loved you," she wrote, speaking for his now-deceased father. The word "loved," written in the past tense, did not go unnoticed.

Just after midnight on Christmas Day of 1988, he was stopped by a Montgomery County police officer for speeding. The cop found an unregistered, loaded .38 caliber Astra handgun in his truck.

The truck's license plate number made the police department's computer light up like a pinball machine. There were charges pending against him by a landlord who had recently rented him a room in his home. The owner of the house, Paul Mahany, claimed Hadden had stolen property and then vandalized his home in the Maryland suburb of Bethesda, near the National Institutes of Health.

The story was familiar. When Mahany had evicted him from a bedroom in the basement Hadden sought revenge, the charges read. Since he was already on probation in Rhode Island for assaulting Flavia, there was reason for Hadden to be concerned.

"My car's coming down Rockville Pike, maybe twelve or one in the morning," Hadden recalled, "I had picked up the gun somewhere else because someone was holding it for me. I was going to my post office box to see if there was any mail there and I had permission to get that handgun and take it to my storage space. I didn't need a permit to do that."

Hadden sounded affronted at being stopped. The Spanish-made Astra pistol had been one of Silas Clark's trophies from his Pancho Villa adventure. Now the police had impounded it, and he was facing a prison sentence. Hadden felt he had been set up.

"My public defender who represented me at the time said, 'Well, if you plead guilty to the destruction of property charges, they won't get you. The state won't take you for the gun charge. I was doing what they told me."

Hadden did not serve jail time for carrying the unregistered loaded gun only because the county courts chose not to prosecute. Destroying and vandalizing the Mahany household was a more serious matter, particularly since a tax-paying citizen was pressing the charges. The events surrounding his eviction seemed, in some ways, too close to what had happened when he had been asked to leave his basement quarters at Geoff's house.

Hadden rented the basement room from the Mahany family in the summer of 1988. Within weeks they asked him to leave, because in their words, he seemed "crazy and evil." There was also another reason. Their twenty-four-year-old daughter, Martha, was returning home from a year in China where she had been a college exchange student. They didn't want Hadden to have even the slightest chance of being anywhere near her.

Their boarder boasted to the Mahanys before he left that he would have revenge, and he did. Within days Hadden killed the two Mahany family cats, skinning one of them. He later boasted to Jesus that he left one animal on their welcome mat, hung by the neck and attached to the front doorknob. The other one was placed in their refrigerator. He also entered the house and sprayed black dye on the living room carpet, then hid rotting fish heads inside their piano, the chimney, and a stove. Paul Mahany called the cops.

"The smell of decaying fish permeated the house and was extremely difficult to eradicate," a charging document would read. Additionally Hadden created a booby trap by balancing a ten-gallon can of oil and water on top of a door that spilled all over a room when the door was pushed open.

"We felt scared," Mahany said. "He told us about how he always got even with people."

Hadden stole dozens of household items, many of them unusable to him and taken simply for spite. There were

Chinese language books, two tape players with 149 audio tapes, a camera, a pair of Reebok athletic shoes, suitcases, women's clothing, and woodworking tools. Paul Mahany got a restraining order that barred Hadden from coming on his property, but soon Hadden showed up again and walked off with a vacuum cleaner and a bicycle.

According to Hadden, he was persecuted by the Mahany family. He said they had rented out rooms to other tenants and since he was there first, they should have permitted him to stay.

"See, I was there longer. And they said, 'You've got to move. We don't like you.' Really, if I had known the laws better, they couldn't have kicked me out like they did. Then they said I did all this stuff that I never did," Hadden remembered.

"So they kicked me out of the house. They kicked me out and I had a job. Okay, actually I didn't have a job at that time, but my rent was paid up. I paid my rent on time every month. They said, 'Well, you're the last to rent here'—they had three rooms to rent. But who had been there longer? I'd been there longer. So one of those people should go before I go. I was the longest tenant.

"And so they put a charge on me when I left the area and went to Rhode Island. When I came back to the area, the police hit my license for something. Maybe I was speeding. Everybody speeds and they caught me."

What did they accuse you of doing?

"They said I damaged their room but I didn't damage it."

Charged with destruction of property, Hadden pleaded guilty as part of a deal which dropped the unlicensed, loaded handgun offense. Again he served no jail time. There was a year's sentence, but it was suspended, with Hadden assigned a probation officer, and ordered to get psychiatric treatment.

*   *   *

By now, Hadden was purposely homeless, living out of both a tent and his truck behind White Flint Mall in Rockville, Maryland. He continued to work in restaurants but was no longer able to get a chef's position, despite credentials from an outstanding cooking school. A seven-dollar-an-hour assistant cook's job at Geppetto's, an upscale Italian restaurant in Bethesda, lasted less than six months with the manager saying he "let him go because of strange behavior." Hadden boasted of trashing the bistro during a clean-up detail.

"I got drunk on a bottle of 151 proof rum and was really out of control," he boasted.

Hadden wanted employment, but was too mentally unstable to keep a job for long. He stayed just three months preparing salads at the Holiday Inn Crowne Plaza in Rockville at $7.50 per hour. He also tried working for a landscaper at eight dollars an hour for a month in April of 1989 before quitting. In between these jobs he took on temporary day work at minimum wage.

In mid-1989, Hadden, now thirty-seven, visited a local veterans' hospital. He was seeking treatment for his mental disorders as required by the court. But he apparently changed his mind immediately after being admitted. His physician's report would read:

> As soon as the patient was brought to the ward, he took off, was brought back by security and had to be put in seclusion and restraints due to his extremely agitated state and ideas of suicide. He was given some Haldol [an antipsychotic medication] over the next couple of days and improved quickly to being less agitated, calmer, and thus was able to come out of the restraints quickly. He continued to ask to leave, but was not released due to his immediate threats of hurting himself. On Monday, July 17, 1989 he was much calmer, appeared in much better control and was allowed to leave

irregularly. Patient was given a one week supply of Haldol and was supposed to come back for an appointment in the Mental Health Clinic on the following Monday.

The doctor's diagnosis for his mental state was "psychosis, with questionable etiology."

When Hadden was first interviewed at the hospital he told a mental health professional he had been constantly depressed for more than three years. He said he was lonely and that recently the depression had increased to the point that he was becoming suicidal. He also admitted to experiencing hallucinations.

"He states that birds and squirrels talk to him and keep him company," the report said. "He said he could not trust anyone although he denied feeling that people are out to get him."

When first interviewed by a hospital doctor Hadden was in restraints and handcuffed, wearing a T-shirt, a helmet, and bicycle racing shorts. The interviewer wrote in his notes that Hadden appeared "extremely agitated. He is a thin, young, white male. He is tearful at times with intermittent outbursts of anger and agitation. He is depressed and anxious. He has paranoid delusions, but no homicidal ideation."

A second psychiatrist called Hadden "a talkative, naive young man who is socially maladept and a victim of circumstances. He is a potential danger to himself through poor judgment and self-defeating behavior."

Physically, Hadden had no serious complaints. He told the doctor he had frequent stomach upsets which he claimed were due to "bad water" from living in the woods, and diarrhea, which he said had presently lasted nine days. Again, he complained about being fired from his restaurant jobs, particularly the one at the Holiday Inn.

"They had food poisoning in this hotel," Hadden complained. "I'm a victim. I lost a good job and I was on time, not playing sick. It was like Geppetto's, saying I did all these things—why didn't they put it on paper? It happens all the time! And I'm fired all the time. The only thing they can say is I was the last one to be hired, but why didn't they give me any warning?"

Hadden was in tears as he told the doctor about his problem.

"They laid me off eighteen days before my probation was up. I tried to do everything right. It bothers me the way they lay me off."

Hadden was worried about an impending court appearance in mid-1989 and in his agitated state, told the doctor about it. He had been arrested in February on several counts of theft. It was the sixth time in four years that he had been charged with a criminal offense.

"I'm going to court tomorrow," the hospital transcript of his remarks read. "I want to get out of it. I don't know what's going to happen. I'm going to go to jail and I did not do it!"

In his final thoughts, the doctor wrote that Hadden "avoids, distracts, projects, and gets away from the reality of the situation by inserting confusion into the scenario."

Hadden's last words to the therapist were chilling.

"I think I have a split personality. I don't like to hurt people, but I do things I am not aware of," he said.

He left the hospital a few hours later. Hadden first asked for more medication but after having lunch he pulled his personal clothing out of a locker, dressed himself, and left the ward. Hadden told an orderly who asked where he was going that he was off to the mental hygiene clinic for coffee and more medication. But when he saw a doctor in the hallway Hadden demanded his Veterans Administration identification card be returned to him and upon getting it, bolted from the grounds. He was marked "Absent Without Leave" by a staff nurse. In all, Hadden spent just five days at the hospital.

* * *

The court appearance Hadden was concerned about involved an arrest on February 19, 1989. This time he had been charged with a seventeen-count criminal indictment. Fifteen were for theft of either over $300 or under $300. More than $300 was a felony and under $300, a misdemeanor. He was also charged with "possession of controlled paraphernalia," since the police had found a hypodermic syringe in his truck when he was arrested. In the most arcane charge, he was also accused of being a "rogue and a vagabond," legal language that perhaps had not been in use since the age of Shakespeare.

What happened to warrant the charges is still remembered by law enforcement circles.

At one o'clock that afternoon Mary Carlin and James Kidwell of the Maryland–National Capital Park Police were patrolling the northern portion of Beach Drive in Montgomery County. The scenic road was in Rock Creek Park, a long, narrow stretch of greenery named for its stone-filled stream that flows from Maryland through Washington, D.C., before emptying into the Potomac River.

Carlin reported that she observed Hadden's white Datsun pickup truck parked on the shoulder of the road, but not in a designated parking area that was just feet away. Hadden Clark, she would say, was leaning over the passenger side of the front seat, fumbling with a green woman's coat and quickly moving items to the storage space behind the seat. Carlin thought the driver at first might be ill and went over to offer assistance, but at the same time telling her patrol partner to run a check on the license plate. But when Carlin approached the truck she saw a black handgun holster hanging from the top of the seatbelt restraints. This gave her pause. She ordered Hadden to exit his truck and walk away from it.

"No. Nobody can go into my truck," he yelled back at her. She went inside anyway, believing that the gun holster and the driver's behavior was enough reason to search the vehicle.

While Jim Kidwell patted Hadden down Carlin took the green coat out of his truck and went through the coat's pockets expecting to find a gun. Instead, a purse fell out. Hadden said it was his purse.

"It's yours?" she asked. Carlin was incredulous.

"Yes," said·Hadden. "I'm a woman."

With that, Carlin stared hard at him. He certainly didn't look like a woman. She rummaged through the purse expecting to find the weapon there. Instead she found some credit cards and a driver's license with a woman's photo on it that looked nothing like Hadden Clark. Her suspect then claimed he had found the purse.

By now, the park police had radioed back and said the truck belonged to Hadden. They also told the two officers that just three months before, he had been pulled over and found to have an unlicensed handgun in his possession. That information allowed the two police officers to look through the truck without a search warrant.

When Carlin continued searching the truck, she was able to pull out more women's coats from behind the back seat together with several wallets, and a thick roll of cash that ranged from one-dollar to twenty-dollar bills. There was also the hypodermic syringe, a woman's dress, a woman's wig, and eyeglasses that appeared to be styled for a woman. The women's identification cards and drivers' licenses were radioed in to police headquarters.

Mary Carlin soon learned that the wallets and purses belonged to fifteen different women. They had been robbed recently while at choir rehearsal inside two suburban Maryland United Methodist churches. One was in Silver Spring; the other, in Chevy Chase. Hadden stole the purses and coats from a cloak room while they practiced their singing. He had committed the robberies while dressed in women's clothing and wearing a wig. Though Hadden may have thought female clothing made him appear less conspicuous, it was hard to believe that a six-foot-two woman would walk through a church unnoticed.

Hadden finally served some jail time. He was inside for forty-five days before posting bond. Hadden would later say that he purposely chose not to post bail because it was February and freezing outside. The prison offered three square meals a day, a roof over his head, and free movies on Thursday nights. For a frugal person like Hadden, prison was preferable to a cold campsite in some woods behind a mall.

Two days after being incarcerated another psychiatrist examined him. The doctor from Maryland's Forensic Screening Program pronounced him mentally competent, fit for trial, and able to tell right from wrong. In court, Hadden's public defender, Brian D. Shefferman, tried to suppress much of the police evidence on the grounds that Officer Mary Carlin did not have probable cause to believe the purses were stolen. Shefferman also said that since the purse hidden in the green coat failed to contain a weapon, there was no justification for checking further. The court disagreed.

"Here, she [Carlin] has what appears to be a man," the Judge, Irma S. Raker, scolded Shefferman, "and she is looking for a gun, legitimately I think, based on what had happened, and the purse falls out of the coat. In response, he does not say, 'It is my sister's' or 'my girlfriend's.' He says 'It is mine.' And he says, 'I am a woman.'

"If you do not think that common sense would dictate to a police officer that that may not be true and require the police to further investigate, then I think you are suggesting the police officer has got to leave his common sense in the squad car when they go out and do these things. I do not think the law requires that."

The fifteen female victims seemed puzzled by Hadden's thievery. On their Victim Impact Questionnaire many wanted to know one fact. Had they been robbed by a man or a woman? Another suggested that he had a fetish for women's military accessories.

"I want to know what this criminal—man or woman—looks like. All I know is that he was living out of his Datsun truck when arrested. I want to know for my own safety," wrote one woman.

"This criminal not only dressed in women's clothing, but apparently he had prior military service," said another victim, Elizabeth Vane. "He recognized my military purse and took it because he was fascinated by my belongings. He had already separated my military I.D., and nursing license from everything else. He could have caused grave harm by attempting to impersonate me through the use of my nursing license and military I.D. I would like to see what he looks like (as a man and a woman) for my own future safety."

Shefferman and the state's attorney's office apparently cut a deal and he was allowed to plead guilty to one count of theft over $300 and one count of theft under $300. Judge Raker then sentenced Hadden to eighteen months in prison at the Montgomery County Detention Center. Immediately after handing out the sentence she suspended all but forty-five days of the eighteen months, the exact amount of time he had served before putting up bond. She also placed Hadden on probation for three years even though he was still on probation in Rhode Island for assaulting his mother and was also on probation in Maryland for his offenses against the Mahany family. Sentencing guidelines called for a prison sentence of three months to two years.

Why such a minimal sentence, particularly in light of so many criminal charges that had been either dropped, not prosecuted, or settled by giving him probation? Raker addressed it tersely.

"The defendant has serious mental problems and is now addressing them in the community," she wrote.

Another of Hadden's public defenders, Donald P. Salzman, was more prescient. Salzman had a letter printed up on his letterhead that contained both the seal of the state of Maryland and the governor's name. Hadden was told to give it to the police the next time he was arrested. The note read:

> **TO ANY POLICE OFFICER:**
> I want the help of my lawyer, Donald P. Salzman, and I want my lawyer to be present before I answer any questions about my case or any other matters.
>
> I do not wish to speak to anyone concerning any criminal charges pending against me or anyone else, or any criminal investigation regardless of whether I am charged.
>
> I do not want to be in any lineup, or give any handwriting samples, or give any blood, hair, urine, or any other samples unless my lawyer is present.
>
> My lawyer's address and phone number are:
> Donald P. Salzman
> Assistant Public Defender
> Office of the Public Defender
> 27 Courthouse Square
> Rockville, Maryland 20850
> (301) 279-1372

Below the letter was a date and a place for a police officer to sign and next to that a phrase that said: "To prove that I have read this statement to you or that you have read it, please sign."

Hadden Clark was a walking time bomb who had a Get Out of Jail Free card in his back pocket. Both the courts and the public defender's office of Montgomery County seemed to think otherwise. They were doing everything possible to keep him walking the streets as a free man.

8

LAURA AND PENNY HOUGHTELING

Penny Houghteling liked to quote from the works of Emily Dickinson, the cloistered poet whose themes were death and immortality. There was good reason. Her life had been one tragedy after another. A younger brother had died in a car accident at the age of two. Her father had suffered financial setbacks, losing his house and land shortly afterward. Just after that, he died and Penny, a tall, slender brunette full of determination, was sent from their home in South Carolina to Richmond, Virginia, to live with an unmarried aunt. Her mother and sister bunked in with relatives two states away.

Penny persevered. In 1952, just after receiving a master's degree in social work from Smith College, arguably the best name in single-sex education, she married for the first time. That husband committed suicide two years later. In 1960, her mother also killed herself.

In 1964, she remarried and had two children, Warren and Laura. She was forty-one when Warren was born and two years older when she delivered Laura into the world, in 1969. Her second husband, Frederic Delano Houghteling was a Washington government lawyer who—if he chose to—could truthfully say that his mother, Laura, was a first cousin of Franklin Delano Roosevelt. Fred Houghteling suffered from depression and at times would disappear for days.

Fred and Penny divorced in 1977 and when their daughter, Laura, was seventeen, he died of cancer. Two months later, one of Laura's closest friends, Lauren Hester, was killed in an automobile collision. The high school senior wrote a class paper at the National Cathedral School for

Girls, the private girls' academy she attended. It was her reaction to their deaths and titled:

> "GOD IS DEAD"—NIETZSCHE
> "NIETZSCHE IS DEAD"—GOD

"When I was five years old we got up the courage to ask our mother if she believed in God," Laura's paper began. "She said no and some things that I didn't understand. When we asked what would happen when somebody died if there was no God, she told us she didn't know and then some more things I didn't understand and something about living in other people's memories. That sounded pretty ridiculous and lonely to me and we were scared because we didn't want anyone to die anymore and we wished that there was a God for our mommy to believe in."

Laura went on to say that Penny was no longer an atheist but now it was she who was afraid God didn't exist and that maybe her mother was right and memories are all one ever had. In the end, she wrote that she had come to the conclusion that she believed in God both then and now. Laura also said she had established her own theology.

"If we are all so great, why is there war and murder and persecution and suffering?" she wrote. "Why is there evil? It's not such an easy question to answer. But the fact remains, that we as human beings are imperfect. We hurt and we destroy and all because we are free to do as we please. There is an evil in every one of us, which is exactly why we truly need God. If we were perfect we would be gods ourselves, and life would be irrelevant."

She added, "Maybe by accepting the evil in ourselves for what it is, we can begin to transcend it. In admitting our imperfections, we can only become better people.

"But in the end, there is always death, which we can't understand because we never really understood life to begin with. I don't know what I believe about death. I know I don't believe in hell, and what's heaven without hell? For the heaven that most people see to work as a concept, everyone there would have to be pretty damn perfect."

Laura apologized to her teacher for using the mild profanity before continuing.

"So Mother Teresa and Gandhi can sit up there in heaven and chat with God but what happens to the rest of us? And what happens to those who never got a chance to become what they thought they might have been?"

Laura talked about the loss of her father and her friend, Lauren, and the pain she felt and how it wasn't right. She ended the essay by wishing she could be with them one more time, but life wasn't fair and she knew that.

Laura got an *A* on the paper, an event no longer unexpected in her short life. There were many *A*'s and she was soon accepted to Harvard University in Cambridge, Massachusetts, perhaps the most prestigious school in America. That was not unexpected either, though she was polite enough to feign surprise.

"She was going to be president of this country one day," said Susanna Monroney, a close friend. Whether she would have occupied that office is moot. Her question of "those who never got a chance to become what they thought they might have been" would, in her case, be a personal prophecy come true.

At Harvard, Laura stood out, partly because she was a statuesque six-foot-tall beauty with long blond hair who entranced her professors, and partly because she was brilliant. Her nickname was Twiggy because of her height, and in addition to academics, she was considered an athlete who was competitive at swimming and tennis.

Her older brother, Warren, was reed-thin and, at six-foot-eight, good enough at basketball to be picked first in an outdoor pick-up game on asphalt. He was a teacher at the Quaker Thornton Friends School in Silver Spring and as close to Laura as any brother could be.

"We would yell and scream at each other and slam doors, too," he once said. "But we knew that there was something between us that could never be broken."

Laura wasn't sure what to do after Harvard. She had majored in history, graduated with honors, and considered herself a feminist. Her professors had at first tried to interest her in other fields—literature and philosophy were two—though sometimes it seemed they simply wanted to bask in her aura. Laura believed she might want to teach like her brother or become a lawyer like her father. She thought she had lots of time to make up her mind.

"Her ability to so interest stodgy Harvard professors often made me jealous," a classmate, Maggie Donahue, remembered.

Everyone sang her praises. It was deserved.

"She had a remarkable ability to reach out to people," said Rachel Allen, her Harvard roommate. "She was always optimistic. She expected things to be better every time."

After Harvard, Laura volunteered at the Women's Law Project in Philadelphia. She was considering public interest law as a career and the stint in the City of Brotherly Love was one way to get her feet wet. When she came home to her mother's house in Bethesda in September of 1992, she still hadn't made up her mind. So she took a job as an administrative assistant at a Washington, D.C., public relations firm, Holman Communications. It fit her feminist ideas—the president was Diana Holman and her daughter, Hilary, was a good friend from high school. It was a place to mark time until she decided what to do with the rest of her life. After all, she was only twenty-three.

Hadden marked time, too, although work-wise it seemed he had been marking time ever since being discharged from the Navy. He wasn't going anywhere as an expert on cookery, despite his Culinary Institute of America degree. Among restaurateurs, the word was out. His résumé was too checkered, his police record too long. No matter how desperate a hotel food service manager might be, Hadden Clark could not be put on the payroll. By the early 1990s he had become a midnight-to-dawn bagel roller at a Washington food shop on Connecticut Avenue called Whatsa Bagel, a retail business trying to ride the newest fast food trend into the next century.

It wasn't the need for money that drove him to such jobs. He still had more than $40,000 in cash, money markets, and checking accounts. Hadden lived as cheaply as anyone could. Rather, it was his need for people. Living alone in the woods and being ostracized by his family had created a social hunger. He needed to be around others.

He would Rollderblade to bars, nursing a Coke or drinking coffee until the place closed. His favorite was a joint above The Dancing Crab restaurant called The Malt Shop, named, not for its excellent milkshakes, but for the many varieties of beer it had available. There he would cajole and badger people around the U-shaped bar until he became one of its local characters. He would stay and watch the NHL or football games, wearing the teams' sports jerseys and jawing with a barmaid named Rosie. The bar was full of colorful patrons. Margaret Gorman, the very first Miss America back in 1921, lived nearby and often wandered in. She was in her eighties now, but deference was still paid and Hadden inhaled her celebrity. Miss America, well, he would like to do her no matter how old she was, he said, and everyone laughed. "To do" was Hadden's way of saying he would like to have sexual relations with a woman.

The Malt Shop, within blocks of several television studios, was loaded with local television talents, sneaking in for a beer and a burger between the six and eleven o'clock news. To Hadden they were celebrities—he might as well have been in Hollywood at the Brown Derby—and he was in the middle of it, sitting at the bar and trading quips. One night the Redskins' legendary quarterback, Sonny Jurgenson, was there. He was a TV broadcaster himself and Hadden asked for his autograph and got it. The Malt Shop could be ecstasy for Hadden on a cold, rainy night.

Hadden would tell the barmaids that he lived in the woods and from time to time one of them would be intrigued enough to ask to see his campsite, not really believing that a forty-year-old man on inline skates was now living alone on nineteen acres of land so close to the junction of two interstate highways that you could hear the traffic buzz by. A few would even go home with him, if riding in a pickup truck to a tent in the woods could be called going home. Hadden would sometimes take their pictures with a camera and the women wound up being stuck to the wall of the cap that covered the rear of his Datsun. Hadden thought of the photographs as family.

These women looked upon him as if he were a six-foot-two child. Hadden wasn't ugly and unlike many of the older customers, there was no flab protruding from his lean body. They liked his blue eyes and trimmed beard. Sometimes there was sex. He was relatively clean, using his privileges as a disabled vet and showering with soap every few days at the Bethesda Naval Hospital. A bit of a weirdo for sure, they would say, but it wasn't like they were ever going to marry the guy.

When he wasn't at The Malt Shop, he hung out at homeless shelters, often dropping in for free lunches at ones run by local churches. Sue Snyder, the president of the volunteer group, Bethesda Cares, a corporation that provided free food and health services for the indigent, often counseled him.

"Hadden was a man to whom friends were invaluable," she said. According to her, he would craft Christmas ornaments out of pine cones for the less fortunate, then hang around and play chess, always willing to help out by emptying the trash or washing dishes after a meal.

At the First Baptist Church of Bethesda, Hadden regularly attended Bible study classes. He yearned for acceptance from the parishioners.

"He came for the social aspects," the pastor of the church, John Burns, would say. "He was a little loud sometimes and made remarks that were immature. He had no social skills."

At times, Hadden would go from business to business offering to distribute flyers or restaurant menus door-to-door on his skates. He called himself the Rockville Rocket. He would chant this nonsensical ditty to recipients:

> I'm the Rockville Rocket.
> I'm the fastest thing on two wheels,
> I'll race you up and down
> the Lincoln Memorial . . .

Hadden wasn't lazy, just lonely. He was willing to take any odd job that brought him into contact with people. Unlike most members of the homeless fraternity, he would be among the first to raise his hand when day work was offered.

One of these women was Penny Houghteling. The little bit of land that surrounded her home was an oasis of flowers. Zinnias and other annuals filled her yard, pachysandra and boxwoods lined her curved walk, and a perfect circle of English ivy surrounded the largest tree. Now in her mid-sixties, with her busy schedule she needed a gardener. Getting a homeless man from Sue Snyder's church-backed group in 1991 seemed to be the kind of humanitarian gesture that was expected from decent people like her.

Her split-level home on the corner of Julliard Drive and Ashburton Lane in Bethesda was modest in appearance, mostly red brick with a smattering of black ones to give it a darker look. There was a one-car garage. The other three houses on the corner were similar except they were either surrounded by tall hedges or chain-link fence. Penny's property appeared more open and inviting. You felt you could walk right up to the front door and be welcomed inside at any hour.

Penny, a psychotherapist with a basement office, knew how to say the things that made Hadden feel as if he were almost part of her family. It didn't take much with Hadden. He pretended she was his mother. She trusted him enough to give him the run of the kitchen where he was allowed to make himself coffee or pour a glass of ice water. He could walk into the house without asking. Things grew so relaxed that Hadden was given his own bathroom when he worked there. It was the one in the hallway next to her daughter Laura's bedroom. Laura, Penny told him, was in Philadelphia working.

But Penny appeared to overlook a lot. When a graduated strand of pearls disappeared, she didn't confront her employee. She didn't seem to notice that her underwear and clothing were being stolen either, one piece at a time. And when she saw him emerging from Laura's bedroom when he was supposed to be outside working, she kept her mouth shut. Penny *had* once complained to Hadden about her garden tools disappearing and then reappearing and he had become angry. Very angry. He blew up and yelled loudly enough to make Penny worry about her accusation and think that maybe she was being too hard on him.

Then Laura came home. Penny had another child now, one she seemed to like more than Hadden. Within days he was plotting revenge.

On October twelfth, Hadden pulled some weeds from the garden, mowed the lawn, and drank coffee from Penny's kitchen. Penny told him that she was going away for a week, giving Hadden the exact dates—from the seventeenth to the twenty-fifth. There was a week-long, New

Age–style conference in Hendersonville, North Carolina. It was called Journey Into Wholeness and combined Jungian psychology with Christian spirituality. The workshop seemed to be the perfect fall break for someone like Penny Houghteling.

On October fourteenth, Hadden visited a Hechinger store, one of a regional hardware chain. He purchased two rolls of duct tape, a coil of braided rope, and three boxes of Mason's Line, a thin braided nylon cord that came in colors. The bill was $21.13. Hadden wrote a check for the exact amount. In the left-hand corner of the check, the place where the word *Memo* was printed, he wrote, "Laura."

Three days later, on Saturday, Laura Houghteling went to the Gold Cup with some friends. The annual event, near Middleburg, Virginia, is a series of steeplechase races widely patronized by millionaire socialites and preppy post-college singles. That was followed by dinner, a party, and a mishap. Laura's misfortune involved her yellow Volkswagen Rabbit—it was towed for being illegally parked. She caught a cab back to Washington and visited her boyfriend who lived on Capitol Hill. He drove her home at two that morning.

The next day, Sunday, October eighteenth, Laura had her brother, Warren, drive her back out to Virginia to retrieve her car. Warren hung around the house and that afternoon the two siblings, together with his housemate Rob Hansen, saw the Washington Redskins edge the Philadelphia Eagles, 16–12, on television. Watching football on a fall Sunday was a national ritual but in the nation's capital, where rabid Redskins fans were a majority of the populace, it was virtually required. During the game, Laura's close friend, Catherine Sheehan, called from Massachusetts where she was a first-year law student at Boston College. The young women chatted for nearly an hour while Laura's brother and his friend focused on the game. Laura wasn't going out that night. There was a big project she was immersed in at Diana Holman's public relations firm and she planned to be into work early the next morning. Besides, she was a little tired from the night before. She went to bed at eleven, wearing a T-shirt and panties.

Just after midnight, Hadden parked his truck on the street next to Penny's gardening shed. He opened the door to the miniature barn-like structure that contained Penny's gardening tools and grabbed the extra house key he knew she kept there.

Hadden didn't look like himself. He didn't feel like himself either. He was wearing a woman's wig—the label said *Paula Young*. This made him look more like Laura than Hadden. Next to his skin he was wearing Penny Houghteling's underwear, which made him feel a little like Penny. He carried a black purse and wore women's flats—heels would have made him too tall to be mistaken for either Penny or Laura. The ladies' blouse and tan slacks Hadden was wearing were covered by a woman's trench coat. Underneath the coat was a .22 caliber rifle that was unloaded, an antique. It had once belonged to his grandfather. Hadden had taken it to a gunshop in Meriden, Connecticut, and had the weapon restored. One of Silas Clark's war souvenirs was again about to be Hadden's helper for an evening of murder and mayhem.

He turned the key to the front door of Penny's house, tiptoed silently towards Laura's bedroom and, once inside, used the gun to nudge her awake. The first words out of his mouth seemed strange, but everything must have seemed strange to Laura Houghteling at that moment.

"Why are you in my bed?" he asked.

Laura was speechless.

"What are you doing in my bed?"

He spoke to her again.

"Why are you wearing my clothes?"

There were tears in her eyes now.

"Tell me I'm Laura."

"You're Laura. Please don't hurt me."

Hadden asked her again, this time forcing her to swear on the Bible that he was Laura. She did. Then, holding the gun on her, he forced Laura to get up, undress, and take a bath. After the cleansing ritual he led her back into the bedroom and had her lie down and turn over on her stomach. His plan was to abduct her, take her to his campsite, and, according to Jesus, "introduce her to Hadden." He bound her wrists with duct tape, then her ankles, then turned her over and covered her mouth, but he became so excited that he couldn't stop and put the tape over her nose and her eyes, winding it around and around her head. She couldn't breathe. Laura struggled until the lack of air suffocated her and she lay motionless.

Hadden said that as soon as Laura became still, he tried to remove the duct tape from her mouth with a pair of scissors. He claimed that he had missed, running the shears into her neck, and causing blood to flow onto her sheets and into the mattress pad. *(Author's note: The assertion of an accident relies on Hadden's credibility.)*

He did a clumsy job of removing the sticky tape from her face and wound up leaving pieces of it stuck in her hair. Fascinated by her earrings, he decided to take them from her as a memento. When he couldn't get the second pierced earring to come off immediately he simply cut it off with the scissors, amputating the lower part of her ear as well.

Hadden sat by the bed and watched Laura for nearly an hour. At times he fondled her breasts and stroked her dead body but has always vowed that in her case he neither raped her nor practiced cannibalism on any part of her remains. Just after three that morning he wrapped her dead body in a queen-size sheet, slung her over his shoulder, and carried her out to his Datsun pickup, exiting by using Penny's side door that was only steps from the street. Hadden put Laura, still shrouded in the sheet, on the narrow bed in the back

of the pickup. He went back inside and gathered up the
bloody evidence—the sheet, mattress pad, and pillowcase—
and carried them out to the truck. He took some trophies.
Laura's high school ring, a crystal unicorn, her camera, and
other jewelry went either into the pockets of the coat or his
purse. He stole her briefcase. Then, after taking a pillowcase from Warren's old bedroom and making sure everything looked tidy he lay down on his victim's bed and
rested. For a few minutes he was Laura.

Laura's killer left the house just after eight that morning.
He wore the wig, the trench coat, the slacks, and the same
women's flats with white socks, carrying the purse. A
neighbor's housekeeper was standing on the corner with a
small boy, chaperoning him while he waited for the school
bus. She had noticed Penny and Laura leaving together
each day for weeks at about that time. Penny would often
drive her daughter to the Metro subway station five miles
away and return. The housekeeper would later say she
thought the person in the trench coat was Laura, leaving
for work alone.

Hadden drove to the North Bethesda United Methodist
Church, less than two blocks away. The church had a large
rear parking lot, containing several paved acres. Hadden
had parked his truck there many times, sleeping under a
large oak tree after dark. He needed to sleep now, he had
to sleep. It had been a big night.

While Hadden slept, Diana Holman began wondering
where Laura was—it was unlike her to be late for work.
She telephoned her daughter, Hilary, who said she had no
idea why Laura wasn't there. Hilary called both of the
Houghteling family's phone lines. The first, the line to
Penny's basement psychotherapy practice contained a recording from Penny, asking the caller to leave a message.
The second line rang continuously. Hilary reported back to
her mother with Diana asking her daughter to drop by the

Houghteling house. Maybe Laura was sick, she said, and wasn't answering the phone.

Arriving at the Houghtelings' Julliard Drive residence, Hilary noticed Laura's yellow Rabbit parked outside. She peeked inside and found nothing unusual. A rolled-up copy of *The Washington Post* was on the front lawn and the mail had been delivered. She rang the doorbell and got no answer. Peculiar. She walked around the house and tried the sliding glass doors at the back. They were unlocked. She went inside. The house was quiet, too quiet. She walked to Laura's bedroom.

The bed didn't look quite right. It was made, but not the way Laura usually made it—the spread wasn't pulled up all the way. Hilary began to get uneasy. She walked into every room of the house and looked around. She saw nothing else that looked out of place. Hilary telephoned Warren Houghteling, leaving a message with his answering service. Warren would return home from his teaching job around five. She didn't yet think Laura's disappearance was important enough to pull him out of school.

When Warren checked his answering machine, he heard Hilary's message and began calling her friends. None of them had heard from her that day. Warren and his housemate drove to his mother's house. It was already dark and when he got there he noticed that the light near the kitchen sink was turned off. That, too, seemed unusual. His mother kept that one on permanently. It was her house night-light and he had never seen it unlit. Like Hilary, he searched the house and found nothing. Warren suggested to Rob that they walk the route to the Metro subway station with flashlights. After walking a mile they saw Hadden Clark driving towards them in his pickup truck. Warren knew the family gardener and waved him down. Hadden, who had hoped to return to Penny's house and go back inside, pulled over. But as Warren walked to the truck to ask him if he knew of Laura's whereabouts, he sped away, pulled a U-turn and

Hadden Clark as the "Rockville Rocket."

MISSING
LAURA HOUGHTELING

LAST SEEN SUNDAY, OCTOBER 18, 1992
PLEASE CALL THE MONTGOMERY
COUNTY POLICE AT (301)657-0112
WITH ANY INFORMATION LEADING TO
HER WHEREABOUTS
6 FEET TALL, 145 POUNDS, BROWN
EYES, BLONDE HAIR

The Houghtelings' neighborhood was covered with these posters days after Laura's disappearance.

The Houghteling residence. WILLIE VOLZ, *THE WASHINGTON TIMES*.

Police photo of Hadden Clark's van in the police garage.
MONTGOMERY COUNTY POLICE PHOTO.

State's exhibit photo of the room where Michele Dorr was murdered. Her blood was under the floorboards. MONTGOMERY COUNTY POLICE PHOTO.

Lt. Michael Garvey, Montgomery County Homicide. ROGER RICHARDS, *THE WASHINGTON TIMES*.

Lt. Garvey and Sgt. Bob Philips worked ten years on the Michele Dorr case. KEVIN T. GILBERT, *THE WASHINGTON TIMES*.

Montgomery County Police Chief Carol Mehrling after the September 1998 arrest of Clark for the murder of Michele Dorr.
ROGER RICHARDS, *THE WASHINGTON TIMES.*

Maryland State police searchers at the wooded area where they found the remains of 6-year-old Michele Dorr in January 2000. She had disappeared in 1986. ROGER RICHARDS, *THE WASHINGTON TIMES*.

Michele Dorr's park gravesite became a shrine after her body was found and removed. The location was within sight of where other children played. GEORGIANA HAVILL.

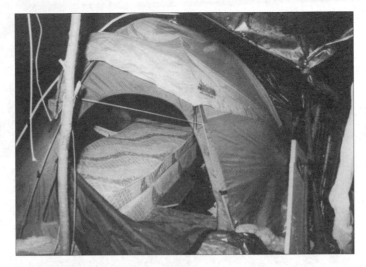

Prosecution photo of Hadden Clark's tented "home" in the woods.
MONTGOMERY COUNTY POLICE PHOTO.

Hadden Clark marked his knives—tools of his trade as chef—with his name or initials. These were confiscated from him and presented as evidence. GEORGIANA HAVILL.

Hadden Clark, in his Kristen Bluefin persona, wears a woman's wig, supplied to him by local law enforcement, and a skirt under his jeans. He is seen here leaving the Barnstable, MA, jail with the FBI. They would spend the day searching for his Cape Cod victims.
VINCENT DEWITT, *CAPE COD TIMES*.

came barreling back towards them. He drove as if the devil were after him and perhaps that was true. Warren's sister's body was still in the back of the truck, concealed by the truck's metal cap and wrapped in the white sheet.

Warren thought Hadden's behavior was a bit weird, but then, he knew Hadden was a bit weird anyway. Maybe he didn't recognize me, he thought. Warren gave him the benefit of the doubt, and continued walking the route to the subway station with Rob, finding nothing.

When they got back to Penny's house, Warren got on the phone and spoke to each one of Laura's friends whom he found at home. The best answer he got was from one young woman who said she had spoken to her on the phone the night before around 10:30.

At midnight, Warren called the Bethesda station of the Montgomery County police. David Shupp, a police officer, drove over and duplicated what Warren and Hilary had already done—searching the house and back yard. The cop wrote down Laura's description as a white female, twenty-three, six-feet-tall, 145 pounds, shoulder length blond hair, brown eyes. He noted that she was in perfect health. Then he told Warren that he shouldn't worry. Statistics showed that ninety percent of all missing persons eventually turn up and are in excellent condition, too, he said.

Warren called Penny early the next morning. She flew home immediately.

Hadden prepared to bury his prize. After running into Warren, he was nervous and frightened. He drove to a spot on Interstate 270, just across the highway from his campsite. Hadden grabbed a shovel, unwrapped her from the sheet, swung Laura's nude body over his shoulder as if it were a sack of flour, and ran stumbling into the woods. Laura was heavy, a hundred pounds more than Michele Dorr, and he wearily dropped her, twenty feet from the shoulder of the road.

He dug feverishly until he had a shallow grave. It was three feet deep and nearly seven feet long. Then he rolled her into it and covered the cavity with tree branches and brush, anything that would disguise the raw earth. In the months to come, animals would detect the body's scent, digging and pawing through the brush, trying to get to the decomposing remains. By spring, Laura's wrists and lower extremities would rise above the ground, the heavy rains forcing her body upwards.

9

HADDEN ON THE RUN

Hadden drove north on Interstate 95. He was anxious to get distance between himself and the murder he had committed less than twenty-four hours before. He tired when he got to New Jersey, pulled off the highway, and found a parking lot in back of a church to park his truck and sleep. He forced himself awake at dawn, got back on the road, and headed for Rhode Island.

He was in Warwick by dusk but had to wait until the next morning to get into a mini–storage locker he had rented there. On October 21, 1992, Hadden deposited the bloody sheet, mattress pad, briefcase, and jewelry items he had stolen from Laura's bedroom into the rented space at Warwick's E-Z Mini Storage compound. He kept Laura's pillowcase. That was the way he would relive the moment while lying in his truck, becoming Laura again while burying his face into the pillowcase as he wore the Paula Young wig and Penny's underwear. If he wanted a bigger thrill, he could always drive back to E-Z Storage and play with the bloody sheets. Hadden drove home to Washington feeling pretty proud of himself.

By now, Montgomery County Police Detective Edward Golian wanted to talk with Hadden. Warren and Penny had both mentioned his name and when he called the description in to headquarters he was told by another officer that the name rang a bell. Wasn't he once a suspect in the Michele Dorr case? When Golian told her about Hadden's criminal record, and that he might be involved in her disappearance, a still-trusting Penny Houghteling poohpoohed the accusation.

"Hadden wouldn't hurt anyone. He's just the gardener," she said.

Warren wasn't so sure. He told Golian about Hadden's unusual behavior when he had approached his truck. He volunteered to call the voice-mail number his mother used that let Hadden know he was needed for gardening chores. His call was returned within an hour. Warren told him that Laura was missing and then asked for an explanation of the truck incident. Hadden said he thought Warren had been a carjacker.

A day later Hadden mailed Penny and Warren a sympathy card. He wrote a note to go along with the printed message.

> Just please give me a call when you are ready to do some gardening again. I can bring you some bagels on Friday, too.

By now Laura's friends were alarmed, already beginning to believe that the unthinkable might have happened. Still, they placed MISSING posters on telephone poles in the neighborhood and at subway stops. Two of her friends went on a television station's six o'clock news to get the story out. Warren himself went on an eleven o'clock broadcast where a reporter asked him to say something to Laura in case she was watching.

"Please call, because we are really worried," he said.

As he spoke, the state of Maryland's computers were spitting out Hadden's criminal record. The gardener, let's find the gardener, Golian was saying. He searched Penny's house and yard over again, looking for clues. This time he went through the laundry hamper, examining each piece of lingerie, looking for blood. He asked Penny if any suitcases were missing. In the neighborhood the police checked out the empty houses that had *For Sale* signs on them. A body could be dumped inside them. It had happened in the past.

Golian called Richard Fallin, a bald, bearded detective in the homicide–sex division. Fallin knew the name Hadden Clark. The Michele Dorr case. Fallin called his boss, Robert Phillips. Phillips had been running the Silver Spring investigative division when Michele disappeared. He too, remembered the name of Hadden Clark.

"Hadden Clark! Absolutely! Let's go!" Phillips shouted into the phone. "Let's get him right now. The son of a bitch got away once."

Golian telephoned Hadden's voice-mail number and Hadden surprised him by returning the call almost immediately. When Golian asked him to stop in for a visit Hadden declined. He said he was getting ready to go to sleep in his truck but promised to drop by the station the next afternoon, October 22. Golian had no choice but to make the appointment, giving him an exact time he wanted him at the station. Before he rang off Hadden asked the cop if he had found Laura yet and if Penny was back at home.

After the call Hadden went back to the North Bethesda United Methodist Church and parked in his usual spot. He went to the rear of his truck, grabbed Laura's bloody pillowcase, and ran into the woods that bordered the parking lot. He threw it by a tree, walked back, and climbed into the cot in the rear of his truck, where he fell into a worried sleep.

Sue Snyder of the homeless group Bethesda Cares walked into the police station with Hadden the next afternoon. Golian was gentle, partly because of Snyder, partly because they didn't have that much to go on yet. He asked Hadden to account for everything he had done and everywhere he had gone on October eighteenth and nineteenth.

Hadden was ready for Golian, giving him a complete account. He had watched the World Series at The Malt Shop above The Dancing Crab on Sunday night, saying he had only drunk coffee there. After that he bedded down at the North Bethesda United Methodist Church and slept until nine the next morning. Then he had gotten up, he said, bought food at a local supermarket, and attempted to do some gardening for a family—except they weren't home when he stopped by their house. He visited a skate shop, went to the Bethesda Cares headquarters twice, and then helped out a homeless man he knew only as John.

He also said he had washed his laundry and taken a shower at the Bethesda Naval Hospital. After his second visit with Sue Snyder, he was on his way back to the church when he met Warren, whom he thought was a carjacker. The incident had so unnerved him that he went to the parking lot of another church, St. Luke's Episcopal, to bed down for the night. Hadden also added a touch that must have pulled on Sue Snyder's heartstrings. He spent most of the evening, he said, working on his Christmas cards. Hadden and his companion left the police station, whereupon he began sobbing. Snyder asked him why he was crying.

"I feel so bad for Penny and Warren," Hadden said.

Two days later a cop showed up at Penny's house with an officer from the canine unit and a trained dog. After the dog sniffed around Penny's house and in Laura's room, they went into the woods behind the parking lot of the North Bethesda United Methodist Church. Within minutes, the canine officer and the dog found Laura's pillowcase. They also found other women's clothing in a clearing between the trees. There was a size 36-B Olga bra, a gray silk blouse, a woman's shoe, and lots of lingerie. All of the clothing would later be identified as belonging to Penny Houghteling. The pillowcase looked fresh. The rest of the items had been there for months.

The police took the pillowcase back to Penny's. It matched the top sheet. It was taken to the county crime laboratory for examination. A quick test showed that the red stains were blood.

That evening, Golian, Fallin, Phillips, and Susan Ballou,

an attractive blonde who was the county's forensic serologist, gathered at Penny Houghteling's home. They examined the mattress closely with Ballou's trained eye catching
what she thought were tiny spots of blood. When it became
dark they used luminol, a chemical that imparts a brilliant
blue light when it comes in contact with iron in the blood.
More than half the mattress gave a bluish glow. Television
cameras outside the house caught the moment while inside,
a technician shot the scene with a high-speed still camera.

Given the amount of blood the luminol indicated, everyone in the room immediately concluded that Laura Houghteling was dead. The next day the blood on the pillow was
confirmed as the same blood-type as Laura's. Hair was
taken from the room and the bed. The strands would later
be confirmed as Hadden's. A single fiber found on Laura's
hairbrush matched that of a Paula Young brand wig. Penny
told the cops that Laura had never worn a wig. The detectives would conclude that Hadden used the brush to style
his hair before setting out the morning after he killed her.

Fallin and Ed Tarney noticed Hadden a few hours later
on East-West Highway in Bethesda and pulled him over. It
was midnight. As they approached him, an aggressive local
television crew that had tailed the two detectives pulled
behind them. When Tarney told him he needed his help to
find Laura, Hadden saw the TV people and began playing
to the camera. He fell to his knees and cried.

"I'm so scared. Oh God, I just want to die."

He told the camera crew that the days of the Rockville
Rocket were numbered and that because of all the publicity
he would never work again.

"I'm just a homeless man," he ranted. "I don't have any
friends. I'll be jobless after this."

Tarney and Fallin took Hadden to police headquarters
and began asking him questions. Outside in the parking lot
cops searched his truck.

"Do you think Laura Houghteling is pretty?" he was asked.

Hadden shrugged and muttered softly that he had never paid any attention to her. Then Tarney hit him with a statement to get his reaction.

"We found the pillowcase in the woods. It had a fingerprint on it. The print was yours."

Tarney was bluffing. While they *had* found a faint fingerprint, it had not yet been identified by the county laboratory. The detective was gambling, hoping for a reaction. He got one.

Hadden began whimpering. Tears filled his eyes. He pulled his wool toboggan cap down over his eyes.

"What did you do with Laura Houghteling?" Tarney growled.

"I don't remember."

That would be his answer to most of Tarney's questions. Hadden did confide to the cops that he liked to dress in women's clothing. He asked to leave and the two cops let him go. They hadn't found a wig yet and they didn't have enough to hold him.

The next day, before the ink was dry on the search warrant, the police seized Hadden's truck for twenty-four hours. They offered to rent him a motel room for the night but instead Hadden sought sanctuary at Sue Snyder's house. She found him a place to stay with a deacon of the First Baptist Church in Bethesda. That Sunday, October twenty-fifth, Hadden dropped a note in the collection plate along with a dollar bill. "Hadden I. Clark homeless," it read. "Is life really worth living any more or is it time to commit suicide?"

Police took hair samples from the truck, copied Hadden's checkbook stubs and a mileage log, and impounded three bed sheets. Copies of the checks obtained from Hadden's bank revealed the incriminating Hechinger purchase, the E-Z Mini Storage existence, and another space he had rented at American Self Service Storage in Kensington, Maryland. Further investigation found that Hadden owned five different post office boxes.

There were a couple of items that would come to fascinate them. The first was something that looked like a hand-drawn map. Was it a map that told them where Laura was buried or was it about someone else? The other item was an eyeglass case filled with soil. The dirt wasn't a kind found in the Washington area. It was sandy and looked like it came from somewhere near the ocean.

Golian went to the offices of American Self Service Storage and was told that Hadden entered the storage space on a near-daily basis. Further, records showed, he had been in the storage space twice on October nineteenth, the day Laura disappeared. That was something Hadden somehow had missed telling Golian when recounting his activities for him.

Tarney and Fallin went to the storage space the next morning and pored through the contents. At first they thought there wasn't much in it but junk. There were some shovels, a photograph album, and a woman's blue suit and slip. The clothing would turn out to be Penny's.

Bakers at Whatsa Bagel, who had seen Hadden's television antics, called in with tips. One slipped the cops the approximate location of Hadden's campsite. Another co-worker, who told the police he wanted to remain anonymous, said Hadden said he wanted "to do" Laura Houghteling.

The woman on Julliard Drive who employed the housekeeper who regularly waited at the bus stop outside the Houghtelings' home also came forward. The maid described the tall woman who had left the house that morning while she stood waiting for the schoolbus with her employer's son. Penny was told about the sighting and immediately concluded, that, whoever it was, it wasn't Laura. Her daughter would never wear slacks to work, she said, and wouldn't ever, ever wear white socks with flats. The new information sent Tarney back to the self-storage space Hadden rented in Kensington. They had done but a cursory search before and there was junk piled to the ceiling. This time they found a khaki trench coat, a pair of women's tan trousers, size twelve women's shoes, and lots of wigs, including a blond shoulder-length style with a *Paula Young* label inside.

Hadden, courtesy of Sue Snyder, continued to stay in the homes of good-hearted church couples who still believed that he was a poor, homeless man who was being persecuted by the police. On October twenty-eighth, Hadden went to see the movie remake of John Steinbeck's 1937 novel, *Of Mice and Men*, starring John Malkovich and Gary Sinise. The classic tale of the wily protector watching out for a sweet simpleton who eventually murders a young woman seemed eerily allegorical.

While Hadden was going to the movies and getting royal treatment in the homes of God-fearing families, Laura's mother and brother were giving up. Penny, pragmatic to a fault, had concluded that Laura was dead within minutes after the police conducted the luminol tests. On October twenty-ninth, Penny, Warren, and some of Laura's closest friends conducted a news conference. They stood in front of her house and addressed a horde of print reporters and local television crews.

"I know in my guts that Laura is dead," Penny said. "It was a very sophisticated murder. For someone to have done this so that there was not any evidence or practically nothing out of place, neither downstairs or in her room, well . . ."

Penny stopped. She was not your typical weeping, hysterical parent who falls into fifty pieces and blubbers for television cameras. Too many tragedies over the years had dried up her public tears. At home, alone, were the times to scream and cry. But not here, not in front of the press.

She was unsparing in her details. She told about the police finding blood in Laura's room and said that whoever had murdered her daughter had cleaned up afterward. She admitted that occasionally she left the side door unlocked but that Laura never did. One of the last things Laura had told her friends after the Gold Cup last Saturday night was that she had to go home to make sure the side door *was* locked.

"Having locked it Saturday night, I don't believe she would have left it open Sunday night. Whoever came in had a key and then left the door unlocked," Penny said.

Warren was already lobbying against the death penalty. He simply wanted Laura's murderer off the streets.

"Many people in this area care deeply about my sister. We want the person who did this to be apprehended. We have no desire to see that person dead, but we don't want this person to do something like this again," he said.

"It's time to mourn," said Penny. "The cliffhanging has just been awful."

While Penny, Warren, and their supporters were giving the hungry press its feeding, the Montgomery County Police Department was forming a search party. Cops were about to ransack Hadden's campsite and the nearby land across the freeway. Using the bagel baker's tip and some photos found in Hadden's storage bin, Bob Phillips found the location using a state-owned police helicopter. They were soon on the ground with cadaver dogs, looking for impressions in the ground, anything that might indicate Laura was below where they were walking. They crossed the road to the other woods, the fifty-four-acre tract of land where Laura was buried. At one point a cop literally stepped over her grave, but noticed nothing. There were the remains of an old stone mansion on the grounds and one of the bagel shop employees said he had heard Hadden talking about a root cellar that was below the foundation of the house. They took the dogs, found the root cellar and searched it, coming up empty.

Hadden was now under covert surveillance by the Montgomery County cops. He knew it and shook them off easily. When Hadden spotted an unmarked police car shadowing him, he let him get close, then slammed on his brakes and let the cop, Don Frietag, bump into the back of his truck. Frietag, his cover blown, cursed while Hadden drove away.

On October thirtieth, Hadden was back on the road in his Datsun truck, headed for Rhode Island and the space he was renting at E-Z Mini Storage in Warwick. He showed up the next morning and had a brief conversation with an employee who knew him, Lila Barchie.

"What are you doing up here?" the woman asked.

Hadden lied and told her he had come to get his father's cremated remains from the storage bin. He was going on to Wellfleet on Cape Cod, he said, to bury the ashes in the family plot. Hadden had buried his father's remains nearly two years before.

When he was concealed inside the walk-in locker, Hadden grabbed Laura's briefcase, the bloody sheet, and the mattress pad. He put her jewelry and the crystal unicorn in his pockets and drove for two hours. On the way to Wellfleet, on Cape Cod, he stopped at a rest area and got rid of part of the incriminating evidence in a Dumpster behind the men's room.

When Hadden arrived at Pleasant Hill cemetery in Wellfleet that afternoon, he drove onto the burial grounds in his truck, found the family plot where his father and grandparents were interred, and backed recklessly into the area, scraping and knocking over headstones and bending grave markers over in a clumsy effort to get as close to the site as possible. Hadden wanted to begin digging. He wanted to remove something very special to him, but was frustrated. He couldn't. There was another woman nearby, praying at her mother's grave, and, well, one couldn't take out a shovel and start digging next to a grave in the daylight. Hadden was confused. He drove out of the cemetery and back to Rhode Island to see his sister, Alison. It was Halloween night and Hadden walked up to his sister's door on West Wind Road near Peace Dale and knocked. The sight of her disheveled and frantic brother arriving unannounced on her doorstep gave Alison more of a fright than any of the trick-or-treaters who had shown up during the early evening.

"They're trying to pin a crime on me because I'm homeless," Hadden told his sister.

Alison asked her brother if he wanted to spend the night or if maybe he would feel more comfortable in a motel. "I'll pay for it," she said. Alison was married, with two children, and trying to lead a respectable life, far away from her scandalous family. Her husband, Bill Huggins, was a graduate of the University of Rhode Island. She was relieved when Hadden declined.

"No, I've got to keep moving," he told her.

Hadden left after a visit that would later seem to be only seconds long. He drove back to the cemetery where his grandparents and father were buried, took out a shovel and began digging. The night was black, the place deserted. Who in their right mind, Hadden thought, would dare to visit a cemetery on Halloween night? Hadden shoveled out a hole, not a grave. He dug down until his shovel struck metal. Then he pulled up the bucket.

Inside the metal container was the story of his life. More than 200 pieces of jewelry, watches, and trinkets that he had taken from victims for more than fifteen years. Some of it had been stolen or purchased at yard sales to be sure, but a lot of it had come from the bodies of the other women he had murdered. Hadden would one day boast to Jesus that he had killed his first victim—a teenager named Debbie—in the summer of 1976. *(Author's note: On the other hand he has boasted to me that his first victim was a boy in 1965. Perhaps males don't count.)* He had picked her up hitchhiking in Pennsylvania and he had killed her because she was, well, "annoying." And his first trophy? That was the delicate silver pin, a winged wood nymph, the one the press would one day call "his angel of death." The pin had been taken from Debbie. He had worn it the night he killed Laura and now he was returning it to this homemade treasure chest on Halloween night. He dropped Laura's class ring and her watch inside the bucket, and brought the container to his truck.

He went back to the site. There was a skeleton under the bucket, the remains of a tiny body. It was another child, a little girl named Sarah whom he had killed and partially eaten in 1985. He scooped up her bones and put them in a plastic bag.

Hadden didn't want to rebury his two treasures in the same place. He wanted the site to be safe. But where? He took the bucket and walked through the woods to the safest haven of all. It was nearly midnight·now and he took his shovel and dug into the sandy soil, burying his treasure at the rear of the property of Silas and Edith Clark's former house. The old estate was still his haven and surely no one would find it there until the day he was ready to commemorate another killing. He kept the remains of the little girl until the next day, disposing of her in another part of the state.

Two weeks after Laura's disappearance, November 1, 1992, a standing-room-only group of her friends packed St. Alban's Church in Washington for a memorial service to honor the still-missing Laura Houghteling. There were platitudes from relatives and the friends who had participated in the search for her.

"I have been searching through the darkness to find the light, and there is a great deal of it here today," a cousin,

Kathy Neusdadt, told the 450 people at the service.

There were readings that featured excerpts from Laura's high school paper on death and the meaning of life. There were many tears and embraces.

"To push aside the horror would be to betray her. We must confront her death, the fear we feel, the loss of trust in others," said her friend Catherine Sheehan in one eulogy.

Penny Houghteling was her usual public self, stoic and composed. She held a flower as she spoke. "I know that Laura is not living in her body," she said. "She was a beautiful spirit, she embodied the spirit of the body feminine."

It was Sue Ballou, the forensic serologist with Montgomery County, who had discovered the fingerprint. The print was on the blood that covered Laura's lace-bordered pillowcase. Sue was waiting to hear from the lab. On November sixth a report came back with the not-so-surprising news that the print was Hadden's. Now all they had to do was find him. He wouldn't go back to his campsite, they were sure of that. Instead, the word was put out to check the churches. A police officer spotted Hadden's truck in the parking lot of the First Baptist Church in Bethesda at 10:17 the same night.

An arrest team of eight cops surrounded the truck, identifying it by its 089-484 Maryland license plate and its Washington Capitals hockey team bumper sticker. An officer looked inside the window of the cap and saw Hadden peacefully asleep, covered by a quilt, with his arms around a one-eyed teddy bear. Another cop banged on the window with a flashlight and told Hadden to step outside. Hadden rubbed his eyes and got out of the truck. He asked them what was going on.

"You are under arrest for the murder of Laura Houghteling."

Hadden shrugged.

"Okay," he said.

None of the cops read him his rights. Miranda be damned, the Constitution be damned, they thought. From now until dawn his butt belonged to them. Hadden was going to tell them where Laura and Michele were before daylight even if it meant pulling out his fingernails one at a time.

10

THE LADIES ASK THE QUESTIONS

In the next seven-and-a-half hours Hadden Clark would ask for a lawyer more than 100 times, with the cops ignoring his every request. The police tactics were not just a violation of law and a knowing breach of ethics, but a violation of his Constitutional rights, no matter how despicable his crimes. The law says that when a person asks for a lawyer, the questioning has to stop. The embarrassed and angry Montgomery County police simply threw the rules out the window. They believed with righteous certainty that Hadden had killed not only Laura Houghteling but Michele Dorr and perhaps others. It grated on them that if they had been more intuitive in the case of the little girl, Laura's death might have been prevented. They had thought that Hadden's intelligence was too low to murder someone, clean up a crime scene, and then have an alibi which all but absolved him. If it hadn't been for the bloody fingerprint that Sue Ballou found, he could have gotten away with this one, too, they thought.

So the courts and the law be damned. An angry group of detectives wanted to know where he had hidden the bodies. And Hadden, more deceptive than they ever dreamed, was determined not to crack.

The police began by redecorating the interrogation room, sliding in a couch, hanging a painting, taking out an institutional gray metal table. The attempt was to make Hadden feel like he was in a homey living room. They chose two attractive female detectives—Paula Hamill and Elizabeth Cornett—as well as the top-ranking woman on the force, Major Carol A. Mehrling, to work on him first. Mehrling would soon become Montgomery County's first female chief of police. The two younger cops' jobs were to flirt with Hadden. They dressed seductively, with above-the-knee slitted skirts and high heels. If Mehrling was needed, she was to act as if she were his mother.

The women began with apologies, saying they were sorry if the handcuffs were too tight, apologizing if their hands felt cold when they unfastened them, and asked him if he would like to use the bathroom. One of the female cops began a vamping process, hoping her friendly approach would get him to talk. She sat down on the couch with Hadden, and moved in close so that their hips touched, speaking soothingly.

"Let me take a look at your wrists. Just relax. I want to make sure that you didn't get hurt or anything because sometimes those guys can be a little rough, even though they don't mean to be. You all right?"

Hadden was wary.

"I'm all right."

"I'm Paula. I've never met you. That's Liz. When you were arrested, did they tell you why you were under arrest?"

"No."

"You didn't hear?"

Hadden told Paula Hamill he had no idea why he was under arrest. One of the female cops asked if he had been awakened when his truck was rushed. Hadden, though, was already aware of the false seduction. It wasn't his first arrest.

"Can you read me my rights? I would like to talk with my lawyer."

The women stalled.

"Well, we will certainly let you do that, but we think that maybe we'll talk to you first. What do you think that your lawyer can do that we can't do for you?"

Hadden asked to talk to his lawyer again and one of the cops asked for the attorney's name.

"Who is he?" Hamill asked.

"Don Salzman."

Paula Hamill ignored the public defender's name.

"Liz and I are certainly going to help you," she said. "I mean, we are not going to do anything to hurt you while you're here with us. What is it that you want to talk to him about that you couldn't talk to us about?"

"He's my lawyer."

"You don't think you could talk to us about what you are going to talk to him about?"

Hadden again proved he could be cunning when it came to legal matters.

"You can talk to him."

The women, with Hamill doing most of the talking, ignored the request. They went back to asking him how long he had been sleeping when the police woke him. They also noticed Hadden's nervousness.

"How come your leg is shaking?"

Hadden stopped his leg from twitching.

"I said how come your leg was shaking? Are you scared?"

Hadden wouldn't answer, so Cornett tried a few words of sympathy.

"I know I'd be scared if they banged on my car while I was sleeping and someone pulled me out of it. I know I'd be scared—so it's okay if you are."

Hamill chimed in.

"What happened to your hand there? Did you cut yourself while you were working? What kind of work do you do? You work with your hands, don't you?"

They were getting nowhere. One tried talking faster.

"Hadden, Hadden, Hadden. Do you work with your hands?"

"Can I talk with my lawyer?"

Hadden thought they might give up if he closed his eyes and pretended to sleep. The women didn't, and Paula Hamill tried to draw him out by bouncing through as many subjects as she could, hoping one would stick.

"Hadden, Hadden, Hadden. Did you work today? Did you go out on your Rollerblades today? I Rollerblade too. Do you fall down a lot? Is that how you cut your hand? Huh? Did you? Is that how you cut your hand or did you do that while you were working?

"What's wrong? Are you scared of me? Liz and I are both here to talk to you, but we're here to try and help you if we can. It's not going to be real easy if you won't talk to us. What are you thinking about? Huh, Hadden? Do you want something to drink? You want a soda or some coffee? You want a piece of gum?"

Paula Hamill had exhausted the menu choices at police headquarters. She kept trying new subjects—anything that might make Hadden talk.

"Did you go to work or not? What did you do today that was fun? Did you hang out anywhere? Did you go to the bar you like to go to in D.C. or what? Did you watch the Caps game on TV tonight? Do you like hockey? Hadden, what's wrong now? Are we bothering you? Hadden?"

Hadden Clark remained still. His was a stony silence, feigning boredom. The women were becoming frustrated.

"I'm here to try to help you, and you are not letting me do that. We're going to try to help make you feel better. Look at us. Look at me. Look here."

Paula Hamill tried to shame him into responding. She delivered a schoolmarmish lecture.

"Hadden, you're acting very childish right now, and that's not the way you should be acting for a grown-up, okay? You are an adult, and two people are talking to you, and we're being very nice to you. I think you should extend the courtesy to us to talk pleasantly, okay?"

Liz Cornett picked up the cue.

"You're being very rude."

Hamill tried again.

"I think you're better mannered and better educated than that, to behave this way. We've done nothing to you. We don't want to hurt you. We want to help you. However you need help, we will try to help you. That's our job. Do you understand what I'm saying?"

When Hadden continued to ignore the two women Hamill became more threatening.

"We're here for the duration. We're not going to call an attorney up at 11:30 at night and have him come in only to see you sitting here, totally unresponsive. So if you want your attorney, you're going to have to behave. You're going to have to act like a man, okay? If you don't, then we won't extend you the courtesy of calling your attorney. Do you understand?"

Again there was silence from their suspect but Hamill knew how to perk Hadden up.

"You've been arrested in reference to Laura. Did you know that? You know Penny? Well, Liz and I are here, and we're here to help her. And we think you can help us help her. Now you understand why you're here. You know it's about Laura. Ask me what you want to know, and I'll tell you."

"Can I see my lawyer?"

That wasn't the question the two women were looking for.

"Well, you can see your lawyer as soon as we get his phone number and when your papers get here from the truck. You told me that the paperwork was in your truck, right?"

"I want to see my lawyer."

"You're going to see your lawyer. But Liz and I talked to Penny, and she asked us to help her because she's helped you for a year, hasn't she? Hasn't she been helping you by letting you work for her? She's been paying you and letting you come to her house and do work for her? Hasn't she been helping you?"

"I want to see my lawyer."

"Do you consider Penny your friend?"

"I want to see my lawyer."

"You're going to see your lawyer."

"I want to see my lawyer."

Hadden and the detectives had become small children on a playground, hurling the same statements back and forth, neither ready to give up. The women tried again.

"What can your lawyer do that we can't do? We're going to try and help you. Neither of us want to see you go to jail, you know that? Neither one of us do. We want to try and help you talk to a doctor, get some help, get whatever help you need, help that a doctor or a hospital can give you that a jail can't give you. That's why we're here, because we don't want to see you go to jail."

"My lawyer—"

Hamill wasn't about to let him get the lawyer sentence out again. She interupted and went back to the Penny Houghteling angle.

"We talked to Penny, and she asked us to help her. She said that she's been helping you. She said you've been doing some gardening work at her house, helping her with some flowers. It's beautiful work. And she's been very nice to you."

Liz Cornett tried holding his hand.

"Is there something wrong with your hand? Let me see it. No?"

They began to focus on Laura Houghteling.

"We want to talk a little bit about Laura. She's very beautiful. Do you think so? Do you think she is?"

"I want to see my lawyer."

"Okay, you will. Don't you think Laura is beautiful? We think she is, and Penny thinks she is, too."

Hadden did his toboggan trick, pulling the cap down over his eyes. The women pulled it back up.

"Do you go to church, Hadden? Do you understand the Bible? Huh?"

And they kept acting like flight attendants.

"Hadden, do you want something to drink? Do you want a soda or some coffee? Just let us know and we'll get it for you—well, within reason. We can't bring in beer, but we'll be happy to bring in whatever—if you want coffee or something. I bet you don't drink beer, though, do you? But you like to go to The Dancing Crab, don't you? I go there, too."

Paula Hamill left the interrogation room to confer with the cops watching through the two-way mirror, while Liz Cornett tried an even more intimate one-on-one. She focused on his hands and religion.

"What's the matter with your hands, Hadden? You look like you're praying. Are you saying a prayer, Hadden? You act like you're looking up to God for something. Are you looking to him to give you some support and some leadership, maybe help you a little bit? Are you thinking about Laura and Penny?"

Hamill returned and tried some free association with him.

"Hadden, what would you like to talk about? You pick a subject matter and we'll talk about it."

Hadden picked a subject.

"My lawyer."

It was getting comical. And the two female cops were getting desperate.

"What else would you like to talk about? The weather? Do you camp?"

If Hadden had wanted to discuss his astrological sign at that moment, they would have welcomed the subject. They took a stab at drawing one of his multiple personalities out.

"What about Judy? What can you tell me about Judy or Lydia?"

They were guessing. The names were from his childhood but not the ones his female side used.

"My lawyer."

"Just because you keep repeating it doesn't mean he's going to show up mysteriously. I want to know about Judy."

"My lawyer."

"That's not what we're here to talk about. We're here to talk about Laura. And I think you can help us."

"I can't talk without a lawyer."

Paula Hamill was frantic from her lack of success. She gave Hadden a long pep talk.

"Yes, you can. You can talk to me and you can talk with Liz because we're going to help you. We don't want you to go to jail, do you understand that? We want to try and help you get a doctor. We're here to help you and we know you can help us to help Penny. There's a big difference between going to jail for the rest of your life and going to a hospital where there are doctors that will help you so you can go out and go back to work and go back on your Rollerblades and go back with your church.

"So what can you tell me about Laura? Can you tell me whether she's tall? Is she tall? Do you think she's pretty? Did she do something to make you angry? Did she hurt your feelings?

"I understand—and so does Liz. We understand if Laura hurt you and it's not very nice if she did. Did she hurt your feelings or make you angry? Maybe she didn't talk to you nice and maybe that made you angry. Did it?"

Hamill decided to tell him they had the evidence to convict him. It was one of her trump cards.

"Hadden, did you know they found a pillow? Look at me. Did you know they found a pillow in the woods with some blood on it? Your fingerprint was on the blood on that pillow. So help us. Help us with Laura. It's only fair that she's be given back to her mother so she can be buried properly. You understand that if you read the Bible. She should be returned back to the earth to go to God. She shouldn't be left somewhere with her family not knowing where she's at. That's what Penny wants. She wants her daughter back so she can be buried properly. As a friend, that's what you should do. As much as she's done for you, if the only act of kindness you show to her is to let her know where her daughter is, then she can properly bury her where she belongs and go back to God. You should at least do that for her. Do you understand that simple concept?"

The detective began pleading with him.

"Tell me about Laura, please. Help me find her. Please."

Hamill was worn out from peppering Hadden with questions. She began to believe that she was perhaps speaking to one of Hadden's other personalities.

"Are we really talking to Hadden? Or are we talking to somebody else? Are we talking to Judy or Lydia? Is there someone else we're speaking with? You don't need an attorney for that, Hadden."

The female cop tried going in another direction.

"Do you have any nieces or nephews? I mean—can you imagine what would happen to them if somebody took them away from someone they loved and they couldn't bury them? Think of the loss. Can you think about going to a church to say goodbye to somebody that's not even there? No body, no casket. Nowhere to take flowers to—can you imagine what that must be like for the family? All Penny wants to do is to bury her daughter."

Hamill brought out the MISSING poster Laura's friends had posted on the telephone poles near the subway stop. She put it a foot away from Hadden's face.

"Look at Laura. She wants to remember you with a smile, but she should be allowed to remember you in a church and then being buried. Look at that beautiful smile. I mean, that's wonderful. Penny brought her into this world; she should be able to bury her in this world. Look at how full of life she is—she's not full of life anymore, is she?"

They thought there was a slight chance Laura was living. Maybe Hadden had her locked up somewhere. The two cops addressed that possibility.

"Look at her. Is she alive?" Hamill asked.

"At least tell us that," Cornett added.

"Tell me she's alive. Can we tear this MISSING off of her? Look at this. Can we take this off? Can we put FOUND on it? Can we do that—get rid of the MISSING and put on FOUND? Is there someone inside you that wants to help us? Is there someone we can talk to?"

Hadden looked at Laura's photo and gave a faint grin. Hamill noticed.

"You're smiling. It's because she's beautiful, isn't she? How do you remember her? Do you last remember her smiling—or was she screaming?"

"Tell me if she did something to make you angry," Cornett requested.

Hamill picked up the motivation theme.

"Did she hurt your feelings? Maybe she wouldn't go out with you? Did she make you mad? I can understand if she did. I can understand you wanting to hurt her, if she made you angry."

Hadden didn't respond. But he kept the goofy grin on as he looked at Laura's picture.

"She's pretty. She's got a beautiful smile and you're smiling because you remember her, right? Did you talk to her when you worked at her house for Penny? Did you used to say hi, and did she say hi to you and Warren? Were they your friends?

"Is there somebody in you that doesn't want to hurt anybody, that wants to help us? Is there someone deep inside you that wants to tell me, somebody that I can talk to—huh?"

Hadden began humming a religious hymn.

"When you saw her last, was it in the daytime? Was it

nighttime? What was she wearing? Was she sleeping? Or was she awake? Did she let you come in because she's your friend and you're her friend and she let you in the house because she wanted to talk to you? And then she made you angry?"

Hadden hummed louder. Cornett began yelling at him. "You're trying to hide from it, and you can't keep hiding. You can't keep running. You're an adult, and adults have to face up to reality whether or not they like it or not, isn't that right, Paula?"

Paula said that was why they were there.

"The reality is that you're going to go to jail if you don't help us. If you do help us, we're going to help you go to a hospital. There's a jail with a lot of men in there, and they're not nice to other people. You don't want to be exposed to that, to men who are like that."

Hadden hummed away, smiling. He took the poster of Laura and shoved it away.

"You can't push her away. Look at this girl. Look at her," Cornett commanded as Hadden averted his gaze. "She's beautiful, isn't she? Did you like her? Did something happen with Penny that made you angry and you took it out on Laura? Did you have a fight with Penny over tools and that upset you?"

Hadden said his head was cold and pulled the knit cap back down over his ears. The move was made primarily so that the detectives couldn't see his eyes. He put both hands on his head and kept them there.

"My lawyer."

"Are you hearing something in your head right now? Is that why you're grabbing your head? Are there people inside your head? Do you hear somebody?"

"My lawyer," Hadden whined.

"Is your lawyer talking to you inside your head? Hadden, talk to me about Laura. Tell me what she had on when you saw her."

Hadden's expression changed. He flashed the two women a look that chilled even them.

"I want my lawyer. What am I being charged with?"

"Didn't they tell you when you were arrested?"

"No. What?"

"Hadden, look at me," Hamill said. "You're being charged with the murder of Laura. We found the bloody pillow and your fingerprint was on it in the blood. And that's why you're being charged."

"How do you feel about that?" Cornett asked. "How do you feel about being in this room with us on a Friday night? Are you angry? Are you happy? Are you sad? Are you confused? That's not a question your lawyer can answer for you. You're probably pretty pissed off that we took you out of your nice truck, aren't you?"

Hadden went back to staring straight ahead.

"Are you afraid of being haunted by Laura? Is she haunting you? Is she haunting you right now? Are you afraid of what Penny may say to you?"

Hadden tensed up when the possibility of Penny confronting him was raised. The other cops behind the two-way mirror noticed.

"I know you're scared. I can tell by the way you were looking, your eyes. You have very dramatic eyes. I can see that. They're very emotional. They are the windows to the soul."

Cornett felt that Hadden was relaxing. She reassured him.

"I think you're actually feeling a little more comfortable with us. I think you can see that we're not intimidating people, and we're not here to throw you up against the wall like on TV, right?"

They began vamping him again.

"I mean, do we look intimidating the way we're dressed in high heels and stockings and skirts?" Cornett said. "Look how pretty Paula's dressed. She's got beautiful clothes on.

There's nothing for you to be afraid of with us. Now if we go get a couple of big burly men in here to talk with you, then I would be afraid."

Their threat was not an empty one. Hadden knew it.

"I only want to know one thing. I just want to know where Laura was the last time you saw her. Was she inside the house or outside the house?"

"Ask my lawyer."

Now they brought in more photos of Laura. They were baby and childhood pictures, snapshots that they hoped would make Hadden feel remorseful.

"Penny wanted you to see these. Look at her—she's like a little Gerber baby. Are you in any of these pictures? Did you get your picture taken with Laura?"

They offered him a picture of Laura to keep. But Hadden dropped it on the floor.

"Would you like this one? That's probably the most recent, what do you think? You can see what a beautiful woman she grew into—don't throw that on the floor, Hadden. You can have that. Why don't you want her picture? I thought she was your friend."

They showed him a photo of Laura in a school play, carrying a sword. They called the sword a knife.

"Did you see a knife with her the last time you saw her? Or maybe, did you have a knife? Was it like the knife down in the kitchen on the countertop? Do you remember that knife when you were in the house?"

"Ask my lawyer. He knows everything about me."

Paula Hamill picked out a photo of Laura and her father, Frederic.

"That's her and her dad. Don't you think she deserves to go to heaven where her dad is? Don't you think that the family needs to be together in heaven? That's only right instead of having Mom and brother in one place and Dad in heaven and Laura in another place?"

Nothing was working.

"Did you help Penny by burying Laura for her? Did you put flowers on her grave? She's very pretty—she probably deserves to have some flowers. Penny would like to put some there. Will you take Penny there? All her friends would like to visit her and talk to her. You can talk to her too."

Hamill gave Hadden some more unsettling information.

"Hadden, we saw you come out of Laura's house wearing a trench coat and the khaki pants and the white socks and the wig. So we know you didn't do it. It's this person in your head. It's this bad one. You need to let the good one come out and tell us what the bad one did so we can take care of the bad one. We have to do it for Penny and Laura and Hadden. The bad one has got to go. So help us. Where is the bad one? What's the bad one's name? It's not Hadden. Hadden's the good one. Is Lydia the bad one?"

Liz Cornett went in a new direction.

"Why did you wear that trench coat and come out of the house that morning? Were you pretending to be Laura? Do you want to be Laura? I can understand why somebody would want to be Laura. You're smiling because you think she's pretty, right?"

Hadden was smiling because they weren't getting anywhere. He was laughing at their frustration.

"Did you want to go to bed with her? Is that what you wanted? Did you want to make love with her?"

Hamill thought she detected a nod.

"You did? Is that a yes? Or did the bad person do it? Where did the bad person take Laura? It's cold out there. She needs to be warm—you don't want her cold. You don't want her hurting. You like her too much. You probably loved her. We know you didn't do anything. Another person did. Was it Lydia or Judy?"

The women took a break, coming back with black coffee with sugar for him. If Cornett and Hamill thought they were wearing Hadden out, they were mistaken. Rather, the opposite was more likely true.

The two detectives tried out other theories. They suggested Laura had caught him going through her mother's lingerie drawer and that the bad person inside his head became angry and lost control. They wanted to know if Hadden buried her in a sleeping bag or had propped her up against a tree. They even tried invoking Laura's ghost.

"She's looking at you. She's saying, 'Hadden, please, please tell them so they can come get me and give me a good burial.' She's saying, 'Hadden, please tell me where I am. I'm cold. I want a blanket.' Remember when I said the eyes are the windows to the soul?"

Hamill shoved a photo of Laura towards him.

"Look at her eyes. She's saying, 'I want Hadden to bring my blanket to me. Could Hadden bring it to me?' "

Cornett put her ghost in the root cellar next to his campsite.

"She's in the root cellar. She's saying, 'Let me out of that root cellar. Let me out. I want to see my mom before I go to heaven. I have to see my mom. I never got to say goodbye to her.' She wants to say goodbye to her mom before she sees her dad in heaven."

They told him Flavia had phoned from Block Island and that she was very upset. They told him his mother needed to talk to him and Laura's mother needed to talk to Laura. Still, Hadden uttered the same well-worn phrase.

"Ask my lawyer."

The women then tried what can only be described as an exorcism. It would go on until they became exhausted.

"Are you going to let the bad Hadden out?"

"Yeah. Let him out."

"Let him out."

"Get him out of there."

"Come on."

"Get him. Time to go, time to leave—"

"Come on."

"Get him out so the good Hadden can help us get Laura and her mom back together one last time."

"Let him out, Hadden, let him out!"

"The bad Hadden knew Penny wasn't going to be home; that's why the bad Hadden went over there. He knew that. He knew where the keys were. He had the keys."

"The bad Hadden is smart!"

"The good Hadden is smarter!"

"And that's why you're going to let the bad one out."

Paula Hamill and Liz Cornett went on this way for another five minutes, doing everything but waving crucifixes and throwing holy water on him. They invoked the coming holidays and suggested that Laura be brought home for Christmas. They said Hadden could call his lawyer, Donald Salzman, and have him meet him at her grave and that they would let Hadden lead the prayer services and light candles for her. They brought in Hadden's one-eyed teddy bear and spent five minutes trying to get him to tell them the bear's name. They told him he could have his bear back if he revealed where Laura was buried. Again Hadden asked for his lawyer. Five more times. Paula tried something new, tried to act tough. Sitting so close, it could almost be called a sexual overture.

"You don't like me sitting near you? Did that upset you, me sitting near you? Were you thinking about Laura when I did that?"

Then she took the opposite tack. She directed him to a chair.

"Get over here and sit down. Sit in that goddamn chair, and stay seated. Act like a goddamn man and stop acting like a fucking kid. Give me the hat. No more hats."

Then they asked him about Flavia. Hadden said he had no mother.

"Is that because she wrote you that letter and said you were kicked out of the family? She probably didn't mean it. Remember how we do things and sometimes we don't mean it?"

The two women made what seemed to be a last try. They asked him to have Laura appear once again and said that if he did, God would reward him.

"When you go to Bible study, you'll say a prayer for Laura and you'll pray that she's happy and smiling in heaven and that's she's forgiven you like God will forgive you. It's an all-forgiving God. He forgives us our sins through Jesus Christ. If you can believe that, you can get help. You can get the bad Hadden out and get rid of him."

Hadden ignored their ploy and once again said he would like to speak with his lawyer. Hamill and Cornett were through being nice. Things were about to get ugly. They had worked him over for three hours and still didn't know a thing.

The two female cops left the room and when they did Hadden finally began talking. He confided in his teddy bear.

"Uh oh," he told the stuffed toy. "Not getting out of this one."

11

GETTING DOWN AND DIRTY

In a room behind the two-way mirror three male detectives were itching to enter the fray. Ed Tarney, who had just been assigned to the case was there with Richard Fallin. But the most eager to get in Hadden's face was Mike Garvey, the cop who had questioned him about Michele Dorr's disappearance in 1986. He would later say that her disappearance had gnawed away inside him for more than six years. Others, with the benefit of hindsight, would respond that if only he had followed up on Hadden Clark then, Laura Houghteling might still be alive. Now, Garvey had no doubt that Hadden was responsible for the little girl's death and couldn't wait to confront him. First, though, he would have to wait for his female colleagues. And the female cops were about to get down and dirty in a desperate last try to get to Hadden.

"We're going to be kind of blunt," Hamill was saying. "What kind of sex are you into?"

"My lawyer."

"You have sex with your lawyer? I don't think so."

The other woman picked up on the sex angle. She couldn't have been more direct.

"Hadden, do you like blow jobs? When you go out—do you date women or men? Who do you prefer?"

"Lawyer, my lawyer," Hadden babbled.

"Do you like anal sex? Do you like to eat pussy? What are you into?"

"My lawyer. I'm into Donald Salzman."

Salzman was ignored. They were going to talk rough and in the kind of language he understood. Their coarseness couldn't have been more obvious.

"If you took me out on a date and we were intimate with each other, would you want me to give you a blow job?" one of them asked. "Or would you rather have a man do that for you?"

"I mean, if we went out on a date, would you be wearing women's clothes or would you be wearing women's underwear? Would you be wearing a dress with a slit like this? Would you want me to dress like a man? What's your sexual pleasure? Would you rather be with a man than a woman? Do you want to be the dominant one? Or would you rather be by yourself and masturbate or jerk off—or get a blow job from somebody?"

Cornett asked him if he was wearing women's underwear at that moment, which caused Hadden to smirk. Cornett said she thought he preferred wearing women's clothing. Hadden answered her by repeating that he wanted to see his lawyer. His statement made Hamill lose her cool.

"You're having a sexual relationship with Donald Salzman? Is he your lover? Is that what it is? So are you homosexual, bisexual, transsexual, or asexual? Or do you just not have sex?"

He asked for Salzman once again. And Cornett wanted to know if his lawyer was also his personal shopper.

"Does he buy you women's underwear? Does he buy your panties for you? Were you wearing women's underwear when you were with Laura? Do you have her underwear?"

Hadden was asked if there had been an intimate relationship with Penny Houghteling. In the most graphic way possible.

"Did you fuck Penny? Did you fuck her and then she rejected you? Is that it? Come on. I'm married. This is nothing that's going to surprise either of us. Did you fuck her and it didn't work out, is that what happened? And to get back at her, you might have taken Laura and fucked and killed her, or maybe cut her throat?"

It was also suggested he might be practicing necrophilia.

"Maybe you're still having sex with her. Who knows? Maybe you're going back and having repeated sex with her after she's dead. Some people do that. It's whatever turns you on. Far be it for us to pass judgment on you."

They took out one of Hadden's photo albums that showed him with various animals and pets. The women were covering all the sexual bases.

"How about these animals? Are you into sex with dogs? Are you into sex with animals?"

The female detectives showed Hadden a photo of him in his Navy uniform, standing by his father's grave. He was told that since he had been allowed to give his father final rites, Penny should be allowed to do the same.

"Don't you think that Penny—whether you fucked her or not—should be allowed to bury her daughter? You got to bury your dad—you know where he is, right?"

They kept on and on, covering incest, mutilation, torture, and other more obscure sexual practices and crimes, asking him if he had sex with his sister or his mother or people at the schools he attended.

"Were you abused when you went to the Wood School? Did some big bully take you in the men's room and butt-fuck you? Is that why you wear women's clothes?"

Hadden smiled at them again. He was becoming amused at their crude tactics. Not that his sarcastic grin stopped the two women.

"Were you sexually abused by a priest? Were you in a choir and some priest pulled you aside one day during practice and forced you to give him a blow job?"

"Let me give Donald Salzman a call," Hadden said.

"He won't answer the telephone. If he's in bed with some woman screwing his brains out, he's not going to take the time to answer the phone and—"

"Yes, he will."

Angry, he turned on the two women. It was Hadden's

turn now. He accused them of lying and harassing him for hours. He said it was "bullshit" that his lawyer didn't want to see him, demonstrating an intelligence that was far above what the female cops had estimated it to be. His interrogation turned into a debate and the detectives automatically lost because they chose to participate in an argument with a killer. He had been grilled for hours and they had nothing. Carol Mehrling briefly tried the mommy trick, which quickly went nowhere. It was time for the men to have at him. The time was 2:52 in the morning when Mike Garvey walked in the room.

Garvey took charge at the outset. He would show Hadden who was boss. Hadden didn't recognize him.

"Can you sit up for me, please? I'm Sergeant Garvey from the Montgomery County police. How are you tonight?"

Hadden didn't answer Garvey's solicitation about his health, instead asking for his lawyer yet again. Garvey stalled, tap dancing around the issue by saying he didn't know Salzman's phone number and then claiming that the phone in the interrogation room had mysteriously broken down. Hadden showed him the Get Out of Jail Free letter that Salzman had typed up for him. Garvey went into a short tirade.

"I mean, I'm not going to call this guy up at three in the morning and have him think I'm some kind of jerk. What's your name—Hayden Clark?"

Garvey deliberately mispronounced the name, hoping for a response. He didn't get one. So he tried again.

"And you're Hayden Clark?"

"Hadden Clark."

"Hadden, okay. You know, you look familiar. Have you and I ever met before?"

"I don't know."

"Do I look like a movie star? Huh?"

"You tell me."

"What do you think, Robert De Niro? Okay. So you're Hayden Clark?"

"Hadden."

"Hadden. I'm Mike Garvey. I think I've met you before. Did you used to live in Silver Spring?"

Hadden's eyes widened. He recognized him now.

"I want to call my lawyer."

The two traded insults on why his lawyer wasn't being notified. Hadden still retained a residue of hatred he had aimed at the two women and he used it up on Garvey. Then the detective went into the reason that he was here and not at home asleep in bed.

"Look at my face, Hayden, look at my face!"

He was going to mispronounce Hadden's name each time. On purpose. He hoped it would rile him up.

"I saw your face."

"So you know who I am, don't you?"

"No, I don't."

Garvey reached into his pocket and pulled out Michele Dorr's missing poster. He put it right under Hadden Clark's nose.

"Do you remember her, Hayden? Remember that little girl on Sudbury Road? Remember her, Hayden? Remember how she walked up to your house and you grabbed her and threw her in your truck? Do you remember her, Hayden?"

Garvey's scenario wasn't quite correct. But his theory was close enough to frighten Hadden.

"Do you remember how your brother threw you out of the house? Do you remember how his wife couldn't stand your guts? Do you remember how you killed this little girl, Hayden? Do you? Do you remember how you killed her?"

Garvey was in Hadden's face now, inches away. When he talked to him, his warm spit sprayed Hadden's face.

"What are you going to do about it? You going to be a man? Look at her. Yeah, you remember her, and you remember me, don't you? Look at her, Hayden. Remember the last time we played this game? You like to play games, don't you? Look at her, look at her. You remember that day, don't you? May thirty-first, 1986. It's been six years. Six years of guilt inside you. Let's quit playing the game. Let's end it all. The game is over, Hayden, over. So take a deep breath. Take a deep breath and just say, 'I did it. I'm sorry, I did it.' Take a deep breath, Hayden. And let it out. Here, hold this in your hand. Hold it."

Garvey put the poster with Michele Dorr's photo on it in Hadden's hands. His suspect tried not to react.

"You held her in your hands before, didn't you? But the last time you held her, you killed her, didn't you?"

Hadden threw the poster of Michele to the floor of the interrogation room. He wanted nothing to do with the image.

"Oh, that's real big," Garvey yelled. "That's a real big guy. Throw it on the floor, Hayden. What's the matter? You can't look at it. You can't look at it because it's eating you up inside. You want to do the right thing? Put it next to your heart. Let her bounce back and forth on your heart a little bit."

After saying those words, Garvey folded the poster and put it in his suspect's shirt pocket. Hadden took it out and let it fall to the floor. Then, in a burst of anger, Garvey grabbed Hadden's one-eyed teddy bear and slammed it to the floor of the interrogation room so hard it bounced.

"Do you remember the day? Remember you were moving out of your house over on Sudbury? Remember Geoff, your brother? Remember the kids: John, Jacob, and Eliza? It's been a bad night for you, hasn't it? But it's been coming for six years. So what are we going to do? How are we going to work this out? I don't buy this act. It ain't never going to go away. This is it. It's time to be a man and own up."

Hadden tried hard not to react. He looked down, attempting to avoid Garvey's eyes.

"Remember those days on Sudbury Road? Remember living down in the basement? Remember when the dog came and killed your little rabbit and you took it out in the back yard and buried it? Remember how pissed off you got when Geoff came to you and said you were going to have to go? Remember all the problems you had there?"

Hadden shrunk in his seat. He was trying to become invisible.

"I've thought about this girl since May thirty-first, 1986. Just about every single day I've thought about her. And I know you've thought about her, too, right? So put her picture next to your heart, Hayden. Why can't you do that? I don't have any problem with that. Do you have problems putting her next to your heart?"

Hadden was wearing a gold medallion of Jesus Christ. It hung from a chain around his neck. Garvey used the religious image for his next gambit.

"How about putting her next to Jesus? You got the medal of Jesus there. Jesus is a very forgiving person. I'm a forgiving person. Mrs. Dorr is a forgiving person. Are you a forgiving person?"

Hadden wanted to ignore the detective, but couldn't. The cop's relentlessness was beginning to make him squirm. Garvey grabbed the one-eyed teddy bear off the floor and left the room, taking it with him. When he came back he had something hidden behind his back.

"Let's play a game. Let's see who can win this little game. You know, you're like a little machine, Hayden. And there are little buttons I can push to make you do things. Watch this. I'm going to put something here and you're going to move your hand."

With that, Garvey took the object he had behind his back and put it next to Hadden's hand. It was a pink OshKosh B'Gosh bathing suit with the tiny polka dots and the ruffled waist, identical to the one Michele Dorr had worn the day he killed her. Someone had purchased a duplicate and stretched it over the torso of a small mannequin. Garvey was not above using it to play mind games in his attempt to break him. Just as he predicted, Hadden moved away from the swim suit.

"Remember this, Hayden? Is that what she looked like? Remember that day six years ago when she was wearing that bathing suit? Here, you want to hold it. Come on, put your hand around it. What's the matter? Touch it, Hayden. How's it feel? You felt that before, didn't you? Put it up on your shoulder and hold her. Isn't that what you did?"

Hadden visibly shuddered. He closed his eyes.

"Six years you've been worrying about this. How many days in six years? What are we going to do now?"

Hadden didn't answer. He groaned and snorted and hummed but wouldn't say an intelligible word.

"Hayden, the memories aren't going to go away. You're going to see them all the time. I'm not going to go away. But you can end the game. You can feel better. Big breath—tell me what happened and let's get on with it. Let's get on with the new Hayden Clark. I'm not going to go away. I'm going to sit right here—me, you, the bear, and the bathing suit. So end the game."

Garvey went on like this for nearly an hour until he began to lose his voice. Once, after twenty minutes of listening to the detective, Hadden placed a finger in each ear in an attempt to keep from hearing the threats. Garvey kept on, repeating his speech, varying it slightly each time. He wanted to know where little Michele was and said he was going to keep it up until his suspect cracked. From time to time Hadden would ask for his lawyer, sounding like a broken record, and Garvey would ignore the request. When Garvey took a break and left the interrogation room, Hadden was so far gone he began talking to the swim-suit-clad mannequin. Nothing he said made much sense.

"Oh, boy. You want to go swimming? They got you a bathing suit? You look good in that bathing suit, you know that? I'm going to take you swimming," was part of Hadden's sing-song soliloquy.

Rich Fallin and Ed Tarney entered the room, replacing Garvey. Tarney's eyes were slits of anger. His mustache had been shaven so thin it looked like it had been drawn on with a freshly sharpened pencil.

The two cops began by threatening to close down all the homeless shelters in Montgomery County if Hadden didn't confess, saying it would be his fault if they did. Tarney said he would get the gas chamber when he was convicted. But if he confessed, he told Hadden, he would be put in a nice hospital where eventually he would be released. Hadden, if anything, was consistent. After each new threat, he asked for his lawyer.

Tarney outlined the choices for him again.

"You're playing a game, and you're playing a very deadly game. You're acting like a hard-ass, and what you're doing is, you're playing with the gas chamber versus a hospital where you can go cook and can go Rollerblading, where you can go get some medicine, where you can get some treatment, and where some day you can get out."

When Hadden continued to ignore them the cops switched subjects. They got into the macabre.

"Ever hear of Jeffrey Dahmer? He's kind of like you. He's killed several people. I don't know whether you ate anybody. You might have eaten some. Did you try any flesh? Do you eat flesh? Do you eat people?"

Fallin picked up the beat.

"You ever drink blood?"

Hadden grinned at the question. Tarney switched subjects.

"If you're sane and competent, you're going to jail for the rest of your life, and if I can show that you murdered this girl, you're going to the electric chair. Two murders make you a serial murderer and means you go to the electric chair. Now you can play the game of asking for Mr. Salzman, who doesn't really give a fuck about you, I'll tell you that right now. Mr. Salzman gives a shit about money and that's about it. Mr. Salzman is in this for the money. We're in it for your good. Just tell me where the body is so we can give it back. That's all we want. All we're going to do is to try and get the damn body back to the mother so she can bury her child."

Hadden tried to stand up to get away from them but Fallin and Tarney shoved him back on the couch. One of them grabbed Hadden by the throat. After Hadden composed himself he repeated the sentence that had already been spoken more than fifty times.

"Call my lawyer."

The two cops took turns insulting the county's public defender, Donald Salzman.

"No. Fuck your lawyer. We don't even like him. He's ugly."

"He's a dick-head! He wants your money."

"He's going to plead you guilty so fast your head will be spinning. We've put 700 man-hours into investigating you since October nineteenth, okay? We even know what size of silk panties your ass wears. Sue Snyder ain't going to come and get you out now."

"Bethesda Cares is gone. Bethesda Cares is no more."

"We're going to kick all your little homeless buddies out."

"It's going to be Bethesda Don't Give a Fuck. Bethesda Cares is history. All those homeless people are out on the street."

The cops kept on about Sue Snyder and the homeless, again saying they were going to run all vagrants out of town and he would be blamed. They said the good people of Montgomery County would now assume that the homeless were criminals and murderers. They said Snyder had done more for him than his own mother but she was history if he didn't confess. When Hadden repeated his mantra of wanting Donald Salzman, one of the cops got personal again.

"What kind of undies you got on, buddy?"

"He's got on girls' undies today. Ain't no doubt in my mother-fucking mind."

One of the detectives reached in and gave Hadden's underwear a strong yank upwards. Hadden grimaced at being given the wedgie, but still said nothing.

"He liked that!"

"Owww, daddy! Jockey ladies. Yeah, they're nice."

"So do you want to make a deal or do you want to fuck your friends? All you have to do is tell us where the body is."

A detective put his hand on Hadden's knee.

"Do you like it when I touch your leg? Does it feel good?"

The cops were out of control. They were threatening to physically molest him. They were on the edge, verbally abusing the two women who had interrogated Hadden.

"Did they look good to you, huh? Did you notice that one had a short skirt on? The other one talking to you was trash."

They noticed every time Hadden closed his eyes.

"You want go to sleep?" one of them asked. "How about if I go over there and rip the nose off your fucking doll? How about if I pretended that was one of the girls, and I just sliced the mother-fucker to pieces, what would you think of that? Hey, do you know who Jeffrey Dahmer was?"

Hadden was disgusted with the crudeness. They had gone through a Jeffrey Dahmer analogy once already. He spoke up and ridiculed the cops.

"Oh, bullshit. What's your favorite movie? *Silence of the Lambs*?"

The cops took the bait.

"Are you serious? *Silence of the Lambs*? Do you know what Buffalo Bill would have done in *Silence of the Lambs* with those women? If Buffalo Bill—now he stuck all of his women in water, but he kind of took their skin off of them. You told some people down at Bethesda Cares that *Silence of the Lambs* was your favorite movie. Of course, you're not good enough to be Hannibal. I think Buffalo Bill, that's probably you. Do you realize they may be making a movie of this one day? You could be famous."

Fallin moved close to Hadden on the couch. He had done that earlier, moving as close as Paula Hamill had, putting his arm around Hadden's shoulder, as if they were a couple on a date sitting in the back row of a dark movie theater.

"Oh, you're sweet."

"He is sweet," the other cop said.

"You are sweet."

"Should I leave you two alone? Do you want to be left alone?" a cop said. They wanted Hadden to react, but he remained studiously neutral. This sent one of the detectives into a rage.

"If someone would stand up in front of the two way window and let me, I would choke the living shit out of you right now. Sit up before I kill you. We're going to take you to jail. Do you have any butt cream? I hope you like taking it in the butt because when the guys at the jail find out that you killed this little girl, do you know what's going to happen to you? I'm going to give them this picture of her. They're going to be fucking you in the ass, you know that? But you might like that."

"And when they undress you over there and find out that you've got on girls' underwear, oh, Daddy!"

"Yes, yes, yes!" another cop chorused.

"Oh goodness, goodness, my goodness," the other chortled.

"Maybe they'll let you prance around in your panties in front of the population over there."

"Oh oh, Daddy!"

Hadden still wouldn't react with words, though his body was shaking. Tarney and Fallin increased their threats.

"I'd like to take this foot right here and slap the dogshit out of you, you know that?"

"You just lost two of what could have been your best friends. You know what? When they walk you down to the gas chamber, we'll be there to watch. We'll come to say goodbye to you. And maybe you'll tell us, right before you die, where the bodies are. But gas is quick. Seriously, I watched a guy die with gas. It wasn't bad. When you start breathing it, your body starts quivering and you quiver for a few minutes. I don't think it's very painful because the guy only screamed for three minutes. So it wasn't bad, and you know, he was singing hallelujah and all that shit going down, but he probably went to hell anyhow."

His partner picked up on the life-after-death theme.

"You need to confess your sins to somebody so that you don't go to hell. The party is over. You're going to jail and your teddy bear can't go to jail. Can I have your teddy bear as a memento?"

Rich Fallin really appeared to want Hadden's one-eyed bear.

"I'll watch out for your teddy bear," he told Hadden. "My daughters all have teddy bears. Maybe I'll take it home to them. And they'll look after it. Will you tell me, 'Rich, you can have my teddy bear'? That way I don't feel that I'm stealing it. What do you think, homie?"

Fallin spoke about Jeffrey Dahmer again. He seemed to know the case well. His premise was that since Dahmer had been found sane, then Hadden certainly couldn't count on an insanity plea to get off.

"What did Jeffrey Dahmer get, life? You see the problem with Dahmer, you know, he got caught with all these dead people in his apartment, and he had cut their hearts and livers out and he put them in the freezer and froze them. He was cooking them and eating them. He had these dead people in his shower and his bed for three or four days, and he was having sex with them. So they eventually caught him and took him to trial. They had this big hearing to find out if he was sane or not. They found him sane. They actually tried him in criminal court and put him in jail for the rest of his life."

Another detective continued when Fallin paused. "That's crazy. Do you believe that, Hayden? He had five people in there. And he had their hearts and livers cut out. And he was sane!"

There was time for one more threat. A cop told Hadden that he was going to let the inmates at the county jail know about him.

"I'm going to tell them that you fucked Michele Dorr before you killed her. I shouldn't do that, but I will. I'm going to tell them that. And when they find out—You may not have fucked her —but if they think you did, oh God. I really don't get pleasure in this. I really don't. It's just that you've pissed me off, Hadden."

They were almost to the end of their verbal torture. Still, they were creative in the way they tried to get a reaction from him.

"Are you still masturbating a lot? Once a day? You know, if you do it more than once a day—"

Tarney finished Fallin's thought.

"—You'll wear out those panties. Those little ladies's panties, they weren't meant for that. They get worn out real quick."

Garvey took some final shots. He believed Hadden had placed Laura's body in the Potomac River and that his team would never find her.

"I mean, if you dumped it in a river, for Christ's sake, we're going to be looking forever. Now, if that's what you did, at least tell me, because I'm going to be honest with you. I have five kids and you know the last time I saw my wife?"

"I've seen his wife since he has," Fallin joked lewdly.

"But she's happy," Tarney added.

"No, seriously, did you put her in the river?"

The cops droned on about how bodies swell up in water and how they come floating to the top without hands because the fish eat the extremities. Tarney related what he said was a personal experience.

". . . His hands were all tied together and when he ballooned up and the damn rope on his hands had these rocks holding him down in, and the skin slips right off the fucking hand. It was unbelievable, gross, stink—God, it stunk. I've got pictures of it. I swear to God the skin came off the hands like gloves. I had to go in the water and pull it out and I'm going to tell you—it was awful. I mean that thing stunk terrible. I'm kind of hoping that you buried it under the ground because, you know, this time of year, the bugs and shit, they eat it up . . ."

The three cops discussed what was more preferable to find, a body in a river or a body in the ground. They ignored Hadden as they argued the merits of which dead body would be preferable. Then they talked about how Flavia Clark had voted for Bill Clinton and how disappointed they were about that and how she had cried when they told her Hadden was a murderer. They talked about Hadden's relationship with his mother as if he wasn't there. Hadden asked for his lawyer again and said he wanted to be taken to jail.

"Look, I don't like your lawyer. Screw your lawyer. Why don't you get a good lawyer, like Barry Helfand, for Christ sakes? Your lawyer's an ass."

It was nearly dawn. Hadden didn't know when they were going to end it. So he threw them a bone. While they were attempting to bring out one of his female personalities for the fourth time, he began speaking in a female voice. He let them pull out where he had buried Laura in dribs and drabs. His female voice told the cops he had taken her to Warren Township, New Jersey, and buried her there, under his childhood treehouse. When they asked him for the location of the treehouse he told them his mother knew. The cops bought the story and finally took him out of the room, booking him at 6:10 in the morning. They were relieved it was over, and thought they would find the body within days.

Hadden was finally booked and put in a cell. He laughed himself to sleep over the deception.

PART THREE

Words are insignificant in light of the magnitude of the loss. The pain is searing. The senselessness of the act is unfathomable. The destruction of her gently loving presence leaves a horrible void in my life, and in the world.

I feel keenly the loss of the contribution she would have made to so many lives. Through her own children she would have added more compassionate members to the human race. Through her gifted and highly developed intellect she would have contributed significantly to any profession she chose to enter, whether it be law, elementary education, or furthering her talents in the arts. Through her spiritual awareness and innately generous presence she would have continued to give profoundly to many people.

—FROM A LETTER TO
THE SENTENCING JUDGE
BY PENNY HOUGHTELING

12

A TIME FOR RECKONING

Hadden's invoking of Donald Salzman's name more than 100 times would be to no avail. The police had discovered that their suspect's net worth was more than $40,000 and that it was largely in liquid assets. Since Salzman was a public defender and only represented the indigent, Hadden was forced to pay for a criminal attorney. Sue Snyder of Bethesda Cares had already walked him into the office of John C. Monahan at the Rockville legal firm of Armstrong Donohue & Ceppos a few days after Ed Golian first questioned him. Hadden was forced to turn over his savings nest egg to retain the attorney.

The brunt of the research for the defense fell to Benjamin S. Vaughan, a strapping, six-foot-four attorney in his mid-thirties. Vaughan had spent his childhood less than a mile from the courthouse where Hadden was scheduled to be tried. He usually defended hospitals from malpractice charges but did not shrink from defending the criminally accused. For him, that was what the law was all about. His altruistic leanings may have been genetic. Vaughan's mother had been a social worker and two of his sisters had followed her into the field. He was the fifth born of six and there had been times his family had despaired, wondering if he would ever have a professional career. Vaughan plunged into the most public case of his life with zeal.

Hadden, held without bond at the Montgomery County Detention Center, was already behaving as his own worst enemy. Three days after arriving at the jail he was given a routine physical examination by a nurse, Christine Bevacqua. The medic didn't know who he was and had never seen him on the evening news.

"I'm not giving out autographs today," Hadden began.

Bevacqua said she didn't know what he was talking about.

"Haven't you seen me on TV?" Hadden asked. "You know, they're not going to find a thing."

After, the nurse took notes of their conversation, adding, "He makes one feel uncomfortable. It's difficult to assess why."

Bevacqua went home and told about her experience to a neighbor in her apartment building. Her listener was a police officer who immediately telephoned Montgomery County's homicide unit.

Although the cops had gotten nothing through their interrogation, Hadden was a chatterbox in confinement. He continued to say all the wrong things in jail, at times blurting out fragmented confessions which were quickly reported. On one occasion, Hadden moped on a bench while a group of prisoners played volleyball. When the ball went out of bounds and came his way he caught it but wouldn't throw it back. When the inmate ran up to him to get the ball Hadden was crying.

"I shouldn't have done it," he sobbed. "I shouldn't have killed her."

Hadden was right when he spoke to the nurse—the cops weren't finding a thing, only spending more man-hours on fruitless searches. On November ninth, the cops and several cadaver dogs spread out in Hadden's old neighborhood in Warren Township, New Jersey. Nothing was found, of course, though a county police spokesman sounded hopeful.

"They found fresh dirt that could indicate there had been a grave, but we didn't find a body," he said. The conned Montgomery County Police Department returned to New Jersey three more times, once with a bloodhound named Sherlock. They dug under the treehouse Hadden had played in as a boy and got nothing but an empty hole. There were several sightings of Hadden's truck in Warren by well-meaning citizens. One, by a dentist and his wife, fueled and the cops' hunt. They said a white pickup truck had been lurking near the Clarks' former home.

"We've seen it a couple of times," said Kathy Alvino, the dentist's spouse. "It was dirty and disheveled. It stuck in my mind."

The police had officially reopened the Michele Dorr case. Embittered, Carl Dorr said he had little hope that his daughter would ever be found.

"They spent too much time focusing on me. They let the killer slip through the cracks," he told the press.

A month after Hadden's night-long interrogation, Ben Vaughan stood alongside prosecutor Kathleen Toolan in a Montgomery County courtroom. The two presented a Mutt and Jeff look to the judge, Dennis McHugh. Toolan was five-feet-one—the top of her head barely reached to Vaughan's shoulders. She wanted more time to prepare the state's case against Hadden. Her opponent was ready to go. It was an unusual proceeding—the opposite was more often true. Toolan wanted to delay the preliminary hearing, saying there was a lot of evidence she still needed to sift through. While her claim was certainly within reason, Toolan was hoping that the cops might soon find Laura's body, making her job easier. The police had told her they were talking with psychics who they hoped would lead them to her remains.

It wasn't impossible to prosecute a murder case without a body in Montgomery County. Her office had just put away a Chinese-American restaurateur, Gregory Tu, for killing his common-law wife even though there was no body or murder weapon. But the Tu case, where prosecutors had to convince a jury that he had shot her while she sat on a sofa in the basement of their home, had been difficult. The first conviction was overturned and the second time around Tu was only found guilty of second-degree rather than first-degree murder. Tu was put away for thirty years, but under sentencing terms he would be eligible for parole long before half his time was served. And Tu was only the county's second murder case without a body in a dozen years. Locating the victim would be a major leap for the prosecution and help to make their case airtight. Toolan asked the court for a continuance while the police continued to search. When the judge asked her how long, she said she would like the time to be open-ended.

"As long as possible," she said. "We have not analyzed all the evidence we have. There is simply a lot of forensic material that hasn't been tested."

Vaughan disagreed. He pointed out that Maryland law mandated a preliminary hearing within thirty days after an arrest.

"Let's keep the continuance to a minimum," he said. Hadden attended the hearing sitting next to Vaughan. He looked drugged, sleepily resting his chin on his open hands. An interested Penny Houghteling was in the front row of the courtroom.

The jurist gave the prosecution two more weeks. Toolan was praying the cops would find her body by then.

In late November, several Montgomery County cops drove to Rhode Island to search Hadden's bin at E-Z Storage. Flavia and Alison met them at the site. One of the items they recovered was the high school graduation painting by Edith Clark that Hadden had stolen from Geoff in 1987. On the back of the canvas someone had scrawled, *To Hadden, from Grandma*. The handwriting was analyzed and turned out to be their murder suspect's.

Three days before Christmas the police again searched the woods where they had found the bloody pillowcase. This time they used leaf blowers and shovels to scrape the ground. A black Labrador dog sniffed the soil. They pumped out a nearby pond, draining it completely. Although the police did find another one of Penny's high-heeled pumps, a poncho, and a videotape from Holman Communications, there were no clues that led to Laura's whereabouts.

While the cops continued searching for Laura's body, Ben Vaughan was preparing a series of thirteen legal motions designed to limit the amount of evidence that Toolan could present to a jury. The prosecution wanted to offer testimony that would say a bloodhound had tracked Laura's scent from a place in the woods where they found the pillowcase and back to Laura's house on Julliard Drive. Vaughan said "dog tracking" was inadmissible as documentation and also irrelevant since Laura could easily have walked most of the course herself a few days before on her way to the subway stop. He also argued that nothing the police had learned from their seven-and-a-half-hour interrogation could possibly be admitted. Wrote Vaughan:

> The State has indicated that it intends to use as evidence a statement made by the defendant to a stuffed bear which had been handed to him by the police in the course of the investigation. The statement was clearly the product of police misconduct.

The next move Vaughan tried to make was to suggest that all pre-trial motions and hearings be sealed and the public, in particular the news media, be barred from attending them. Vaughan argued that the media's reporting on the case would divulge Hadden's other crimes and that any reports by the press on Hadden's personal life would prove to be humiliating and embarrassing. Additionally, the lawyer said that information about Hadden's cross-dressing had to be excluded, saying it was prejudicial. He also asked for a list of Penny's patients in order to develop "other suspects."

Finally, Vaughan wanted any testimony by the nurse,

Christine Bevacqua, to be suppressed because she was "an agent of the state" and thus should have given him a Miranda warning before talking to him. That request was denied.

Vaughan's plea to seal the information discussed during the preliminary motions was also refused. The "dog tracking" motion was not immediately ruled on. Patient confidentiality rules were used to bar Vaughan from getting access to Penny's psychotherapy appointments. Only the clearly illegal interrogation by the police was ruled inadmissible, with even the prosecutors appearing embarrassed by the dialogue contained in the tapes.

"He almost immediately asked for a lawyer," admitted Assistant State's Attorney Robert Steinheimer. "One was not provided. The statements were involuntary."

Steinheimer also said that Hadden never received his Miranda admonition. The remarks were considered unusual. It was rare for a prosecutor to chastise his own police department, even slightly.

The press appeared to be shocked by the interrogation. *The Washington Post* wrote a long editorial on the subject, saying in part:

It is astounding that in this age of nightly repetitions of Miranda warnings on television, in both police dramas and true-crime reenactments, law enforcement officers in a place like Montgomery County would fail to deliver the caution. But they did. They also ignored the defendant's repeated requests to see an attorney, a failure that would surely sink any confession subsequently given. The average ten-year-old, we would guess, knows these rules.

Why did these officers slip up so egregiously? It is reasonable to accept the word of Mr. Clark's lawyer that a policeman sat on the defendant in order to keep him in his seat and that at some point the lawmen threatened him with death in the gas chamber and urged him to commit suicide.

Official police spokesmen have not denied any of this. But what are they doing to set the officers straight and to see that this kind of conduct is never repeated?

Rich Fallin, in court testimony, disagreed. He said it was all for the greater good—which he defined as the attempt to find Laura's body.

"We planned the interrogation that way," he said. "We felt that we could locate the body of Laura Houghteling."

Hadden was indicted for first-degree murder on December seventeenth. His trial was scheduled for June of 1993.

Ed Tarney had studied the map found in Hadden's truck and concluded that it was a blueprint which would lead to a body. After conversations with the Wellfleet police he learned that their suspect had been spotted in the vicinity of the Pleasant Hill Cemetery on or about Halloween.

Rushing to the scene in early January, the police found the overturned cemetery markers and the freshly turned dirt. They brought in a cadaver dog named Dan and dug a hole six feet deep. The dog pointed at the new mound of dirt. This made the cops believe that there had been an unembalmed body there and that it had been recently removed. They were correct on those assumptions, but would falsely theorize that the body was that of Laura Houghteling and later that of Michele Dorr. Their belief was that Hadden had driven to Wellfleet on October twenty-first, and then returned on Halloween to dig her up and rebury her when he realized Tarney had found his map.

"He's trained to 'alert' to two things—blood or decaying human flesh," Richard Rosenthal, the Wellfleet police chief said of Dan, their cadaver dog. "Before we touched the site, we let him go out there. He had the whole cemetery to choose from and he went to the disturbed site and started digging. This dog does not know how to lie."

Newspaper reports about the cemetery search led two local men to tell the police that they had seen Hadden's truck on the outskirts of Wellfleet. The spot was near the woods that were part of the Cape Cod National Seashore, two miles from the cemetery. This sent the Montgomery County Police Department back to Wellfleet where they searched 100 wooded acres in late January. This time dogs from the Massachusetts State Police joined the search. The ground was largely frozen, making it a temporary tundra and virtually impossible for the dogs to detect anything that was underground. Still, Police Chief Rosenthal thought they were close.

"I believe the body is here," Rosenthal told some shivering reporters. The cop never said which body, but added that the two men had seen Hadden walking on a path into the woods and acting "in an unusual manner."

"They had a sense that something was not quite right," Rosenthal added, claiming Hadden's map was accurate. "I would have drawn it the same way."

When Flavia Clark was contacted by a reporter about the search, she weighed in on her son's situation. His mother was more than ready to testify on behalf of the prosecution, denying he had any multiple personality disorders.

"Any time I was dealing with Hadden, I felt I was dealing with Hadden," his mother recalled. "If I was dealing with somebody else, I wasn't aware of it."

Flavia also said she had gotten past Hadden's murder charge. "I had a lot of anger for a bit, and then terrible shock."

Flavia claimed not to have known that Hadden was living out of his truck. She said she knew nothing of his many arrests, but when told he had stolen the choir ladies' purses while dressed as a woman, admitted she had seen him wearing female clothing around the house on at least two occasions.

"I didn't know he was homeless," she said. "He had a mailbox drop and a telephone answering service, but I didn't think anything about it."

Hadden was "a brain-damaged baby," she remembered. "He would often be very hyper or he would become so frustrated, he would withdraw and go to his bed for hours," Flavia recalled. She told her interviewer that Hadden didn't have any friends as a child and that doctors had never been able to diagnose his disability.

His mother said she had visited with her son at the Montgomery County Detention Center three times since his arrest for murder. Flavia was hoping the police would find Laura Houghteling's body, hoping that "then there will be a sense of closure for both families. The end might not be the way you like it but you can pick yourself up, accept the facts, and go on."

On one hand, Hadden seemed to be enjoying his star status at the Montgomery County Detention Center. He had made ten drawings in jail and was gifting the counselors in the psychiatric unit with some of them. He signed each piece, "The Rockville Rocket." Other inmates were asking for his autograph, he told Flavia, adding that he was considered a celebrity in his new home.

By the spring of 1993, the Montgomery County Police Department hadn't come close to finding Laura's body, though it wasn't for lack of trying. In April they were back in Massachusetts, this time in Provincetown, a resort destination on Cape Cod's northern tip that catered to artists and gay tourists. Again, with trained dogs, they searched an area around that town's cemetery. The hunt was initiated because of a local who came forward and said he had seen someone who resembled Hadden carrying a body through the cemetery on Halloween night. They found nothing.

Their newest theory was that Hadden had dug up Laura after discovering that the cops had the map, and reburied her in or around Provincetown. The police assumptions went against all FBI statistics. The Bureau's numbers said that killers like Hadden were generally territorial, and almost always buried their victims a short distance from where they lived so they could visit the grave to relive the act. Perhaps they felt Hadden Clark was a new kind of criminal, and disposing of a body nearly 800 miles from where he was residing was a fresh type of murderer profile as yet undiscovered.

As the June trial date drew near, the prosecutors began to get cold feet. In truth, they had one piece of real evidence, the fingerprint on Laura's pillow. Any statement Hadden made to the police or Christine Bevacqua might be able to be explained away if the defense was able to convince a jury that Hadden's mental state was suspect and he was liable to say anything under pressure. They could easily concoct a story about the bloody pillow, saying Hadden found it near his truck and took it into the woods. His hair samples from Laura's bedroom could easily be explained. Penny herself had already said she saw him in her daughter's room without permission on at least one occasion. Hadden's criminal record and background would be excluded, unless he took the stand, which was unlikely. In his mental state, he was likely to say anything. And there was no body, so the prosecution would have the additional burden of proving that Laura was dead. Juries were unpredictable. Who knew what arguments they would buy?

With days to go before the trial began, Kathleen Toolan offered Monahan and Vaughan a deal. She would allow him to plead guilty to second-degree murder. Hadden accepted the offer with Vaughan adding a condition—Hadden must be allowed to serve his time at Patuxent Institution, a Maryland prison that was also a psychiatric hospital.

Toolan went to Penny Houghteling and gave her the

terms. Penny agreed. As a psychotherapist, she knew more than anyone that Hadden Clark was not of sound mind.

Less than twenty-four hours later Penny and Hadden were in Courtroom Thirteen in Rockville. As a formality Kathleen Toolan informed Irma S. Raker, the judge, that she had been informed Hadden wanted to plead guilty to second-degree murder and that the state of Maryland was accepting his plea.

"Do you understand the crime of second-degree murder?" Raker asked him.

"Yeah. I understand what I did," Hadden said. His voice was sullen, his face that of a petulant child who had been caught at a prank.

Raker weakened Vaughan's demand for a stay in the Patuxent Institution by saying that, while she would recommend it, being sent there was not guaranteed. Admission was up to the staff of the hospital, she said. Then Toolan rose and showed photos of the bloody pillow and the luminol evidence, arguing that if the case had gone to trial she would have won anyway. She went into Hadden's hair fibers, which were found in Laura's bedroom, and the wig fibers on Laura's hairbrush. She took special care to establish that Laura wasn't just missing, noting her passport was still at home and no earnings had been reported to Social Security since her death. Vaughan and Monahan made no objections. Hadden was asked if he would like to make a statement. He stood up and read rapidly from a piece of paper that had been prepared by his lawyers.

"During the early morning hours of October 19, 1992, I entered the home of Laura and Penny Houghteling. I found Laura alone in her bedroom. I killed her by means of suffocation while she lay there in bed. I moved her from her home and buried her. I was not assisted by any other person and suffered no delusions at the time of this crime. I committed the crime of my own free will.

I profoundly regret my actions and wish to extend my deepest sorrow and regrets to the family of Laura Houghteling with all my heart. I am pleading guilty because I am guilty and for no other reason."

Penny Houghteling was sitting with Warren in the front row. As Hadden spoke she touched his shoulder gently. Behind Penny were Flavia Clark, her brother, Brad Scranton, and his wife, Jane. They did not react. Sentencing was set for June twenty-fifth, two weeks later.

After the guilty plea, Penny Houghteling held another news conference where she wore and held fresh-cut flowers. She said the flowers symbolized how short Laura's life had been. Penny told the press she still wanted Laura's remains returned to her—giving back the body had not been part of the plea deal—but she seemed somewhat resigned to not getting her wish.

"On another level, it doesn't matter," she said. "She was here, we loved her, and we know she is dead."

Flavia implied that she, too, was a casualty.

"There are many victims," she offered. "There is much healing to take place on both sides. I've been harassed, my son Geoff's been harassed, even though we're not guilty of anything. People call all day asking, 'What do you have to say?' Well, what is there to say? In a case like this, we're all victims."

Within hours after pleading guilty, Hadden told his lawyers where they could find Laura. Toolan, Vaughan, and Monahan drove to the site, just minutes from the courthouse, with Vaughan finding the grave and Laura's nude, decomposed remains. A television station helicopter's camera caught the body bag being loaded into a hearse.

Monahan praised his client. "If Mr. Clark didn't want to disclose this, he could have taken it to his grave," he said.

Penny and Warren issued a joint statement saying, "This

brings a sense of closure to one level of this tragedy."

The Montgomery County State's Attorney's Office had not forgotten Michele Dorr, though it seemed to hold little hope of ever finding her. Andy Sonner, its chief prosecutor, said it would be "raw speculation" to link Hadden with Michele, a view certainly not held by Mike Garvey or the other detectives in the county police department. Sonner did say that Hadden "will always remain a suspect."

Eleven days after his guilty plea, on June 25th, 1993, Hadden was sentenced. The county moved the event to Courtroom One, the largest space in the judicial center. A full house was expected and the regular circuit court rubbernecks were not disappointed. Penny, her sister Mary Runnels, Warren, and three of Laura's friends from school sat together in the right front row. Flavia sat three rows behind with Geoff and Stephanie Clark on one side, and Ed Tarney and his wife on the other. Flavia was dressed festively. She wore a flowered suit and a green blouse. Carl Dorr was there as well, watching attentively. Monahan gave another plea for his client to be housed and rehabilitated at Patuxent Institution. He also employed some pop psychology.

"Hadden has said to us, 'I want help.' He doesn't want to be released until he is well, until he is cured. That is what he told us and that is what he would tell you if he stood up now," Monahan said. He claimed this excuse as his client's motive.

In Hadden's crazy, mixed-up world, Penny became a replacement for his mother. When Laura came home, there was a reason, obviously misguided, that he discerned as a threat to this relationship and that is why he did what he did. Quickly said, this explanation may cause two mothers in the courtroom to start to blame themselves. He doesn't want this and we certainly don't. The guilt for what happened to Laura Houghteling is with Hadden Clark and not with Penny Houghteling and not with Mrs. Clark. It would be awful for them to continue to blame themselves for what he did.

The phrase "continue to blame themselves" hung in the air, angering both Flavia and Penny. Though Flavia had indeed disowned her son, with little communication between the pair for more than five years, she would not take the blame for Hadden's crime. The extroverted, alcoholic mother of Hadden believed that not one percent of blame could be laid at her feet. Penny was infuriated as well. The implication was that she had been too trusting, too informal with Hadden, and that her friendliness had cost her a daughter.

John Monahan then revealed that a Dr. Gary Kay from Georgetown University Medical Hospital had just examined Hadden. The report indicated that there was a malfunction in the left lobe of his brain, Monahan said.

Ben Vaughan asked for a ten-to-twenty-one-year sentence, saying that Hadden's disclosure of where he'd buried Laura was "a meaningful act of remorse." Kathleen Toolan countered by asking for the longest sentence possible.

"With regard to the actual sentencing, the maximum potential penalty in this case is thirty years," she said. "The state is asking that you impose every day of the maximum that you are allowed. I have had enough of listening to Hadden Clark's problems. There is another person who is not here, Laura Houghteling, to say what she has gone through."

Toolan went on to recount the suffering of the Houghteling family and the elaborate deception schemes Hadden had devised, including his telling the police that Laura's body was in New Jersey. She read letter after letter that Laura's friends had written supporting her demand for the maximum penalty. She finished by saying that Hadden felt no remorse. His only regret was being arrested and being forced to plead guilty, she said.

Hadden, who was wearing a green-and-blue turtleneck shirt, spent the morning chewing gum, flipping pencils, and generally looking bored with the proceedings. He got up to speak but his statement, written partly by him, only backed up Toolan's assertion that he had little contrition. He spoke without emotion, reading his speech as if forced to do so.

"I'm sorry for all the pain and suffering I have caused Penny, Warren, family, and friends. I have hurt a lot of people by taking a life they can never replace, someone they love very much and they will never see her again, and I'm sorry for hurting Penny, Warren, family, and friends' feelings and putting them through all this grief, shock and insecurity. I especially apologize to Laura Houghteling."

When Hadden said "they will never see her again," tears filled Laura's friends' eyes. The remark had struck home and in his final moments before them, he was causing additional pain.

"I apologize for not releasing the body sooner and for prolonging the anguish to Penny, Warren, family, and friends and making Penny, Warren, family, and friends suffer by not knowing if they would ever recover Laura's body. I'm sorry for putting Penny, Warren, family and friends and the community through this horror and shocking experience and making them feel they are unsafe in their homes."

Hadden spoke the phrase "Penny, Warren, family, and friends" each time as if the passage were one long word. He seemed eager to finish his statement.

"I deeply regret my wrongdoings to Penny, Warren, family, and friends for killing Laura Houghteling and taking her life away from Penny, Warren, family, and friends, people who loved her very much, people who will never see her again. It is something that can never be replaced."

It was time for Judge Irma Raker to have the final say.

Within three months she would be appointed to the Maryland Court of Appeals, only the second woman to get the nod. She had been a trial judge for more than a decade, and a prosecutor before that. Raker wasn't hesitant to express her fury by going back on the deal Vaughan thought he had made.

"You have taken Laura Houghteling's life in the cruelest way," Raker said. "You pose a great danger to society. Having considered all the previous extensive psychiatric treatment and their inability to help you I will not refer you to Patuxent Institution for treatment. You may petition for admittance on your own. It is the sentence of this court that you be remanded to the Department of Corrections in a maximum-security facility for thirty years. And it is the hope of this court that you serve every day."

Laura Houghteling's remains were cremated, with her ashes buried in a cemetery in Fairhaven, Massachusetts, where the Houghteling family had a summer beach house. Ironically, the main road running through Fairhaven was U.S. Route Six. It ran north on to Cape Cod and into Wellfleet, which was an hour's drive away.

Like the Clarks, the Houghtelings also had a family plot near the sea. Nearly forty friends showed up to pay their last respects. Laura's physical remains were inside a black, plastic box with Penny commenting that her daughter's cremation ashes were more like large chips. The box was put into a freshly dug hole near her father's grave and in the late afternoon the guests filed by each dropping a spadeful of dirt on top of the black box until the opening in the earth was filled.

There were many posthumous memorials to Laura. A weeping birch tree was planted near her dormitory at Harvard, her photography was exhibited, a teak bench was placed with her name on it near the tree, and a scholarship fund was established for Harvard students wanting to teach at the elementary school level. None of her friends believed it was enough.

Hadden Clark was sent to a medium-security prison on the Delmarva peninsula. Despite his thirty-year sentence, he was to be eligible for parole after serving twenty-five percent of it—November 2000.

13

TIGHTENING THE NOOSE

Hadden failed to adjust to his new life at the Eastern Correctional Institution—ECI was the Delmarva version of WCI—and at times seemed to be begging for further punishment. There were incidents in the prison chow hall where he would spit into the coffee of an inmate or deliberately pour salt into someone's beverage instead of sugar. These acts resulted in a beating by a gang of convicts within days. Prison officials didn't want his murder on their hands and kept putting him into protective custody, a type of privileged solitary confinement, once for more than a year. Ed Tarney asked him how he survived so long living alone.

"Correspondence chess. That was the only way I could play. It's fun. You correspond and he writes back. Two of the people I was playing with, they might send cards or add a little something. One guy I played, his wife sent me a card, a Christmas card and an Easter card. My family don't send that to me."

Does that bother you?

"It bothers me some. But you just have to deal with things. Like you've got to understand what I've put them through, and I want their forgiveness. But that doesn't stop me from sending them a card."

Are you closest to Geoff?

"I don't know. He don't answer my letters. I can understand why. I've put him though a lot of problems, you know."

Does anyone in your family ever write you back anymore?

"No. I don't ask, 'Will you write me?' but I will ask

questions in the letter, like say, 'How are you doing?' That's like saying, 'Answer my letter.' But the answer is no."

Flavia Clark was still hoping the police would find Michele's body even if it meant another murder conviction for her son.

"If that's the way things are going to be, I want to get it over with," she said.

A month after Hadden arrived at ECI he wrote a letter to his mother. Flavia had just learned she was in the beginning stages of breast cancer, a disease that would soon metastasize and kill her.

"One day, more like a few months down the road I would like to tell my side of the story. What made Hadden do what Hadden did. But right now you'll have to wait," he wrote, adding, "Please don't throw out my ladies clothing. I like my ladies clothing. I don't know why, I just like it. Maybe I'll get rid of them when I get out."

He also asked his mother for his address book but she never mailed it. After time had passed Hadden told a cellmate that he believed Flavia would never give it to him. He said his mother knew he would write to everyone in the book, telling them he was in jail and she didn't want him to because she was ashamed of his situation.

Flavia never responded to any of her son's letters from prison. She died on September 17, 1995, at the age of sixty-five from complications of the cancer that included pneumonia and septicemia. Like Hadden's father, Flavia was cremated.

Her will stated that not only was Geoff to be the executor of her estate but that he would receive all of her tangible personal property including the house on Block Island, the contents of her checking accounts, and any cash. Flavia's land and house were assessed at $204,632 for tax purposes. While it was understandable that Brad and Hadden received nothing, her total omission of Alison was viewed as perplexing. The will, drafted in May of 1994, contained a codicil that gave only this hint as to her thinking.

> My children have, and probably will have in the future, unequal assets. I love them and my grandchildren, and wanted to have some fair division of property. If it is not accepted or is thought unclear, consult with the attorney who drafted the will, Elliot Taubman, for an interpretation.

To be fair, Flavia may have taken care of both her imprisoned sons before her death with a small trust. According to a penal official, small money orders are sent every few months to Hadden's prison spending account from a mysterious source in Maine. Geoff sporadically sent money. Hadden said he isn't sure of the origin of the funds from Maine.

Geoff kept the property and though he sometimes vacations there, he also rents the house out to summer visitors. His asking price, according to a Block Islander, is $8000 a month.

In August of 1994 Hadden was sent from ECI to Patuxent Institution to undergo a six-month evaluation. According to him, he was rejected from entering into any long-term psychiatric program.

"Hedda Barry, the director, she said, 'We're going to accept you in. We're going to accept you in the Patuxent program,' " Hadden recalled. "I never got accepted. They said I was too old for it. Here I'm trying to get help and they say I'm too old, but a month later they accept a guy that was fifty-four years old. And then a year later the guy that I was turned down with, well, he had a grievance and

I had a grievance. He won his grievance and I was told I had to wait three years."

He was asked about the criteria for getting into Patuxent.

"Well we had a group and the psychiatrist," he recalled. "They said, 'If you participate in the program, you'll get accepted.' Well, I know lots of people who participated in the program, but they didn't get accepted.

"This is the way I explain it. It's like, if you apply for a job as a sergeant and you have a thousand people apply for that position, but only one person's going to get the job. Well, it was the same way with being evaluated."

While Hadden whined about not being accepted into Patuxent's long-term psychiatric program, the Montgomery County police were putting new efforts into either finding Michele Dorr's body or getting enough evidence to charge him with her murder. In October of 1994, the Warwick, Rhode Island, police again searched Hadden's packed-to-the-ceiling bin at E-Z Storage after first talking with their Maryland counterparts. They impounded two women's bathing suits, a large towel that looked as if it had blood-stains on it, and some photographs of small children, one of whom looked like a pudgy version of Michele. When they showed the items to Carl Dorr, he couldn't identify any of them. Too much time had passed.

In September of 1995 the Montgomery County police went back to Wellfleet yet again, this time with five cadaver dogs, police investigators from Massachusetts, and FBI agents from Quantico, Virginia. The Bureau brought along Sonar and other imaging equipment that could detect objects under the ground. They were acting on a theory that Hadden must have buried Michele somewhere on Silas Clark's formerly owned seven-and-a-half acres of land. When the cadaver dogs all keyed on the same twenty-five-foot-square section of land, the police cordoned it off with yellow tape.

"I think this is probably the best lead we've had so far," an enthusiastic Ann Evans, the Montgomery County police spokesperson, told reporters just before digging. The police dug several holes, each one seven feet deep, at times getting down on their hands and knees to sift the earth with their bare hands for bone fragments. They found nothing. The cops were puzzled. They believed the cadaver dogs to be infallible, a theory that had been somewhat disproved when dogs had searched within several feet of Laura's shallow grave in Maryland and missed it.

"The example they gave me was of a woman buried in a landfill in New Jersey," explained Jim Cumming, a Massachusetts State Police lieutenant. "They went there with a dog and found her, despite all the chicken bones and garbage and everything. She'd been missing for fifteen years."

After blanking in Massachusetts once again, police from both Montgomery County and Rhode Island went onto Flavia's former property on Block Island less than a month after her death. They searched both the barn and the pumphouse where Hadden used to sleep. Again cadaver dogs were used, if only to establish that there were no bodies buried on the land. It appeared that Geoff Clark, the estate's new owner, encouraged the search.

"Geoffrey was very cooperative and indicated he had noticed that Hadden stored things there," said the Block Island police chief, Bill McCombe.

By now the police had figured out that besides being a serial killer, Hadden was also a pack rat, and if they went anyplace where he had once lived they were certain to find something. They were not disappointed on Block Island. In the barn they found a pair of Hadden's blue jeans, a windbreaker and two pair of gloves that were stained, possibly with blood, a cop said. They also found a passport, a duffel bag, and some of Hadden's personal writings. But what got the cops really excited was the discovery of a large collection of knives—twenty-eight in all—ranging in size from a butcher knife to smaller ones like fillet knives. There was also a straight-edged razor. Nineteen of them were in a tool chest, seven in a smaller container, and two were in a small box.

The Montgomery County police didn't neglect the Maryland suburbs either. They searched for Michele Dorr's body in the same area where they had found the body of Laura Houghteling, continuing to comb the county for nearly four years. As late as February of 1998 they were using radar to scan underneath the ground near Laura's gravesite, bringing in a front-end loader to dig even deeper holes.

The local police began to think that if they couldn't indict Hadden for Michele Dorr's disappearance, perhaps they could find him guilty of other crimes. They began circulating a photo of a woman who they hinted was someone he may have met at The Malt Shop bar above The Dancing Crab restaurant. The photograph, taken by Hadden, showed the woman at Hadden's campsite, partially obscuring her face with her arms. They questioned patrons at the bar, wanting to know if any of the regulars had suddenly vanished.

Ed Tarney began gathering evidence as to which tools and items had been stolen from the Mahany family when Hadden lived with them. Maybe they could add some years there. In that case, he had only been put on probation for destroying property. If they could get a conviction in a court for theft, that could be good for another ten or twenty years. Seeing that Hadden never walked free became their priority.

Minutes after Hadden pled guilty to murdering Laura Houghteling, Rich Fallin had taken advantage of the press corps to speak his mind. Fallin said there was no doubt that Hadden had killed the little girl but admitted he couldn't prove it either.

"Sergeant Phillips, Detective Garvey, Detective Tarney, and myself have looked over the whole Michele Dorr file and from what I've read and found, I feel as strongly about him doing Michele Dorr as I did about him doing Laura Houghteling. We just don't have a fingerprint or any physical evidence at this time."

Tarney and Fallin went back and reread the Michele Dorr file. This time they finally understood what they had been missing for years. Carl said he last saw his daughter at 2:10 in the afternoon and Hadden punched in at 2:46 on a time clock. So Hadden couldn't have killed her, tidied up, hidden her, and driven to work in thirty-six minutes. What they had missed, they concluded, was that Carl Dorr probably was lying and too embarrassed to tell them he had let his daughter out of his sight for so long. What if the last time he saw her was noon or even one o'clock?

Fallin reinterviewed Carl Dorr. Michele's father quickly recanted his statement. Sure, he said, it could have been as early as noon. Fallin told him he had lied. Carl claimed he hadn't. He just wasn't sure and never had been. With Hadden's alibi destroyed, the cops could go further with the case.

At Patuxent Institution, Hadden was hurting himself. Literally. He began openly boasting that he had killed Michele Dorr, telling and retelling his story so many times and in such graphic detail that several prisoners on the 32-cell evaluation tier where Hadden lived became disgusted. It didn't take them long to calculate that relaying such information to a law enforcement agency might make them look good when they appeared before a parole board. Heck, they might even wind up with a reward, they thought.

Hadden's beefy, thirty-two-year-old cellmate, Benton Chambers, in Patuxent for drug distribution, was one of the first to be so inspired. Chambers, and another inmate, John Fridley, a convicted burglar, decided to tape-record Hadden as he bragged about killing Michele. Using an old boombox radio and tape-player that they rigged to record instead of play, they inserted an old Ozzy Osbourne rock tape and recorded over it. Chambers sent the tape with the incriminating evidence to his wife, who gave it to the police. It soon wound up in the hands of Ed Tarney. The detective paid a visit to Ben Chambers and John Fridley.

"He found her in his niece's room playing with dolls. He went in and slashed her with a knife," Chambers told Tarney. Fridley's version was that Hadden told him he at first thought there was a burglar in the house and he got a butcher's knife from the truck to kill him. When he saw Michele he became out of control. Both said there was a lot of blood, with Hadden telling them he had wiped the floor clean.

When the word got around Patuxent that Hadden was openly flaunting his murder of a six-year-old girl, it didn't take long for prison justice to be administered. An inmate gave him a brutal beating using a makeshift blackjack. The weapon had been fashioned from an athletic sock that had a steel padlock inside. The blows split open the back of Hadden's head and caused a huge cut over his eyebrow. He was sent to the prison infirmary for stitches and then put into protective custody.

Using the information they got from the Patuxent cons, the police received permission to go into Geoff Clark's house and search for bloodstains in Eliza Clark's bedroom. Other detectives began interviewing previous occupants of the house to see if there ever had been any unusual bleeding in the room.

In September of 1995 Montgomery County's blood expert, Sue Ballou, and her technicians began lifting up the floorboards in Eliza Clark's room and the carpeting in the hallway outside it. The cops came up with nearly 100 different samples of blood, but since they were almost a decade old, the evidence was considered too degraded to be of any use for nuclear DNA analysis, which might have found the blood to be Michele's.

Instead Ballou sent the blood evidence to an FBI lab for mitochondrial DNA analysis. Mitochondrial DNA or mtDNA was a newer, much more sophisticated forensic typing that had been developed to identify the bodies of missing soldiers in Vietnam. Nuclear DNA had components of just two copies per cell but mtDNA contained between several hundred and as many as thousands per cell and could be found more easily in degraded blood. Since mtDNA was inherited from the mother, and Dee Dee was still alive, Carl's former wife could provide a reference sample. But mtDNA was not absolute evidence. It was viewed differently from nuclear DNA by the courts. For example, it was more susceptible to contamination, and in a few cases, unrelated people have been found to carry the identical mtDNA. So it was considered imprecise and most courts would not allow it to be used as evidence. Ballou, though, had no choice but to gamble. The new science, prosecutors thought, might be enough to get an indictment.

Getting the blood evidence analyzed took nearly two years. The FBI lab had a long waiting list for mtDNA analysis. Ballou was eventually forced to ask for her samples back. She then sent them off to the Laboratory Corporation of America in Burlington, North Carolina, one of only four private labs in the country qualified for the new science. LCA promised it back in ninety days. The wait was in vain. While the blood appeared to be Michele Dorr's, it wasn't definitive enough to be certain. Sue Ballou could not testify in absolute terms that Michele was murdered in Eliza's room. She could, however, testify that there had been a lot of bleeding in the room and that it certainly didn't come from any previous occupants in the house.

Hadden had been bounced out of Patuxent and transferred to Roxbury Correctional Institute in Hagerstown, Maryland,

when Ed Tarney brought him back to Montgomery County
to be charged with the murder of Michele Dorr. Before he
started reading the indictment, Tarney made a final try at
talking to Hadden and winning his confidence. He worked
hard at getting him to tell him where he had hidden the
items he had stolen from the Mahany family. If he could
recover just a few of the woodworking tools, that particular
prosecution would be made a lot easier. According to Hadden, Tarney's opening hello that day at the prison wasn't
exactly charming. The detective started out by playing
tough guy by tearing Hadden's hat off and throwing it to
the ground. He finished up by punching him in the testicles
while patting him down. *(Author's note: When asked if this
were true, Tarney wouldn't comment.)*

Back in Montgomery County, the detective put him in
the same interrogation room where the cops had worked
him over in 1992. With the furniture rearranged, Hadden
didn't recognize the setting. He was still afraid that Tarney
was going to come in and rough him up again. To quell
his fear, he began singing hymns and reciting the alphabet
in his high-pitched, sing-song voice:

"I'll be perfect according to his plan,
Fashioned by the Master's hand."

"You all right, bud? Are you singing?" Tarney asked as
he came into the room.

"Yeah, singing to God and he can hear me," Hadden
said. Tarney asked him if he wanted coffee and his prisoner
said he would take it black with sugar as long as he didn't
have to spit his gum out. He knew Tarney wanted to find
out something and he was determined to play with him for
as long as he wanted. Hadden seemed to set the ground
rules during the first five minutes of conversation.

"A lot of people ask you certain questions and you give
them the best answer you can," he said. "So if you ask a

stupid question, I'm going to give you a stupid answer. It says so in the Bible."

Tarney asked how he was getting along in prison with Hadden saying he was helping other prisoners to learn to read. Tarney allowed as that was a pretty nice thing to do.

"You've been a decent guy all your life. You've just made a few mistakes."

"Yeah," Hadden answered. "That's what people in prison have done; they've made a few mistakes."

Tarney attached himself to the philosophy, implicating himself. "That's pretty much what everybody does, though, Hadden. There's not anybody who goes through this life that doesn't make a lot of mistakes."

"Right."

"Some make more than others and some make bigger ones than others. But we all do it to one degree or another. You're just paying for yours now."

"What?"

"I guess you're paying for one of your big mistakes now."

"Yeah. But I'm doing positive things, making myself a better person."

"That's a big plus," Tarney said.

Hadden began complaining to Tarney about a long article on his case in *The Washington Post* magazine that had run in 1997. He said the reporter had lied to him by promising to mail him an expensive cookbook for the interview and then had reneged on the promise.

"I said, 'There's one book I'd really like to get but I wouldn't ask for it because it's real expensive.' He said, 'Oh, that's no problem. I'll get it for you.' The book is seventy bucks. It's like this culinary dictionary. He told me he was going to get it for me. He lied. Just a sucker punch."

Hadden was willing to talk about any subject that wouldn't incriminate him. He complained to Tarney that he had never gotten help for his mental problems.

"I tried to get into the VA hospital. I drove my car all the way up to a friend's because I couldn't leave it in the parking lot while I was in the hospital. I took it all the way up the East Coast and came back. My doctor wasn't there. The doctor that was interviewing me said, 'Where do you live?' and I said, 'Well, I guess since I'm homeless I don't have an address right now.'

"He said, 'Well, if you really want some help—' and I said, 'No, I'm coming—I'm supposed to be in the hospital right now. I'm supposed to be getting therapy.' They see a lot of homeless people in the winter who want to get out of the cold. I wasn't doing that. So it's 'Well, you go out,' and that's why I lived in the woods and survived. So I never got any help."

The answer was so convoluted and disjointed that Tarney had a hard time following what Hadden was saying. He eased into the Mahany matter in a manner that was as subtle as a bull in a china shop.

"Remember when we were talking earlier about people forgiving people for things?"

"Yeah."

"Okay. I know the Mahanys have no hard feelings towards you because I've talked to them. And I know they have forgiven you and you have forgiven them, so everything is done and over with."

"Right."

"Uh, just as a favor, Mr. Mahany would like to have his tools back. Can we get them back to him? There's some tools that left with you."

Hadden was a large fish who wasn't biting.

"I wouldn't know where that stuff is. If I had them, I wouldn't know where they are at this time."

"Are they in your storage stuff?"

"I wouldn't know."

"Does Geoff have them?"

"I don't know. I wouldn't know how to answer that question."

"Well, he just wants his stuff back."

Hadden fenced with Tarney, never incriminating himself, never admitting he stole anything from the Mahany family. Tarney wanted to focus on finding the tools so he could get Hadden an extra ten years. Hadden wanted to change the subject.

"The old fellow wants his tools back."

"I really can't answer those questions. See, my mind is focused on doing positive things now. All the other stuff that I've done I'm forgetting about because I'm trying to work on this new slate for me. I'm wiping everything clean."

"Listen, one good way to wipe the slate clean . . ."

It was a nice try but Hadden was having none of it. He interrupted, and went into a long *non sequitur* on fishing, talking of how he had plastic lures saved in a locker and that the salt water he had fished in wouldn't harm plastic. It was a crazy, manic riff and Tarney couldn't get him back on the subject.

"I just don't understand what that has to do with Mr. Mahany's tools. Is it worth us looking for it? Just yes or no."

"He might have given that stuff away. I don't know where that stuff is—if I did have it, well, I wouldn't know if I had it. I'm trying to be honest with you. So I don't know."

Tarney tried another tack.

"How about the suitcase with the family's tapes and stuff, the cassette tapes, their daughter's clothes?"

Hadden seemed agitated.

"I don't remember that. I don't remember. I don't even know what you're talking about. He said something about a booby trap, oil or something."

Tarney tried to get back on Hadden's good side. He

appeared to praise him for killing the Mahany's pet cats.

"I know one thing you did do that I think is funnier than hell. Those damn cats."

"What cats?"

"Their cats."

"I don't know what you're talking about."

"Just from your grin—I think you remember. The cat fur looked pretty good."

"I don't know what cats you're talking about."

"That's the first time I've seen you smile today," Tarney said.

Hadden went back to religion. In his mind, the Bible had already absolved him for his evil deeds.

"I'm not going to say I hate you," he told Tarney. "I can't do that. It's against my religion. In the Bible it says you have to forgive people even if they've done something bad. In order for God to forgive what I've done bad, I have to forgive people who have done bad to me. So I can't hate you, that's just the way it is."

Hadden also appeared to be pardoning Tarney for the punch to his testicles. He asked Tarney if he would be spending the night at the Montgomery County Detention Center. He wanted to go back to the state prison in Hagerstown.

"Nobody is treating you bad here, are they?"

Hadden didn't answer. Tarney tried to get information from Hadden about his trips to Wellfleet in October of 1992 and only got evasive answers. The only questions Hadden would discuss were on movies, religion, and his philosophy of life. He said his favorite actress was Maureen O'Hara. He claimed he had never seen *Silence of the Lambs* until he got to prison.

"I've seen a lot of the world, and I'm happy with the way I've lived my—Well, I'm happy with how I've lived a lot of my life and not happy with a few things I've done. A few things I've done have been very bad, and maybe if

I got the proper care or people hadn't abused me, I might not have done what I have done."

"Who abused you?"

"I've been abused by society lots of different ways. I'm going to be abused when I get back to prison. I know there's news reporters out there. It will be on every channel tonight."

"You're a pretty famous guy. Someone could write a book."

"About what?"

"About you. I mean, it would be interesting."

Hadden said he was going to write his own book. Then he claimed he couldn't do it while he was in prison.

"I'm going to deal with my problems," he told Tarney. The detective agreed with him.

"You have to deal with the cards that you've been handed."

Tarney asked him if he wanted something to eat, saying it was five o'clock and time for the standard pre-prepared prison meal. Hadden went into Hannibal Lecter–ish musings on what he would really like for dinner.

"Fuck that. I don't want to fuck with you feeding me. I don't care if you feed me. Boneless steak . . . baked potato, sour cream. Hm-m-m. Asparagus. Hm-m-m. That's a good meal. And a cannoli for dessert."

Tarney wasn't quick enough to ask him if he wanted fava beans on the side. His menu choice was more pedestrian.

"We've got a bagel in there," he said.

Tarney asked more questions, trying his best to pry some real information from Hadden. He wanted to know about an ax, asking him if he had ever chopped someone's head off with it; he asked about a photo from the bar above The Dancing Crab; he showed him Michele Dorr's picture and asked questions about the little girl. Tarney got mostly nonsensical responses that would be meaningless in court.

Hadden wanted to clam up entirely on the matter of Michele. "My lawyer told me not to talk about that."

Tarney told him there were inmates in prison waiting to testify against him. Hadden stayed calm.

"I don't know where she is. Prisoners will talk about anything."

The detective gave up.

"I'm going to read something to you. This is a warrant, an arrest warrant, charging you with first-degree murder."

He read the entire indictment, which went on for more than a thousand words. The last words seemed to strike home.

"Your applicant believes that Michele Dorr, the deceased, was murdered in the bedroom at 9125 Sudbury Road, Silver Spring, Montgomery County, Maryland, by Hadden Irving Clark."

Tarney left the room and Hadden began speaking in broken, nonsensical phrases again. He made up a new poem on the spot.

Oh well, I'm the Rockville Rocket
The Rockville rocket, that's me.
This could be a bunch of bullshit,
To try and break me.

Tarney came back in appearing genuinely concerned.

"Hadden, you're white as a ghost. You okay?"

"Just tired."

He refused dinner when it was offered again. When Hadden continued to mope, Tarney knew how to make him smile.

"I'll tell you what, I still like what you did to the cats."

"Yeah, I know you do. I'm going to hear about those cats all the way back to Hagerstown."

14

THROWING AWAY THE KEY

The Montgomery County State's Attorney's Office gave the task of putting Hadden Clark away for good to a pair of its most experienced prosecutors. Both the Mahany theft and the Michele Dorr murder were assigned to Debra Dwyer and Jim Trusty, lawyers who were thought to have synergy with each other. The bond was genuine. Each had graduated from the same Montgomery County high school and, after joining the state's attorney's office, they had been held up at gunpoint together.

Trusty, who had the face of an aging frat boy, liked to tell the story of how he and his colleague had once pulled up to a Burger King drive-through window while at a prosecutors' convention in Houston. A gunman had walked up to their car and put a gun to Trusty's head while asking for their money. Dwyer quickly pulled all the money from her purse and gave it to him, but Trusty later cracked jokes about it, saying the burger run had been Dwyer's idea.

"My life was in danger over Debbie's Whopper," was the punchline.

Trusty, in his mid-thirties, tried to stay in shape by jogging and running the occasional 5K road race. Dwyer, nearly five years older, was a physical marvel. She was an aggressive golfer and strong enough to pedal fifty miles of a city-to-city bike run to raise funds for AIDS research. Still, she liked a good Irish beer. She believed it an omen when she had visited Ireland on Saint Patrick's Day, walked into the first bar she saw, and found out the pub was called O'Dwyer's. That was good for an extra Guinness.

Before getting Hadden's case, her biggest legal challenge had been to convict Bruman Alvarez, an Ecuadorian immigrant who had alternately stabbed and used a hammer to kill five people, after he was discovered raping a fifteen-year-old girl. Four of them were members of the same family. The other was Alvarez' boss, a painting contractor who walked in on him during the rape. Alvarez received six life terms, five of them without parole.

Both had imperfections. Trusty had a habit of wisecracking his way through the most serious of cases with one-liners, sometimes using his scathing wit to ridicule defense witnesses. Dwyer was the opposite. Earnest aggression was her forte and she tended to punctuate every 100 words in her opening and closing arguments with the phrase, "ladies and gentlemen" whether the jury members were or not.

Dwyer and Trusty were given nine months to prepare the murder case. They would have half that for the Mahany theft trial which was scheduled for the last week of May 1999.

There was one preliminary hearing after another during the spring of 1999. Most were on procedural matters in the Michele Dorr case but there was also a hearing in the Mahany theft case in which Hadden, for only the second time in a Montgomery County court, testified on his own behalf.

Brian Shefferman, Hadden's other public defender in addition to Donald Salzman, put his client on the stand in an attempt to prove the cops had illegally searched his truck in 1992. If he could get a court to go along with that, then he could make a case that the items found in the storage bin belonging to the Mahany family were improperly found. Shefferman's argument was that Hadden's storage lockers would never have been discovered if the cops hadn't gone through his truck without a search warrant while he was being questioned. Hadden was whiny in his responses.

"I wanted to leave but they wouldn't let me," he said.

Hadden was a bad witness. Just by sitting at the defense

table, he became the prosecution's best weapon. Wearing an old turtleneck with jeans, his graying face, sunken cheeks, and intense stare made him look like a movie version of a serial killer as envisioned by Central Casting. On the stand, his choppy hand gestures looked violent. Though his testimony was in front of a judge without a jury present, his agitated manner and long, self-pitying explanations seemed to amplify the public defender's worst fear. It wasn't just that Hadden resembled the public's conception of what a convicted murderer should look like, but that he looked as if he would kill again willingly. His demeanor left little room for sympathy. Shefferman lost the motion.

At another hearing Hadden managed to expand on the abuse he got from Ed Tarney in 1998, adding that Tarney had put on the handcuffs too tight and said he wouldn't loosen them until he talked. He claimed that Tarney had choked him and then, as he put it, "punched me in the nuts up in Hagerstown." Nobody in the courtroom, except perhaps Salzman and Shefferman, seemed particularly saddened by the claim.

His public defenders tried to get the case dismissed on the grounds that Sue Ballou had given false testimony about the DNA samples in Eliza's bedroom. Ballou's sin was more of omission than design. The mtDNA showed that the blood samples could have belonged to five people other than Michele, something Ballou had left out. Judge Michael D. Mason, who was scheduled to preside over the trial, called the motion "absurd." Salzman then called the prosecutors "zealots."

Hadden's attorneys also argued prior to trial that none of the 1998 interrogation by Ed Tarney and his assistant, Detective Craig Wittenberger, should be admitted into evidence. They said the illegal 1992 interrogation had so traumatized Hadden that he may have made incriminating statements to Tarney because of his fear of being beaten and abused. Judge Paul Weinstein appeared to disagree.

"Mr. Clark said six ways to Sunday his lawyer told him not to talk about the Dorr case and he didn't," Weinstein told the bushy-haired Shefferman. "Did you see anything at all that shows they got involuntary statements out of him? I didn't."

When videotapes of both interrogations were shown in open court, a new rain of criticism fell upon the police department. This time *The Montgomery Journal* editorialized:

> It is the responsibility of the police to know the law and to uphold it, even when it's inconvenient or when an especially horrific crime is involved. Police are supposed to keep us safe from the bad guys, not jeopardize the community's safety by taking shortcuts in hopes of closing a case faster.

Carl Dorr, in court for many of the preliminary hearings, began telling the press he wanted the death penalty for Hadden. He said that a kidnapping charge could be added to the murder indictment, which would give prosecutors a better chance for an execution.

"There are people you have to look out for," he offered. "There are perverts, predators out there who go after young girls. Clark was not right psychologically. He clearly fit the profile."

During Hadden's theft trial, the prosecution was not allowed to mention the names of Michele Dorr or Laura Houghteling and thus prejudice the jury. It was a case of stolen goods, plain and simple, though it seemed hard to believe that the seven-man, five-woman jury had never heard of Hadden Clark and his many misdeeds.

"Sometimes things are just as simple as they appear, and that is what this case is all about," Trusty said in his opening statement. Salzman countered with the argument that too much time had passed since the Mahanys had had their items stolen.

"George Bush was Vice President of the United States," Salzman told the jury, with current events very much on his mind. "Bill Clinton was just a governor. And Monica Lewinsky was thirteen years old."

Trusty and Dwyer countered with what seemed damning evidence. Did not some of the tapes taken from Hadden's storage unit have Martha Mahany's name inscribed on them? Were not many of the items—like the Chinese books and a rare carpentry tool called a spokeshave—so unusual that the owners would not forget them? Salzman had a hard time arguing against that. Still, he claimed that Hadden was just an eccentric collector who may have mistakenly taken a few items when he left the Mahanys' home.

Debbie Dwyer, fearful that the court was again going to let Hadden off with another gentle rap on the knuckles, begged the jurors for the maximum sentence. "There is no doubt, no doubt, that Hadden Clark stole the property. Do not go into that jury room and plea bargain with this man," she said.

Brian Shefferman saw his client differently. "Hadden Clark did not intentionally steal. Mr. Hadden Clark is a pack rat. He is not a thief," he said, keeping a straight face.

Surprisingly, the benevolent jurors entered a split decision, convicting him of stealing from Martha Mahany but unable to reach a verdict on the theft from her father. Dwyer was conciliatory.

"We respect the difficult job the jury had, and we don't think there was a miscarriage of justice," she told the press. Trusty said it was a victory.

"No matter what, we have exposed Mr. Clark to another felony charge for a crime he did, and also exposed him to another fifteen years in prison," he said.

At the sentencing, Shefferman recited most of Hadden's troubled life history, telling Judge Weinstein that Hadden was unable to speak until he was five and had been diagnosed as a paranoid schizophrenic in the Navy. While he did so, Hadden attempted to engage Debbie Dwyer in a staring match. He testified during the sentencing phase and Dwyer asked him about the rear-end collision he had had with the cop in 1992, adding "was that after you murdered Laura Houghteling?" Hadden shot her a chilling look that would have made many run away. Dwyer didn't.

"The state feels this man is a dangerous and calculating individual," she argued. "Hadden Clark has repeatedly preyed on this community."

Judge Weinstein did not give Hadden the maximum, sentencing him to ten years that would be added to the thirty he was serving for killing Laura Houghteling. According to the law, Hadden was still eligible for parole, now moved forward three years, to 2003.

Trusty and Dwyer's murder case against Hadden was far from a certainty. None of the interrogation tapes from 1992 and 1998 could be used, the courts had ruled. Neither could the tape made by the convict, Ben Chambers. It was against the law in Maryland to record someone's voice without permission. They also didn't have a body. Worst of all, there was another suspect, Carl Dorr, whom the defense could paint several shades of black. After all, hadn't he confessed to murdering his daughter on more than one occasion? They couldn't mention Laura Houghteling's name or go into any of Hadden's other crimes unless he testified, because the court would deem it to be prejudicial.

Hadden testify? Fat chance of that.

The two prosecutors had developed a false but potent hypothesis. Trusty and Dwyer believed Tarney's theory that Hadden murdered Michele, took her body to Massachusetts immediately after killing her, and buried her within a few feet of his grandfather. Then, they theorized, on Halloween he had dug her up as if he were a dog with a bone and reburied her elsewhere because he knew Tarney had found his map. They certainly had the circumstantial evidence to imply that to a jury. If they could make that case, it would certainly make Hadden appear diabolical, even bordering on the satanic. And if the jurors wanted more proof of that, all they had to do was look at him.

On September 26, 1999, more than 250 prospective jurors filed into Courtroom One, the same chamber where Hadden had been sentenced for killing Laura Houghteling in 1993. The judge, Michael Mason, was fifty. His brown hair was combed to the side, so that it covered part of his forehead, giving him the air of a prep school professor. He had a habit of typing in his trial notes on a laptop computer as arguments raged in front of him, often pulling his glasses down to the tip of his nose and looking over them at the lawyers. The first question out of his mouth that day allowed a dozen potential jurors to escape.

"Does anyone have a moral objection to convicting someone of murder if the body is undiscovered?" he asked. If a juror chose to remove himself capriciously, perhaps he couldn't be blamed too harshly. The prospects, whose stipend was to be fifteen dollars a day, were told the trial would likely last three weeks.

A jury of seven women and five men was selected. In gender, it was the mirror opposite of what had been chosen for his theft trial four months before. Trusty gave the opening statement, knowing only too well that to interest a jury from the start he had to tell an interesting story.

"The case that brings us here, a case that is going to occupy and consume all of us for the next three weeks is really a book, a story with many chapters. Those chapters begin on May thirty-first of 1986 when the man sitting across from you, Hadden Clark, murdered a six-year-old girl named Michele Dorr."

Trusty moved towards the jurors while Hadden glowered.

"Now there are many chapters that flow from that moment in May of 1986. Unlike a book of fiction, it is not going to be a perfectly smooth read. There are going to be moments of fits and stops and starts. That is the sign of a true story rather than a fictional one."

Trusty had a large photograph of Michele Dorr on an easel for the jury to see as he spoke. He looked towards the picture.

"This is my star witness. She is the only witness to the murder of Michele Dorr. She cannot tell you about that hot May day in 1986. But you will hear her voice throughout this trial, as it comes out firmly from the testimony of parents, the teachers that knew her, and even from her blood."

At the defense table, Hadden, wearing a long-sleeved navy-blue shirt appeared bored. Trusty went on, defending Carl Dorr, telling how her father had rented *The Little Mermaid*, and, like a good attorney, omitting *Death Wish 3*.

"It is your classic night of excitement and fun for a six-year-old. She is with Daddy. She got to play. She got some sweets. And she is going to stay up late watching a movie with her daddy."

Trusty tiptoed gently around Carl's neglect of Michele on the afternoon she was killed. He did not absolve him, however.

"This is his cross to bear. It is not something that is easy for a parent to live with. That is, if I had just been outside, or if I had checked every half-hour or every hour, then my child could be a nineteen-year-old in college today."

Carl Dorr, seated in the courtroom, tried not to react. Hadden looked his way, too, a lazy stare. Trusty didn't have to do much to demonize him. The accused was doing it to himself. The prosecutor went through Carl's breakdowns, trying to preempt the attack that was surely going to come from the public defenders. He began talking about one of the bit players of the long saga, Ed Jagen.

"Now these are some of the things that come out of that breakdown. There is a guy named Ed Jagen, all right? And I do not think he is actually the devil, but Ed Jagen was somebody who kind of injected himself into this case, who—and I don't know if he worked for some kind of child find organization—he kind of linked up with Dee Dee as an advisor to try to help her figure out what happened. Jagen was very much at odds with Carl Dorr and so when Carl Dorr lost it, he was saying things like, 'Ed Jagen is the devil. She's buried in my basement. She's going to rise from the dead. I'm Jesus.' "

Trusty went through his version of Michele's murder, saying she had wandered up to Eliza's bedroom and Hadden came along and murdered her with a knife. He went into Hadden's interrogation and tried to defend the Montgomery County Police Department with this left-handed compliment.

"The police are not a bunch of knuckleheads or Keystone Kops," he said.

It was hard to jump over Hadden's Laura Houghteling history. But Trusty had to or face a mistrial. So he went straight to the scenario of Hadden burying Michele's body in Wellfleet. He referred to the directions that led to the cemetery as Hadden's "treasure map." Trusty described the disturbed earth, the cadaver dogs, the earth in the eyeglass case which he said was identical to the earth at the gravesite. He hinted, painting word pictures, laying the initial groundwork for Debbie Dwyer's closing argument. She was to conclude that Hadden must have first buried Michele in Massachusetts, and then reburied her elsewhere.

Trusty began defending the former convicts whom he thought were his best witnesses. He knew their credibility was suspect and he dealt with it directly.

"You might be wondering, 'Well, gosh, I don't want to

believe these guys. Why would I believe somebody that is in jail themselves?'

"But there is a code that says, 'Hey, I did some bad stuff. You did some bad stuff. But you do not kill a child.' You do not kill a child. And some of these guys, I looked at them and said, 'God, is he a jerk. He did something horrible.' But when Mr. Clark made comments to them about how he broke that code, they felt compelled to bring it forward."

Trusty emphasized that no deals had been made, saying the inmates got nothing. Nor were they going to get anything, he claimed.

"You are going to hear from a guy who breaks into houses, a kid who steals cars and set fire to a building, a guy who raped somebody, and somebody who committed murder. I'm not saying these are angels. I am not saying, 'Folks, to believe them, you have to invite them over for dinner at the end of the trial.' We are not that naive.

"Do not dismiss them by saying, 'Oh, they are all jail-birds. Oh, they are all a bunch of snitches.' Because they are not snitches. They are informants.

"Now there is an old saying, and I guess that is kind of where we are, 'Sometimes you have to go to hell to catch the devil.' You are going to meet some people that have done some bad things, but they did not kill a child."

Trusty described a female private investigator who had taken it upon herself to correspond with Hadden, saying he had written her a letter that implicated himself. Then he went into the blood evidence. His first sentence belied his argument that the police were not knuckleheads.

"Well, for the first time in 1995, the police say, 'You know what? We should check that out.' So they go to Eliza's room, that tiny little room, that tiny little floor, and they use a tool called luminol."

The prosecutor described the properties of the chemical and how it would luminesce when it came into contact with blood. The blood would make it glow, Trusty explained.

"It is not on the top of the floor. This is how we know it was cleaned. It is not at the top of the floor like a sitting lake of blood. It is in the cracks and the grooves, the places that you would not be able to soak up as you furiously wipe a towel across it, and as you try to stem the bleeding. Sue Ballou is seeing the floor light up like a Christmas tree—crack upon crack upon crack, and she gets down on her hands and knees and she is swabbing the ground and trying to capture this blood inch by inch. Blood, blood, and more blood scattered across the grooves and surfaces."

Trusty knew that none of the techicians could state with certainty that the blood was Michele Dorr's or even that it was human. So he spun it, putting the best face on the issue.

"No expert is going to come in here and tell you that to a reasonable degree of medical certainty Michele Dorr did not bleed on that floor. And that is important on its own, obviously, right? They cannot contradict that—there was blood on the floor."

Trusty began wrapping up.

"There is a chapter that is left and I cannot write that. You write that last chapter. God knows Michele cannot. You will have the option of either writing a last chapter that ends in chaos—"

"Objection!"

"Sustained."

"You can write a chapter that says justice for Michele."

Shefferman was on his feet, objecting again. Judge Mason felt compelled to give the jurors a lecture.

"Sustained. Ladies and gentlemen, please do not understand Mr. Trusty's remarks as an appeal to you for sympathy, pity, or passion. You must decide this case fairly and impartially. Only in this way do you write any final chapter."

Trusty bounced off Mason's remarks as if they were a cue.

"We will ask you to decide it fairly and impartially. Keep the common sense that you had when you came here last week over what will be an arduous three weeks. And we believe if you keep that common sense, there will be justice."

After a recess, Salzman came back and tried to pick apart the prosecution's case. His theme was that the police were desperate for a conviction but had chosen the wrong man

"Nothing chills the soul of a police officer more than hearing the words, 'My daughter is missing.' Protecting the weak, the vulnerable, the young, that is what leads someone to become a police officer in the first place.

"The Montgomery County Police Department did everything and anything that they could think of to try to bring this sweet little girl back to her parents' family. And as the days turned into weeks and the weeks turned into years, the Montgomery County Police Department has not and does not have a higher priority than finding the person that they assume must be her killer. Over the years, that police determination became a sense of urgency, and eventually it turned into desperation.

"It is that desperation that has led the police to accuse the wrong man of murder. Hadden Clark is the wrong man. Hadden Clark is falsely accused of murder. Hadden Clark did not kill Michele Dorr. The trumped-up case against Hadden Clark is nothing more than a mirage. It is a mirage put together by people who are desperate to solve the mystery about this little girl. And at the end of this case, when all the evidence is in, the only thing that will be left is a mirage. We will be left with the puzzling, troubling mystery about what happened to this sweet little girl."

Salzman was acting as a lawyer should; he was sworn to defend his client to the best of his ability. He knew Hadden was a convicted murderer. He knew of his other crimes. But he wasn't about to just go through the motions.

What he really believed about Hadden would remain his secret. Today he was to be his advocate, and it was his duty to provide him with the strongest defense possible.

"The police have spent thousands and thousands of dollars searching for this little girl. They have spent hundreds of thousands of dollars, probably millions of dollars trying to prove a case of murder. They have enlisted the help of the FBI, police in other states—Massachusetts and Rhode Island—and they have enlisted local police. And here we are in court with Power Point demonstrations, laptop computers, sophisticated courtroom demonstrations. Who knows what we are going to see?"

"Your Honor, I am going to object," Trusty said.

"Overruled."

Salzman began focusing on his straw man.

"It is fair to say that from the beginning and for several years at least, the police investigation focused on one man—Carl Dorr, Michele Dorr's father. The police suspected Carl Dorr because he told them he had no idea where his six-year-old, shy daughter had gone from almost four hours in the middle of the day. The police suspected Carl Dorr because of his behavior. They began to look at his marriage to his wife Dorothy, who also goes by the name of Dee Dee."

Salzman was off and running on Carl Dorr, painting him as a suspect, giving every possible reason that it was he who was Michele's murderer and not Hadden. Carl, sitting in the courtroom with his new wife, Margaret, tried to look unconcerned.

"Part of his story did not add up, none of it could be corroborated by the police. They felt at the time that his bitter dispute with his wife might have been enough to make him do something with Michele."

Salzman switched to the convicts who were going to testify against Hadden, calling them "honorable gentlemen," making the phrase ring with sarcasm.

"The inmates who were living with Hadden Clark heard broadcasts, read newspaper articles, and then the teasing began. 'Hey, Hadden, tell me where you put Michele so I can get out of here. Come on, Hadden, tell me what you did with her so I can go home.'

"These honorable men had honorable reasons. One of them, William Yates, told the police, 'I had a daughter who died recently. I know what the parents must be going through.' What could be more honorable than that? Now, some of you may be troubled by the fact that William Yates never had a daughter who died—not recently, not ever."

Salzman, his voice rising, tried to knock down each of the prosecution inmates as if they were bowling pins. He did so with derision, with facts, with scathing voice inflections. Trusty made several objections, but most were overruled. Salzman went on to the subject of the so-called "treasure map." He was on more solid ground here.

"Let's talk about disturbed earth and dogs. The prosecutor forgot to tell you something. In 1991 Hadden Clark and his mother wanted to bury his father's ashes because he had died in 1986. And the ashes, the urn had been with his sister. Hadden and his mother decide to bury his father's remains. They were cremated remains. He sent the funeral home a map showing where his family plot was in the cemetery. You will see that map and it looks like this map. The reason they needed the map was they needed to make arrangements with a local gravedigger to dig a hole so that Hadden and his mother could bury the ashes. That is why the map was drawn. This is not a treasure map. It is a map that was sent to a funeral home in Wellfleet, Massachusetts, in 1991. To say it is a treasure map, is turning it into something, a mirage. Something it is not."

"Objection."

"Overruled."

Encouraged by Mason, Salzman continued with the theme.

"It is simply a mirage. It is a pretty big leap to say that because a dog did something in that cemetery that Michele Dorr is buried there. But desperate people want you to take big leaps."

Salzman attacked the blood evidence, implying that even if what Sue Ballou had found was blood, she could not even say it was human blood. He said that three dogs and several hamsters had lived in the house, and lots and lots of people over the years. Salzman was a smart lawyer. He was doing his duty, spreading reasonable doubt at every step of the way.

The timeline was his last subject. He said the cops were presenting two options.

"Obviously one option is to say, 'Well, Carl Dorr was wrong when he said that he saw his daughter at 2:10 in the afternoon. It must have been earlier. The second way to say it is, 'Hadden Clark was not at his work at 2:46 that afternoon.' "

He attacked Carl Dorr and the witnesses who were going to back up Michele's father's changed story. He finished by returning to his theme.

"All of the prosecutors and the police leads in this case are a mirage. They shimmered. They offered promise. They offered hope. They offered anticipation. But in reality, there was nothing there."

Hadden stifled a yawn.

"For those who are desperate to convict Hadden Clark for murder, they will follow that mirage, a mirage that has obscured the truth for those who do not want to see it or cannot see it—the truth that the police have followed the wrong man for years. And you will see the truth—Hadden Clark is innocent. He did not commit this crime."

Hadden looked towards Ed Tarney, seated in the front row of the courtroom, asking for recognition. He didn't get it. Next to Tarney was Michele's mother, Dee Dee, who did return the gaze. With it was all the hatred she could muster.

15

END OF THE LINE

In another county, in another state, Hadden Clark may have likely gone unprosecuted for the murder of Michele Dorr. Few jurisdictions in America have the resources to allow the man-hours or to spend the money to investigate a thirteen-year-old murder in which there is no body or hard evidence. An eleven-year-old case for the theft of household odds and ends is usually forgotten. Montgomery County, Maryland, despite the mistakes of its police department, had the tax revenue to not only prosecute Hadden for both crimes, but to do it right, flying in Michele Dorr's former kindergarten teachers from as far away as Florida just to offer positive personality assessments. At times, the educators seemed to be putting her up for sainthood. While one of them, Gayle Komisar, said she had witnessed an intense argument between Carl and Dee Dee, no defense attorney would dare to contest the angelic traits of an innocent six-year-old.

After the teachers finished their parade, Carl Dorr took the stand. Trusty used a ploy that would bring any bereaved father to tears. He handed him Michele's overnight bag that she had brought to his house on Sudbury Road the night before she was killed. It had sat in a police department storage locker since 1986. Trusty asked Carl to identify the contents.

"These are her roller skates. These are her shoes," he said in a shaky voice, tears welling in his eyes.

"Did you kill Michele?"

"I did not."

"Did you have any responsibility for her death?"

"I did not."

Shefferman tried to take Carl apart.

"You say she ate lunch with you that day?" he asked.

"Yes."

"You didn't mention that when you were questioned in 1986, did you? Didn't you threaten to abduct Michele from school or her babysitter's home?"

Carl denied he had ever made the statement even though Dee Dee had alleged that he had in court papers. In fact, Dee Dee, in the front row of the courtroom, was offering silent support by dabbing at her eyes with a tissue while he spoke, a spectacle few jurors missed.

Shefferman accused Carl of laughing when he first spoke to detectives about Michele's disappearance. He disagreed.

"I did not laugh. It was not a laughing situation," Carl said.

"Didn't you say to her mother that you would be behind bars for the rest of your life if they found Michele?"

"I don't recall saying that."

Dee Dee backed up Carl. She had a different story from the one she had filed as part of her divorce documents in 1986.

"I did not take those threats regarding Michele to heart," she now said. "I knew he loved her and I knew he would never hurt her."

Hadden shot Carl a stare as Dee Dee testified. He was spending his days in the courtroom either gazing out at people in the chamber or trying to intimidate witnesses. When Mike Garvey began to testify he shot the detective one of his better evil-eye looks and mouthed the phrase, "You're lying," over and over again.

The only really new evidence that seemed to challenge Hadden's timeline alibi came from Pat Generao, a neighbor who lived on Sudbury Road. Generao said she saw Hadden's truck parked at Geoff's house just before three in the afternoon as she drove to her shift at a nearby hospital. When Salzman asked why she hadn't reported the sighting until late 1998, Generao had a ready answer. It didn't make the police look good.

"Because I had never been asked that question before," she said.

The second act of the prosecution's play consisted of witnesses who buttressed their theory that Hadden was someone who had driven to Wellfleet twice—the first time to bury her and ten days later to dig her up and rebury her. Alison testified, as did a Massachusetts state trooper, Kathleen Barrett, who said that Dan, the German shepherd, had pawed at the ground near Silas Clark's grave. The woman who saw him there on Halloween day, Andrea Slade, also verified Hadden's presence.

"The marker in my mind was Halloween," she said. "I personally detest Halloween."

A Wellfleet policeman, Arthur A. Parker, Jr., said that the disturbed ground was forty-two by fifty inches and inconsistent with the surrounding ground.

"The soil was a mixture of sand and dirt and below the surfaces were shells that looked like they came from the road, with oak leaves, too," he told the jury.

Other members of police departments took their turns on the stand, all describing the disturbed earth and dogs that were trained to sniff cadavers. None could say with any certainty whether or not a body had ever been present or whose body it might be.

The most dramatic testimony came when the parade of convicts told their tales. John Fridley, sporting a gold hoop earring, with a tattoo gracing his forehead, was graphic. He used his hands to make slashing motions across his chest.

"He told me it was a twelve-inch butcher knife," Fridley said to Debbie Dwyer in a matter-of-fact voice. "He told me he almost decapitated her."

The revelation caused several members of the Dorr family to bolt from their seats and run from the courtroom. Their loud sobs all but drowned out Fridley's words. The trio included Carl Dorr, his wife, and his sister, Susan Schellinger. Dee Dee, sitting in the front row, stayed, as did Tina, Michele's half-sister. While the Dorr family wept outside, Tina shed tears in the courtroom with Dee Dee staring straight ahead, her eyes fixed on Hadden. The cause of all this grief tried to look bored, almost to the point of falling asleep as the drama played out. Fridley wasn't through.

"She was pretty much in shock," the former convict said of Michele. "He went in and slashed her. She bled a lot. He said he had to clean up and get rid of things that had blood on them."

He said Hadden wanted to write a book about himself. Fridley had claimed he knew an author. The ex-con told the court the book was a ruse to get Hadden to talk about Michele.

Fridley, on parole, said he had not received early release for his testimony. In fact, the opposite turned out to be true. Salzman handed him some documents that showed he had actually been kept in prison an additional nine months, serving nearly six years of a ten-year sentence while the police digested his information. He could have been out in five, Salzman pointed out. Upon learning that, Fridley threw the letter down and left the stand in a huff, understandably upset.

Another inmate, William Wayne Yates—the convict whom Salzman said had no child—had a different version which seemed even more horrific. Yates claimed that Hadden had said he had raped Michele and told him he'd killed her because he was afraid she would tell.

"After hearing that, I didn't want anything to do with him," Yates testified. "He told me if I said anything to anybody about it, he would kill me."

Yates had an unusual life story. He said he had a child who had died in a car accident in 1997, but then later learned he wasn't the father. He remembered the mother's name was Tammy and that he had lived with her for three years but somehow couldn't recall her last name. However, the experience of losing a child had inspired him to come forward, he told the jury. It was a tale Hadden's attorneys had a hard time refuting.

"I knew the pain and suffering I was feeling," Yates told the court as Hadden glared at him. "I felt remorse to the parents of this little girl that Clark killed."

Finally, Ben Chambers came forward. With good reason. While he was out on parole, he had already been arrested again for possession of heroin and was facing another trial. A conviction could put him behind bars for another five years. He needed something to balance the ledger.

Chambers said he had heard the same words as Fridley. Hadden told him what he was going to put in his book, he claimed. Chambers was much more graphic than the cons who had testified before him.

"He said he slashed her across the chest and she fell down. And he like, straddled himself over the top of her and took the knife and just pressed down on her throat and it like, went all the way through, almost cutting off her head. He said that the blood had squirted all over the place—on himself, on the floor. It was a hard-type floor. The blood was just laying there, all puddling up."

When Salzman suggested he might be testifying to get a deal on the latest charge, Chambers pointed with his finger toward Debbie Dwyer and spoke dramatically. It was right out of an episode of *Law and Order*.

"I'm not doing it for them," he said, looking at the two prosecutors. "I'm doing it for the little girl and the little girl's mother."

He also said Hadden had given the cops false information when he hinted he had buried Michele in Rhode Island and in New Jersey.

"He wanted to send you on a wild goose chase. He got a kick out of it because he hates you all really bad," Chambers said, looking at some of the cops in the courtroom. "I got to know Clark and I could tell when he was telling the truth and when he was giving people some bullshit to throw them off."

Hadden was excited by Chambers' retelling of his murder of Michele. He became so stimulated that during his next bathroom break, he began masturbating in the stall, with the sheriff's deputy assigned to guard him having to halt his prisoner before culmination.

The prosecution also produced the private investigator, Sharon Weidenfeld, who had corresponded with Hadden. In one of the letters to her he had written, *God and I know the terrible things I have done. I'm sorry I did it.* Of course, Hadden could have been referring to Laura or even another deed, but the prosecution's inference was that he was talking about Michele.

Salzman and Shefferman focused on the timeline in their defense of Hadden. They brought in a former chef from the Chevy Chase Country Club, Peter Stogbuchner, to testify that Hadden had clocked in at 2:46 that afternoon. Debbie Dwyer tried to ask him about employees who clocked in for others, but there was an objection, with Judge Mason finally ruling that there had to be direct testimony on the matter. Unless the prosecution had an employee who would testify that he had falsified a timecard, the accusation couldn't even be suggested.

The public defenders then attacked the blood evidence. Megan Clement, of the North Carolina lab, said that five samples of the blood had produced DNA, but none of it matched Michele or Hadden.

Salzman also seemed to relish going after Ed Tarney on the matter of the map, suggesting the police had altered it for their own purposes after it came into their possession. He showed video tape from a 1993 television newscast and then compared it with the current map. It appeared that an arrow, a question mark, and parentheses had been added.

Trusty argued that substantive features were found on both maps.

Debbie Dwyer gave the closing argument for the prosecution. She had a habit of swiveling nervously in her seat at times, so she immediately rose to address the jury. With her best friend seated in the courtroom, she went through the case step-by-step, saying it was other people who tried to convince Dee Dee that Carl killed Michele.

"Ladies and gentlemen, eighteen days ago Mr. Salzman stood before you and said this was a trumped-up case. They want you to believe that Carl Dorr killed his daughter. But Carl Dorr came into this courtroom and with tears in his eyes said he did not kill Michele Dorr and I ask you to remember that."

Rather, she said, it was Hadden who killed Michele, and he had several hours to clean up and dispose of her body.

"Some of the others, like the psychics, said Michele was here, or Michele was there, and some of them, like Ed Jagen, I submit to you, ladies and gentlemen, were corrupt charlatans who eagerly convinced Dee Dee Dorr that Carl Dorr had killed Michele."

She made the case that Hadden had buried Michele next to his grandfather.

"He knows the police have an eyeglass case with soil in it, and ladies and gentlemen, he knows that the police have this map. Hadden Clark knows that it is only a matter of time until the police find that cemetery and the police go there. Ladies and gentlemen, ask yourselves, why is Hadden Clark carrying this cemetery map in his possession? Because he knew the police had it and he knew the police would wind up there. So Hadden Clark does what any guilty person would do when they know the police are onto them. Hadden Clark runs. Hadden Clark hides, and, ladies and gentlemen, Hadden Clark tells more lies."

Dwyer's recitation of what she believed to be facts was

flawed, but she was resonating with the jury. At times they had seemed on the verge of falling asleep during the trial, but today they were riveted. Particularly when Dwyer picked up the theme of a clandestine grave. Though the prosecutor never said so directly, she painted the picture of Michele's body being buried and reburied so well, the jury members couldn't miss the implication. She then defended the inmates, saying they had come with baggage but had told the truth. Sheila Weidenfeld's letter from Hadden was a confession, she said.

"Ladies and gentlemen, this letter is devastating. The letter is a confession to a heinous and grisly crime. It is a confession to Michele Dorr's murder. Read it up, down, sideways, it still says the same thing. It is devastating evidence from his own hand."

Confident that she had sold Weidenfeld's evidence to the jury, Dwyer made a plea for a conviction, not just of murder, but murder in the first degree.

"Ladies and gentlemen, premeditation does not have to be days. Premeditation does not have to be hours. I submit to you, ladies and gentlemen, it can be the time it took for Hadden Clark to walk out of that house, walk to his truck, open a toolbox, get out a knife, go back inside and slash Michele Dorr's throat. It can be the time between a slash to the chest and a plunge of the knife into her throat.

"Come from that room with the final chapter!" she exhorted. "Ladies and gentlemen, Madam Forelady, you tell Michele Dorr and you tell Hadden Clark that justice delayed will not be justice denied!"

Exhausted, Dwyer sat down. Judge Mason declared a recess. It would be up to Brian Shefferman to counter her closing.

"Many people are drawn to celebrities, and in his own way, Hadden Clark was a celebrity who was in prison," Shefferman said. "People didn't want access to Hadden Clark for his autograph. Having access to Hadden Clark meant you had leverage to get what you wanted—a reduced sentence or maybe something else you wanted like medical treatment. That is what prompted the former inmates you heard from to contact the police about Hadden Clark.

"Hadden Clark should not be here because he did not kill Michele Dorr. There is no way that he could have killed a person on Sudbury Road and possibly gotten to work at 2:46 in the afternoon."

With that established, Shefferman began pointing the finger at Carl Dorr again. He knocked down the prisoners' testimonies one by one, calling Fridley and Chambers "corrupt conspirators" who had formed a team to get their sentences reduced. He said their stories weren't consistent and that it didn't make sense because the police had searched Eliza's room in 1986 and found nothing amiss. Knocking down the inmates' testimony seemed to be his prime concern. Despite their built-in lack of credibility, their stories had been powerful and perhaps the prosecution's best weapon.

Shefferman made a good case that Hadden wouldn't have hired someone to provide him with a hole for his father's ashes if Michele Dorr's body was anywhere nearby. After all, the cemetery employee could have accidentally dug up Michele, he reminded them.

"He did not bury Michele Dorr at that location. Nobody who had done that would have brought in this gravedigger to dig in that same area. Who would ever do that?"

Finally, as he had all through his rebuttal, he came back to Michele's father.

"Carl Dorr's confessions are not made to dishonest criminals but to police officers and his ex-wife, and again, that is something you simply cannot ignore. Many people here are still desperate to solve this particular case. It would be convenient to convict the man who has been charged. It would be, but it wouldn't be right. Hadden Clark did not kill Michele Dorr and the only proper verdict is not guilty."

Trusty had the final word. While Debbie Dwyer at times wept, his presentation was short.

"Carl Dorr did it! Carl Dorr did it! We knew that was coming. We brought it out in the opening, and they went at it for a while, and then they went with an alibi defense."

He defended the convicts once again, saying it wasn't fair to portray Fridley and Chambers as two-headed monsters. Shefferman objected but was overruled by Mason.

"It is heaping insult upon insult because it is desperate. Throw it up against the wall and see what sticks. These two guys spoke the truth."

Trusty used one-liners to destroy a defense expert witness, Dan Craig, a scientist who had disparaged the abilities of the cadaver dogs. Trusty called him "the monkey doctor" because Craig had conducted experiments on primates.

"The monkey doctor deserves a little ridicule. Did you really think that was a spontaneous, credible doctor, or do you think this guy might have some issues? That he might be a little bit of a quack? And he was a quack. This man tries to tell you that from his great thesis work of getting baboons high and radiating monkeys to study their vomit, that he has something to tell us about this case. I mean, he probably trained a dog to fetch marijuana for a baboon because that is the only way he could tie in his experience to this case."

Dwyer continued to cry along with the Dorr family members in the courtroom. Trusty finished with these thoughts.

"You have to focus on evidence, not speculation, and that is a difficult task. That is not easy. I know that, but that is why you are here, and that is your oath, and I believe that when you write the final chapter, in the moments before you come out here to announce that final chapter, I believe and hope that that firm quiet whisper of truth will be in your head—that firm quiet whisper of a shy child killed on a hot day in 1986 that says, 'He killed me. There is a murderer amongst us and it is not the daddy I love.' "

Counting the weekend, the twelve jurors deliberated over four days. They had little doubt about Hadden's guilt, instead debating the merits of first-degree versus second-degree murder. Carl Dorr was worried, though. When the four alternates were released, two had said they would have voted to acquit.

In the end, the jurors decided on a second-degree conviction. They said they had no proof that Hadden had planned the murder. Some seemed to blame Carl for Michele's death, while others spoke negatively about the police.

"He was a negligent father," Karen Schwartz, one of the jurors, said of Carl. Another, Jerry Talen, said he didn't put a lot of credence in the inmates, but at least they had forced the cops to go into Eliza's bedroom and look for blood.

"The police did not follow up in 1986 when Hadden Clark got sick at the police station," he said, echoing the thoughts of many.

Debbie Dwyer said it was the proudest day in her career and Jim Trusty said he had prayed about it over the weekend. Sentencing was set for a week away.

On October 20, 1999, Salzman went through Hadden's life again, focusing on his handicaps and the abuse he had suffered. He said he had physical injury to the brain, was beaten by his father, and on and on, making both Trusty and Dwyer angry. He asked that any sentence Hadden received be concurrent, and not the maximum. Trusty got up, furious.

"You know, I am struck by how we have become invaded by psycho-babble in this courthouse. It is expected and routine. We expect to hear, 'Oh, well, he had a terrible birth. He had a terrible childhood. He was picked on by kids.' Forceps deliveries are now being used as an expla-

nation for killing people and I am struck by how absurd it
is. I guess I look at the report on this person, which is
damning, and that tells this court that this is a psychotic
man.

"This is a man who will take any excuse, any perceived
injustice, such as being asked to leave an apartment, and
turn it into twisted revenge. If someone doesn't return his
amorous attentions like Laura Houghteling, they are murdered. If a six-year-old wanders into his grips, they are
murdered. And I guess I look at this report, and I say sar-
castically, 'Thank you for the help, people of the forensic
psychiatry world.'

"I don't care what happened in his childhood. I don't
care if he had a mean father or a mother who drank too
much. I don't care if his family was dysfunctional. Maybe
this sounds callous, but I don't care if his brother is serving
a sentence for murder in California.

"What explains this man is the old-fashioned notion that
he is evil, that he is twisted, and that he acts upon that in
the most evil, most outrageous way you can imagine. This
man is emotionally volatile, he is not emotionally vulnerable. The real constant in his life is not one of victimhood,
but of being a victimizer."

Trusty went on, letting Hadden and the public defenders
know his own feelings more than the court required. He
was frustrated that, after nearly fourteen years, and millions
of dollars in taxpayers' money, Michele Dorr's body had
yet to be found.

"The one issue left is the inability to bury Michele or
the remains that are Michele. I wasn't sure of my feelings
about this until this morning. I knew how part of the family
felt. There is a general feeling of resentment towards Mr.
Clark, a feeling of 'Sir, take it to your own grave. You
have no power over this family. You have no power over
this community. You have no power over Michele Dorr.' "

Hadden put his head down on the table and pretended

to sleep as Trusty berated him, saying he wouldn't beg for her body. He pointed out some of Hadden's unusual behavior during the trial.

"There were comments about, 'Look at this emotionally vulnerable man,' and I am reminded by the fact that, in the midst of the trial, as a mother sat crying, this man stared towards her and smiled. The same man that was staring at jurors and staring at prosecutors and then feigning vulnerability during closing arguments, that same man had the gall to look at this mother and do that.

"That is not psycho-babble. That is not bad upbringing. That is twisted and evil."

Hadden was asked if he wanted to say anything. He didn't. Judge Mason sentenced him to the maximum, thirty years. Hadden now had a total of seventy years to do, of which he had served just six.

16

OTHER BODIES, OTHER PLACES

After Hadden told Jesus where he had buried Michele and Jesus got the word to the cops, the police searched the wooded area he had described for them but kept missing the exact spot. So they picked up Hadden from WCI, and drove back to the site in early January. Hadden told them he had put an old mattress on top of the body and near the base of a tree. Ed Tarney nearly tripped over a spring from the mattress, pulled on it, and soon glimpsed a frayed piece of Michele's pink-and-white swim suit. The site soon became a shrine, with people who had followed the case bringing flowers, crucifixes, and stuffed animals to the place. A border of sticks was arranged to mark where she had remained buried for almost fourteen years.

"Hadden wouldn't talk to anyone before the search," Tarney recalled. "He beat his head against a wall and was talking in a crazy language. The problem was that his alter ego Kristen told him not to tell us where Michele was buried."

"It was a very intense moment," said Debbie Dwyer, who was one of those at the scene when the body was discovered. "Once they found human bone, it was very solemn and silent. A number of people embraced, but it was still very sad."

There was a proper funeral on January 15, 2000, with Dwyer, Jim Trusty, and several Montgomery County cops—Ed Tarney, Mike Garvey, Bob Phillips, and Ed Day—asked to be pallbearers. Tarney and Garvey had to decline as the date conflicted with yet another trip to Cape Cod, this time with Hadden and Jesus. Police business came first. More than 400 attended; including most of the county's politicians. A photo montage of Michele greeted them at the church.

"We dare not allow the dark evil that she encountered for a few brief moments of her life consume our thoughts," Charles L. Updike, a Baptist minister, told the throng. "She lived in a beauty and innocence and grace that touched many people in her life. The good qualities of Michele shine as bright and fair as ever."

On the way to the cemetery the funeral procession stopped near the woods where she had been buried by Hadden nearly fourteen years before. Carl Dorr and members of his family got out and said a prayer. Dee Dee had visited the site earlier. Michele Dorr was buried on the side of a hill at Fort Lincoln Cemetery, which borders Maryland in Washington, D.C.

After Michele was interred, there was a lot of posthumous fingerpointing. James G. Zumwalt, the son of the Vietnam War hero, admiral Elmo Zumwalt, was the first to weigh in with an editorial-page column in *The Washington Times*. Zumwalt, one of Ed Jagen's many supporters, blamed Montgomery County authorities for not only failing to link Hadden to Michele's murder, but, he wrote, "eleven other victims to whom Clark has now alluded." He said Ed Jagen had conducted an independent investigation that fingered Hadden but the evidence was ignored because of professional jealousy by the police. Zumwalt claimed Jagen had interviewed a neighbor who offered to help Hadden load a navy duffel bag into his truck, which he suggested may have held Michele's body. He also said that Jagen had met with Hadden, convinced that he had a multiple personality disorder, and eventually turned over the results of his investigation to the police and was ignored.

Why was this evidence ignored? It appears the investigation the police were conducting was pointing elsewhere—to Michele's father . . . The police were so certain they were on the right track with Mr. Dorr, they failed to follow basic police procedure in pursuing all leads.

Zumwalt claimed that Jagen had corresponded with Hadden, encouraging him to allow his feminine side to emerge. Jagen told Hadden to ask the police to let him wear a dress, Zumwalt said, and thus implied that he was at least partially responsible for Michele's body being found.

Mr. Jagen knew the key to getting Clark to confess to Michele's murder was to crack through his multiple personalities. He knew Clark's personalities were both male and female—with the former having no recollection of Michele Dorr while the latter did.

The piece by Zumwalt, titled "It Takes a Village to Save a Child," brought a quick response from Debbie Dwyer. She was apoplectic in her letter to the newspaper.

I, as one of the prosecutors of Hadden Clark, am left completely speechless at his complete disregard for the truth about Edward Jagen and the role he played in the search for the killer of Michele Dorr.

Mr. Jagen never, at any time during this investigation, told the police he suspected Mr. Clark as the murderer of Michele. To the contrary, he did everything he could to convince the police that Carl Dorr, Michele's father had killed her.

Dwyer concluded that Jagen was nothing but "a man with a big ego who will stop at nothing to promote himself, and his pocketbook."

This brought a reply from an ally of Jagen's, Gwendolyn Gregory, who said she, too, observed that evidence submitted to the police which pointed to Hadden as Michele's murderer was ignored. She wrote that Laura Houghteling and other victims "might be alive today if the evidence had been handled in a more professional manner."

> I saw firsthand how Michele's parents interfered with the police investigation. The enmity between the parents was deep long before Carl Dorr neglected to watch over Michele on May 30 [sic], 1986. It is a good reminder to us all that abuse of children is not always about abduction at the hands of a stranger. I watched while the mother, in her anger, told everyone within hearing that Mr. Dorr was the murderer and refused to accept Clark as the killer in 1986 and while Mr. Dorr admitted to that charge at times, just to assuage his terrible guilt and grief. I lived through the histrionics of faked suicide attempts, his and hers, lying to the authorities, and real threats against one another. Though my sympathies lay with Mrs. Dorr initially, I gradually realized that not many of the parties involved with the investigation really were thinking of Michele.

Zumwalt also responded to Dwyer's letter, suggesting a challenge. He wanted the detectives involved in Michele's investigation and Ed Jagen to undergo joint polygraph testing to verify if evidence had indeed been given to them in 1986 that implicated Hadden. He said that if the lie detector test proved Jagen wrong then he would apologize, but if the results supported him, then Dwyer should retract her allegations.

A month later, Carl Dorr himself responded to the stories with his own editorial-page column. The article appeared to be professionally written, and one could suspect that he had help with the piece. After writing that Jagen, Zumwalt, and Gregory were part of a group who had hounded him since 1986, he ended his article with these words.

Based on my personal experience and some of his past performances in the last fourteen years, I believe that Edward Jagen is a potential menace to the very fragile feelings and mental health of grieving parents everywhere.

Finally, the village needs to let James Zumwalt, Gwen Gregory and Edward Jagen know they are in no position to cast stones at anyone outside their own group who investigated my daughter's tragic death.

In Wellfleet, the police appeared to be certain that Hadden, in a dress, accompanied by the man he believed was Jesus, could quickly lead them to body after body. The combination of cross-dressing and Christ attracted media crews from around the nation, particularly when it was topped off with charges of cannibalism. The psycho-babble by some of the cops had to have made Jim Trusty grind his teeth.

"Hadden Clark wanted to become the women and girls he killed," said one. "He consumed them quite literally."

"He has no other source for acting out his psycho-sexual fantasies except in talking about them," said another, describing him as Hannibal Lecter come-to-life. If Hadden were a celebrity killer in Maryland he was even more so in New England. Criminal investigators from Rhode Island, Connecticut, Pennsylvania, and Vermont, as well as Massachusetts and Maryland, all vied to speak with him.

One of the girls he was suspected of killing was nine-year-old Sarah Pryor. She had disappeared from her home in Wayland, Massachusetts, in October of 1985. Hadden claimed credit for her death by saying he was in the area visiting his father that year. He asserted that his dad had stood him up and made him angry. He cut off her head and ate part of her, he said, but had really wanted to kill her mother. Another possible victim, Cathy Malcolmson, sixteen, had vanished while riding her bike to an after-school job in Stow, near Wayland. Hadden was linked to her disappearance but doesn't remember committing that crime. His grandmother, Edith Clark, had died in Wayland in March of 1985, and Hadden's father had lived in the area just before his death, so both deeds were possible. Part of Pryor's skull was later found but the rest of her remains have never been recovered. When Hadden was shown her picture among a package of similar photos he couldn't pick her out. (*Author's note: Hadden has since claimed to me that he took her remains and buried them near his grandfather's property.*)

An older woman whom Hadden was suspected of killing has been known for decades as "the Lady of the Dunes." Her nude body, with a pair of Wrangler jeans folded neatly beside it, had been found in July of 1974 by a thirteen-year-old girl walking her dog near Race Point Beach in Provincetown, Massachusetts. What was distinctive about the corpse, believed to be that of a mid-twenties female, was that her hands had been chopped off, and thus no fingerprints could be taken. An attempted decapitation had been botched. The torso was so badly bitten by dune flies that further identification was impossible. Hadden was working in Provincetown restaurants at the time she was found. The state police, when asked, would not rule him out.

Most cops on Cape Cod had concluded the woman was Rory Gene Kesinger, a twenty-four-year-old drug user and recent prison escapee who was awaiting trial in Massachusetts for robbery and assault before escaping. She had also attempted to shoot a police officer—twice. Someone had slipped her a hacksaw blade, and she cut through the bars of her window, using tethered sheets to slide her way down the building and escape. But there were details about her that made it unlikely. The nude body had thousands of dollars' worth of gold crowns as part of her dental work and her toenails had been recently pedicured and painted pink.

The grave marker of the unidentified woman, at Saint Peter's cemetery in Provincetown became a bit of a tourist attraction, with flowers often anonymously dropped off on the anniversary of the discovery of her body. The headstone read "Unidentified Female Body Found Race Point Dunes July 24, 1974."

Hadden led a search for the two severed hands at Race Point Beach, Herring Cove Beach, and through some dunes on April 11, 2000. But it was like looking for the well-known needle in a haystack. When the police were asked by reporters if they suspected Hadden of murdering "the Lady of the Dunes," they issued a terse "No comment." Hadden says he did kill her, claiming to have whacked her with the heavy end of a large fishing pole and then, after she was dead, to have used two of the fingers as experimental fish bait.

When he was taken to Cape Cod for a second time with Jesus, this time in female attire, the local wags labeled it "Hadden's Spring Break." He was described in press accounts as wearing "a below-the-shoulder brunette wig," an improvement over the red hairpiece he had worn in January. By now Hadden was flashing his own personal signature. He would raise two manacled hands, put up a finger from each hand and make a cross which he told cops was the sign of hope. Wellfleet senior citizens who remembered the Clarks as having been one of their more distinguished resident families appeared more than a bit embarrassed at all the hoopla accorded the celebrity serial killer.

"Silas Clark was a nice gentleman," said Richmond Bell, who had once served on a Wellfleet financial committee with Hadden's grandfather. "He was a far cry from the younger generation. This doesn't tie in with his reputation at all."

Andrea Slade, who had testified at Hadden's trial, recalled some uncomfortable moments riding in an automobile with Flavia, Hadden, Geoff, and Alison. "They are vague childhood memories," she said. "I do remember that the vibes in the car were very scary. It was the low point of my day."

The former owner of the Moors restaurant in Provincetown, Mylan Costa, also had some unusual recollections of Hadden. "He was a good employee," Costa said. "He was sort of slow, learning-wise. He never impressed me as a dangerous person." He told a reporter Hadden used to live with other summer employees near the restaurant.

The restaurateur also remembered a few of his peculiarities. "He did have a couple of odd habits, like dressing up as a woman. He fished a lot, but just as often as not he left the fish outside to rot."

It was also noted that he liked to drink blood that had been drained from beef. The local *Cape Cod Times* described Hadden's visits as "a gothic horror story, a sort of Stephen King meets Thomas Harris, author of *Silence of the Lambs*."

Hadden's memory just wasn't that good anymore. He couldn't recall the full names or surnames of many of the women he had killed. In other cases, he would take the police to a location only to find it was asphalt, and part of a parking lot. In Meriden, Connecticut, he claimed he had buried two girls near West Mountain. When they took him to the area and Hadden described how he had lugged a body up a hill with a shovel, the cops challenged him, saying the incline was too steep and the body too heavy for him to do so. But they searched anyway, using two cadaver dogs. They also reopened the files of three young girls there. Dawn Cave, fourteen, and Mary Mount, ten, had vanished thirty years before. The third, Doreen Vincent, twelve, had disappeared in June. 1988. Hadden couldn't recall any names for this area.

"We don't know that he's not leading us on a wild goose chase," Ralph Carpenter of the Connecticut State Police told reporters. "What we do know is that he has provided enough information that we think that possibly, there may be someone in the Connecticut area where he may have been involved."

Michael O'Keefe, an assistant district attorney for Cape Cod, took the allegations that Hadden had murdered others seriously. But he doubted that the bodies would ever be found.

"This has not been easy," he said. "It has been more than two decades since the killings, the topography had changed, and Clark is an individual with a number of difficulties who has been in and out of institutions."

James Plath, a Massachusetts state trooper, seconded O'Keefe, pointing out that not only had the topography of the land changed but that even the sand dunes had shifted. Still, he said, the time spent wasn't a total loss. "It was a very productive day. We had additional conversations with Clark and he pointed out additional areas of interest."

Peter Gulotta of the FBI admitted that the Bureau had a serial killer file on Hadden, but said it wasn't just New England. He told reporters it was in many states. "We're working with everyone, looking to see if Clark is responsible for additional victims. If we can possibly link him to someone else, we will," he said.

Hadden, for his part, became increasingly agitated with the lack of success. In June, after he confessed to the police that he had spirited two women off the Block Island Ferry in 1982, killed them, and burned their bodies on a beach, the police investigated, but told him he couldn't go with them on the search. Hadden then wrote six-page letters to the editors at *The New York Times, The Washington Post, The Boston Globe* and the *Boston Herald*. He told the media that he was doing his part but the police weren't pulling their weight.

(*Author's note: In one face-to-face interview with Hadden, I asked him how many people he had actually killed.*

*I told him most estimates were between ten and thirteen.
Hadden smiled at the question. "A lot more than thirteen,"
he said, grinning.)*

Perhaps the police chief of Block Island, Bill McCombe,
spoke for many by mouthing a few words of his own. He
seemed a bit disgusted. "This guy's a whacko. He says a
ton of stuff, but the problem is you can't discredit it all."

Still, Derek Baliles, current police chief of the ever-
accommodating Montgomery County, was more than willing to help Hadden. "So he likes to wear women's clothes,"
he said. "If wearing a woman's wig makes him happy and
he can help us, I'll get him the wig myself."

EPILOGUE

As of this writing, Jesus is still at WCI. During the summer of 2000, both the FBI and the Montgomery County Police Department lobbied for his release at the state's attorney's office in the Delmarva county where he was convicted of murder in 1974. The consensus was positive, provided that Jesus reside somewhere other than Maryland when and if he was released. However, the local authorities said that the state's chief executive would still have the final word. Renewed efforts were made with legal aides of Parris Glendening the hard-nosed governor of Maryland.

In January of 2001 his request for parole was rejected by a judge with a short, one-word denial. Because of his association with Hadden and his cooperation with the FBI, Jesus has to be kept in solitary confinement. There are no plans to allow him back into the general population. Thus Jesus, too, can be seen as an unwitting victim of Hadden Clark. He will be eligible for parole again in 2003.

Ed Tarney has retired from the Montgomery County Police Department. He works on a horse farm near Frederick, Maryland.

Hadden has been moved away from Jesus to the Maryland House of Corrections in Jessup. During a recent visit with him there I asked if it were his parents who had made him become a criminal and murderer or did he think he was just born that way?

"My parents," he answered without hesitation. When I asked him which one was most responsible he had no problem fingering his mother.

"She abused me. She carried liquor with her everywhere and nobody knew it." He said she lied about his beating her up on Block Island, claiming she had fallen down the basement stairs instead.

Hadden requested that I give him the addresses of some of his victims so he could write letters of apology to their parents. His demand was rejected.

I now have a stack of several dozen letters from him, some with statements so over the top, they cause my eyes to widen each time they are read. One doesn't know what is dementia and what is real when reading paragraphs like:

> I didn't give them everything last year. Kristen is very unhappy with the police and if the police thinks they are going to get any more bodies they are crazy. Kristen doesn't like how she was treated and she's not going to help them unless they help me get help for my mental problems everyone tells me I have.

> Kristen is now pissed off and I don't know if she'll tell me where that body is. She comes and visits me off and on and brings her daughter Nicole with her sometime.

At WCI, Jesus has a new cell which faces the tall green mountain, where he looks forward to the weekends. It is then that he can watch a new phenomenon. Scores of hang-gliding enthusiasts soar freely across the face of the peak, far above the prison, disappearing into the clouds. He says he can watch these daredevils all day long.

Jesus continues to tell me about Hadden and recently, after I sent him an old magazine article on Laura Houghteling's murder, he wrote this in a return letter:

> Thanks for the story on Laura. It really caused me some sad feelings and I wanted to beat Hadden up. But that's not a problem. I've felt that way many times!

I have offered to buy Jesus a hard-shell Maryland crab dinner and to share a pitcher of beer with him if he is ever released. He says he is all for it, especially if the restaurant is close to the Chesapeake Bay, with a view of sailboats gliding past and gulls diving towards the waves, searching for their food.